The Meaning of Life

The Meaning of Life

Questions, Answers
and Analysis

edited with an introduction by
Steven Sanders and David R. Cheney
Massachusetts State College at Bridgewater

PRENTICE-HALL, INC., Englewood Cliffs, New Jersey 07632

Library of Congress Cataloging in Publication Data
Main entry under title:

The Meaning of life.

Bibliography: p.
Includes index.
CONTENTS: Tolstoy, L. My confession.—Schopenhauer,
A. On the suffering of the world [and] On the vanity of
existence.—Stace, W. T. Man against darkness. [etc.]
1. Life—Addresses, essays, lectures. I. SANDERS,
STEVEN (date) II. CHENEY, DAVID R. (date)
BD431.M469   128'.5   79-22360
ISBN 0-13-567438-7

Editorial/production supervision by Virginia Rubens
Interior design by Les Bodian
Cover design by Infield/D'Astolfo Associates
Manufacturing buyer: John Hall

Printed in the United States of America

10   9   8   7   6   5   4   3

PRENTICE-HALL INTERNATIONAL, INC., *London*
PRENTICE-HALL OF AUSTRALIA PTY. LIMITED, *Sydney*
PRENTICE-HALL OF CANADA, LTD., *Toronto*
PRENTICE-HALL OF INDIA PRIVATE LIMITED, *New Delhi*
PRENTICE-HALL OF JAPAN, INC., *Tokyo*
PRENTICE-HALL OF SOUTHEAST ASIA PTE. LTD., *Singapore*
WHITEHALL BOOKS LIMITED, *Wellington, New Zealand*

Contents

XI
Linguistic Philosophy and 'The Meaning of Life'   129
Kai Nielsen

XII
The Absurd   155
Thomas Nagel

Preface

The Meaning of Life: Questions, Answers and Analysis contains some of the most important philosophical writing on the problems of the meaning of life. The views that are considered in these essays are (1) that life has no meaning, (2) that questions of the meaning of life should be given "cosmic" or "extraterrestrial" answers, and (3) that life is given meaning through individual human choices. The major differences among these views, and some of the main themes to be found in the essays, are discussed in the Introduction.

Two principles have guided our choice of selections. First, we sought essays of high quality which deal primarily with the meaning of life from various points of view. Second, we wanted essays which would be comprehensible to the reader who has had no previous exposure to philosophy. Adherence to these principles has led us to exclude many essays which deal peripherally with the meaning of life. Other essays have been excluded on the basis that they are largely unintelligible to the reader who is encountering philosophy for the first time.

Three forms of philosophizing about the meaning of life are to be found in this volume. The first involves *raising questions* about the meaning of life. The second consists of *providing answers* to questions about the meaning of life. The third is not directly concerned with asking or answering questions about the meaning of life; instead, this line of inquiry involves *examining* key concepts and presuppositions of claims about the meaning of life. These forms are distinguished rather sharply in the Introduction for the sake of expository clarity and in order to guide the reader in his or her own exploration of the problems. In practice, however, these forms overlap in the work of any particular thinker. Nevertheless, it is easy enough to find in this collection a core of essays directed primarily at providing answers to questions about the meaning of life, a group of essays preceding them which could be considered preparatory to answering those questions, and a third group intended principally to clarify questions and claims about the meaning of life.

By bringing these essays together, we hope to correct some misconceptions—for example, the belief that all questions about the meaning of life are nonsense questions; or that writings about the meaning of life are invariably obscure. We hope that, in addition to correcting these misconceptions, our book will have two other results: first, that readers will reexamine their own questions and assumptions, and second, that philosophers will address themselves to these questions and carry on the work that remains to be done.

Following the Introduction and the selections themselves, the reader will find notes on the contributors and an annotated bibliography detailing alternatives and further developments.

We are grateful to Professors Joel Feinberg and Howard Pospesel for their support and encouragement of this project. Our thanks also to Joe Yokelson and to readers of earlier versions of the manuscript for their helpful comments.

S.S. and D.R.C.

Notes to reader:

1. Some of the essays in this book appear in exerpted form. When material has been omitted, this is indicated by a series of three dots at the point of deletion, followed by an extra line of space to the next paragraph.

2. A dual footnoting system has been used in the essay selections. Footnotes preceded by a number are those which appeared in the essay as originally published; those preceded by an asterisk are notes added by the present editors.

INTRODUCTION

Raising, Answering, and Analyzing Questions about Life's Meaning

Steven Sanders
and David R. Cheney

Raising Questions about Life's Meaning

In his monumental study of Nietzsche, Karl Jaspers writes, "The question of the value and meaning of existence is unlike any other question: man does not seem to become really serious until he faces it."[1] On this important point, a conflicting view is expressed by Freud: "The moment a man questions the meaning and value of life, he is sick. . . ."[2] With whom should we agree, Jaspers or Freud? If we consider the autobiographical work *My Confession* by the great Russian novelist Tolstoy, we will find enough material to illustrate the claims of both Jaspers and Freud.

For nearly half a century, Tolstoy lived the good life, adorned with wealth, literary fame, nobility, and a handsome family. Then came the "arrest of life," the prolonged, tumultuous pause about which he wrote, "I felt that what I was standing on had given way, that I had no foundation to stand on, that that which I had lived by no longer existed, and that I had nothing to live by." What brought Tolstoy to this grave condition which he likened to that of "any person who falls ill with a mortal internal disease"? What haunting turn of fate left him under a shroud of seriousness for the remainder of his life? He tells us that it was due to his inability to avoid or to answer these questions: "What is the meaning of my life? What will come of my life? Why does everything which exists exist, and why do I exist?" *My Confession* displays the circumstances of his quandary and records the long journey in search of an answer.

---

[1] Karl Jaspers, *Nietzsche* (Tucson: University of Arizona, 1965), p. 333.
[2] Sigmund Freud, *Letters of Sigmund Freud* (New York: Basic Books, 1960), p. 436.

We can consider a case like Tolstoy's from either of two points of view, the psychological or the philosophical. The former arises when personal inquiry about life's meaning coincides with an emotional upheaval. The psychotherapist regards such disruption as indicative of an abnormal state of mind, and his intent is to determine the cause of this condition. As Freud's remark suggests, the psychotherapist may consider distress over the question of life's meaning to be merely symptomatic of an underlying malady. To detect such sickness and its causes and to promote the restoration of health are the tasks of medicine and psychology. Thus it is the illness and not the question of the meaning of life which is the primary concern of the psychotherapist. On the other hand, the philosophical concern is with the question itself, detached from any emotion accompanying its asking.[3] Philosophy attends to the point of such questions, their intelligibility, and the rational scrutiny of answers to them. As Jaspers' comment indicates, to face up to questions about the meaning and value of existence is to take both the questions and life seriously, and to do so is one way to philosophize. Thus, to take questions about life's meaning seriously is to pursue the truth, not about the pathology of the questioner, but about life, its meaningfulness or lack of it. Certainly the need for finding meaning in life is felt intensely by many people. But the intensity of the need for finding meaning in life does not prove that the need can be *satisfied.* Even by proving that meaning in life is indispensable for living happily, one proves merely that meaning in life is a necessary condition for a happy life. One does not thereby establish that the condition is, or even can be, satisfied. The fact, if it is a fact, that we must have meaning in our lives if we are to avoid arrest of life, does not guarantee that we shall not be confronted with the void.

The purpose of this collection of essays is to present philosophical, not psychological, perspectives on the problem of the meaning of life. The philosopher's task is not simply to answer questions about life's meaning. Initially, one must ascertain exactly what is in question. A clearer understanding of the questions will surely aid any attempt to provide answers. Moreover, this will help determine what considerations would be relevant to discerning the truth or falsity of any particular answer.

One way to begin this overall inquiry is to ask why questions about life's meaning arise in the first place. In doing so, the philosopher seeks to identify the reasoning that accompanies such queries. In perusing the essays of Tolstoy, Schopenhauer, and Stace, we encounter one common thread that runs through the diversity of their reflections. Questions about life's meaning tend not to be asked unless one doubts *either* that life is meaningful *or* that one knows what the meaning is. But the point and the doubting run deeper than this. Such doubts arise most often from the suspicion that one's

---

[3]This is not to deny that the philosophical resolution of an issue may bring peace of mind to an individual previously troubled by it. Cf. R. M. Hare, " 'Nothing Matters' " in this volume.

belief in the meaningfulness of life is incompatible with certain factual observations about the conditions of human existence. If this is the case, then we
need to ask: What are the conditions of our existence which are thought to
challenge belief in life's meaningfulness? Is there, in fact, an incompatibility
between acknowledging these conditions and believing in the meaningfulness
of life? Pursuit of these inquiries provides a basis for understanding that which
determines the meaning of life. With this, we begin to see how the matter of
life's meaning is intertwined with other concerns and convictions about the
world and living within it.

The world of literature—autobiographical and fictional—is an especially
rich resource for our effort to understand the context of concern from which
inquiry about life's meaning arises. As an example, let us turn again to the case
of Tolstoy. Perplexity about the meaning of life appears in the novels of
Tolstoy written a decade prior to the period of his own personal disquietude,
as recounted in *My Confession.* The characters Pierre Bezhokov in *War and
Peace* and Constantine Levin in *Anna Karenina* display grave preoccupation
with life's meaning, as each ponders the loss of loved ones or the inevitability
of one's own death. Indeed, Tolstoy's own concern for meaninglessness
appears as a sense of futility derived from his thoughts on the unavoidability of
suffering and the common end of all in death. Here we begin to encounter the
sort of factual observations which are thought to be incompatible with the
conviction that life is meaningful. Confronted with this contest between fact
and belief, Tolstoy realized that the next, and final, consideration was what to
do with his life. Concern about the meaning of life is not only a matter of
interrelating our beliefs and discerning the true from the false. Also at stake is
the tie between our beliefs and our actions. In other words, what consequences does life's meaning or lack of it have for the way life is lived? Tolstoy
considers the possibility that since nothing matters and it is irrational to
pursue our desires, perhaps suicide is the only justifiable act. The character of
these musings and their connection with what it is reasonable to do in life and
to believe about the meaning of life is graphically presented in the excerpt
from *My Confession* reprinted here.

In searching for a way to resolve his bewilderment, Tolstoy recognized that
the exercise of reason follows two courses, one through science, the other
through philosophy. In science he found a closed universe and the quest for
explanatory principles which leave no room for an overriding purpose or a
confirmation of value. In philosophy he encountered echoes and extensions of
the judgment of Solomon in *Ecclesiastes*, "all is emptiness and chasing the
wind." Tolstoy turned in despair to observe the simple, but fundamentally
untroubled, life of the Russian peasant and came upon another option, the
Christianity of the Gospels. The life of faith afforded Tolstoy an end to his
perplexity in that it related the finitude of man to the infinity of God. But, as
he noted, "from faith it followed that, in order to understand life, I must
renounce reason, for which alone meaning was needed." Traversing the

ground of philosophy, science, and religion, he found refuge only in the last.

The experience of Tolstoy is by no means atypical and leads us to inquire: What are the provisions of science and philosophy such that they provoke, rather than resolve, questions about the meaning of life? What can religion offer to end this dilemma, and must the price be the denial of reason? Is the conviction that life is meaningful possible only through religious belief? The selections by Schopenhauer and Stace provide some response to the first of these questions. The other queries are among the central concerns of the essays which follow.

Philosophical perspectives on the human condition are diverse, as the essays themselves reveal. But the strain of thought to which Tolstoy appealed is unmistakably pessimistic. This tradition is best exemplified by the force-ful writings of one of Tolstoy's primary sources, Arthur Schopenhauer. Schopenhauer's writings constitute a devastating critique of the optimism of eighteenth century Enlightenment philosophers. It was the firm belief of the typical Enlightenment philosopher that the world was a rationally coherent whole, and that the exercise of reason would inevitably lead to both moral perfection and the contentment of humanity. Contrasting the Enlightenment ideals of the attainment of human happiness, the inevitability of progress, and the perfectibility of man with his own pessimistic observations on human nature and the circumstances of our existence, Schopenhauer calls into ques-tion the very prerequisites for the belief that life is meaningful.

Much of Schopenhauer's anti-Enlightenment critique focuses upon the spectacle of human wickedness, vanity, and folly. Another equally important aspect of that critique lies in the claim, reminiscent of the teachings of Buddha and the Upanishads, that human relationships and achievements are by their very nature impermanent, transitory. "The vanity of existence is revealed in the whole form existence assumes: . . . in the contingency and relativity of all things; in continual becoming without being; in continual desire without satisfaction; in the continual frustration of striving of which life consists." Schopenhauer here sums up that critique of human existence which pessi-mism makes its point of departure.

Schopenhauer's critique of the human condition attains its most extreme development in nihilism—the conviction that human existence is without meaning, value, or purpose. In "Man Against Darkness," Walter T. Stace finds that the threat of nihilism issues from the perspective of science as well. In this essay, Stace considers first the extent to which the conviction that life is meaningful rests upon religious belief with its guarantees of a divine plan, an unshakeable foundation of morality, and a measure of human freedom. With this he contrasts the attitude of science with its assumption of determinism and its pursuit of causal explanation within the natural order. In a careful examination of the details of these two postures, he weighs the compatibility of theism's promise of meaningfulness with the world portrayed by science.

The Search for Meaning

The selections from Tolstoy, Schopenhauer, and Stace provide somber descriptions of the human condition. These descriptions focus on the constancy of individual and collective endeavor to fulfill goals, to achieve something of value. Such efforts nearly always provoke some measure of struggle and suffering. In the midst of all this, doubts can arise about the prospect of achieving one's goals. We realize that time and death inevitably win out over any undertaking. The world appears neither to sustain our values nor to support our projects.

Although these reflections may originate with attention to one's own life, they eventually encompass the whole order of things. Their weight may lead one to wonder about the point of it all, thereby initiating a personal search for life's meaning. Such quests usually culminate in the seeker's adoption of one of three types of viewpoint: *metaphysical* or *religious* views, which find meaning beyond the bounds of human life; *secular* or *humanistic* views, which insist that meaning is created solely through human activities and goals; and *pessimistic* or *nihilistic* views, which claim that life is without meaning. Since many of the essays included here consider the merits of one or more of these three viewpoints, let us examine each type a bit further.

Metaphysical and religious views, however they may differ, commonly seek to discover life's meaning in something which embraces or transcends all existence. Occasionally, expressions of such views do little more than offer assurance that life is meaningful, while giving no indication of what the meaning is. The eminent Jewish theologian Martin Buber is a case in point. Writing of the individual's encounter with the Deity, he observes that "there is an inexpressible confirmation of meaning. . . . You do not know how to exhibit and define the meaning of life, you have no formula or picture for it, and yet it has more certitude for you than the perceptions of your senses."[4] Occasionally, individuals have certain unique experiences or visions which leave them with an affirmative answer to the question "Does life have meaning?", though what that meaning is remains a mystery. But, if the meaning is not, or cannot be, given, what exactly has one affirmed life *to have* in saying only that it has meaning? Content to rest with the faith found in such experiences, many people, including Buber, offer no further response. However, the British philosopher H. J. Paton, commenting on Buber's view, notes that religion assures the individual that his life "is not something isolated and ineffectual, but is part of one great enterprise . . . part of a wider teleological whole."[5] This comment provides the general view shared by most metaphysi-

---

[4]Martin Buber, *I and Thou* (New York: Scribner's, 1958), pp. 108-112.
[5]H. J. Paton, *The Modern Predicament* (London: George Allen and Unwin, 1955), p. 171.

cal and religious theories of life's meaning. In this context, the differences among metaphysicians and theologians derive largely from alternative accounts of what the "one great enterprise" is and how being a part of "a wider teleological whole" ensures meaning.

Nearly all of us are familiar with at least one typical and prominent version of this sort of view, namely theism. Essentially, theism amounts to the belief in an infinite, personal god who is the creator and sustainer of all things. Such belief has served not only as the foundation of several major religions—Islam, Judaism, and Christianity—but also as the prototype of many metaphysical theories. In stating their version of the great enterprise theory, theists commonly claim that only God can provide a cosmic plan and ensure its fulfillment, only God can sustain good against the threat of evil, and only God can save human life or achievement from annihilation. These are not things which can be achieved through human effort alone; so without divine assistance, human life is meaningless. As you will recall, only the promise of Christian theism gave Tolstoy peace of mind, putting an end to his search for meaning.

Of course, personal acceptance of the theistic view of life's meaning requires that one also adopt certain religious beliefs—that God exists, that He has a plan, and so forth. With this in mind, several questions require our attention. Are the religious beliefs upon which this account of meaning depends true? Is the theistic account of meaning sound? Is it true that without God all possibility of meaning vanishes? Does acceptance of the scientific world view—as opposed to the theistic—provide us with a reason for saying life is meaningless? In his essay "The Meaning of Life," Kurt Baier considers these questions and offers a critique of the theistic position which has implications for other metaphysical or religious views.

In order to comprehend Baier's responses to these questions, it is necessary to understand his distinction—important to many of the later essays in this anthology—between two senses of 'purpose'. In the first sense, to have a purpose is to choose some goal toward which one's efforts and activities are directed. Usually, our lives are filled with many such purposes, though a person's life could conceivably be devoted to a single purpose. In the second sense, to have a purpose is to be made or used as a means toward the achievement of some objective. If the meaningfulness of life is a matter of having a purpose, then distinguishing these senses of 'purpose' shows that there are two ways of understanding the claim that life is meaningful. First, there could be meaning *in* one's life whenever one elects and pursues some purpose. Second, there could be a meaning *of* one's life if the whole of one's life were created or used for some purpose beyond that life itself. If all life were created or used for this same purpose, then this would be the meaning of all life, not only one's own life. It is the latter account of meaning, using the second of the sense of 'purpose,' which Baier discerns to be the basis for the religious view that if life has no purpose it must therefore be meaningless.

Baier's critique of the theistic view, especially the Christian version, falls into two parts. The first concerns God's plan and its relation to humanity, and the second, the connection between an afterlife and this earthly life. In regard to the divine scheme, he questions both its plausibility, given the sort of scientific data previously discussed by Stace, and its morality, considering that the plan reduces man to being merely a means to God's purposes. In addition to considering the credibility of the doctrine of immortality, he asks why an afterlife is thought necessary to give our earthly existence purpose. This leads Baier to question the Christian's tendency to harshly evaluate our earthly existence by comparing it to the promised eternal bliss of an afterlife.

Historically, pessimistic or nihilistic theories tend to result from the loss of confidence in metaphysical or religious views. As we noted, theorists of this sort typically insist that life's meaningfulness depends solely on a great cosmic enterprise which includes human existence. As the German philosopher Nietzsche observed: "The nihilistic question 'for what?' is rooted in the old habit of supposing that the goal must be put up, given, demanded *from outside*—by some *superhuman authority.*"[6] If life's meaning depends on the existence of such a cosmic scheme, or even if we only believe that it does, then a convincing challenge to the claim that such a scheme exists will undermine the conviction that life is meaningful. Indeed, pessimists and nihilists are convinced that life's meaning depends on such a scheme and that no such scheme exists. Given these convictions, their reflections focus on the darker side of human existence, resulting in judgments that life is pointless, meaningless, absurd. Since, in their view, nothing matters, they are inclined to doubt that life is worth living. In practice, suicide is the ultimate conclusion of this line of thought. This disparaging view of life is examined in the selections by Camus, Taylor, Edwards, and Hare.

Taking one's life is considered by Camus in relation to two questions: Does life have meaning? Is life worth living? He assumes that if life is not worth living, then one has good reason for committing suicide. Thus, the main issue becomes: does life have meaning, and if it does not, does this necessarily imply that life is not worth living? Camus cautions that any response to this question must deal squarely with our sense of life's absurdity. Working with this notion, he first portrays the feeling of absurdity and considers the sorts of occasions in which it arises. But since feelings, no matter how intense, are often nebulous, Camus attempts to clarify the idea of the absurd which is occasioned by such feelings. This brings us to the question of whether life is, in fact, absurd. Human beings want and expect to live in a world which confers

---

[6]Friedrich Nietzsche, *The Will to Power* (New York: Random House, 1967), p. 16.

meaning, unity, and value on their lives. But Camus finds no evidence that there is any sort of supreme being or universal scheme which fulfills these expectations and needs. We are left then with a sharp and absurd contrast between what we seek in life and what, in fact, life offers. The suicidal renunciation of life under this condition stems from a failure to realize that we can live in conscious defiance of this absurdity. And Camus claims that acts of defiance create value, even nobility, in our lives, making them worth living.

In Richard Taylor's essay, "Does Life Have a Meaning?," we find a detailed examination of the phenomenon of meaninglessness. Taylor suggests that we look at human existence from various perspectives and in contrast with diverse forms of animal life in order to facilitate the distinction between meaningful and meaningless existence. If we had nothing to do in our lives, then life would be meaningless. If we did the same thing over and over again, but to no purpose, then it would be meaningless. But it is not evident that either of these fates is necessarily ours. There is much that we can do; there are many objectives that we can pursue. But what is the point of our endeavors if they never culminate in anything lasting? Taylor finds this question to be the fundamental source of the meaninglessness that threatens our lives. In pondering the matter, Taylor asks if the threat of the annihilation of our achievements is really so crucial to living meaningful lives. In the end, his answer resembles the advice given by Alyosha to Ivan in Dostoevsky's *The Brothers Karamazov:* ". . . love life above everything in the world. . . . love it, regardless of logic as you say, it must be regardless of logic, and it's only then one will understand the meaning of it."[7]

In the selection by Paul Edwards we find an appraisal of pessimism which parallels Baier's critique of Christian theism. Since pessimists and theists generally agree on the conditions which must be fulfilled if our lives are to be meaningful, many of the objections raised against Christian theism can also be levied against pessimism. The difficulty Edwards finds with both pessimism and theism is the insistence that life is meaningless if it does not contribute to an ultimate cosmic goal which includes individual survival after death. Edwards asks why death and the absence of such an ultimate purpose should be thought to completely nullify the meaning and value of life. He finds the answer in a variety of confusions the pessimist makes about the relevance of the future to judgments concerning the meaning and value of our lives in the present. These confusions especially arise in conjunction with the pessimist's estimation of the significance of death and what it means for something to be worthwhile. Beyond attempting to sort out these muddled ideas, Edwards questions the pessimist's standard by which the value of life is measured. His challenge is similar to Baier's criticism of the standard which Christians use to judge the worth of our earthly existence.

[7]Fyodor Dostoevsky, *The Brothers Karamazov* (Garden City, N.Y.: Literary Guild, 1953), pp. 172-73.

R. M. Hare's " 'Nothing Matters' " was written on the occasion of his encounter with a troubled young friend who, having read Camus' novel *The Stranger,* had become convinced that nothing matters. This conviction can be taken as synonymous with the realization that life is absurd, without meaning—in other words, as an affirmation of the truth of nihilism. In response to this situation, Hare seeks to clarify the notion that nothing matters. He begins by asking what it means to say "nothing matters" and what the world and one's life would be like if it were true that nothing matters. His answers constitute an important alternative to the understanding of the problem of life's meaning as discussed by Camus and Taylor. In Hare's view, the problem is not that the world fails to fulfill expectations which must be upheld if life is to have meaning. Indeed, it is nonsensical to look to the world to discern what matters; instead we must attend to our lives, our choices, and actions to see what matters.

Secular or humanistic views on life's meaning begin, as nihilistic and pessimistic theories do, by rejecting the ideas of a supernatural presence in the universe, an all-encompassing purpose, and immortality. However, according to the humanist these denials do not leave us with a pointless existence, since we can establish meaning in our lives through the goals we choose to pursue and the values we live by.[8] In the conclusion of his essay, Baier espouses this view, drawing upon the first of his two senses of 'purpose'. He notes that we can create meaning *in* our lives by endeavoring to fulfill purposes of our own design. It is true that human beings cannot establish a purpose for their lives which transcends and embraces all existence. But religious and metaphysical views as well as nihilistic and pessimistic theories are mistaken in claiming that the latter is the only sort of purpose which could give life meaning. In rejecting this religious and nihilistic claim, the positions of Camus, Taylor, Edwards, and Hare all point in the direction of some sort of humanism.

In her essay "The Far Side of Despair," Hazel Barnes presents an existentialist version of the humanistic response to the concern about life's meaning. She combines a defense of that version against those who have criticized or misunderstood it with an account of the existentialist critique of both theistic and nihilistic views. She considers the problem of meaningfulness to be primarily a question of the pattern of our lives. Either we live within established patterns or we create our own patterns. Both theistic and nihilistic theories concur that life can have meaning only if the former option holds. In opposition to both theories, the existentialist maintains that the prospect of meaningfulness rests solely with the possibility that we are free to create our own pattern in life, intermeshed with the patterns created by others.

Overall, Barnes' position is similar to Baier's, and she offers an account of

---

[8]For an account of humanism, see "What is Humanism?" by Paul Kurtz in his *Moral Problems in Contemporary Society* (Englewood Cliffs, N.J.: Prentice-Hall, 1969).

how it is possible for life to have meaning despite three obstacles: (1) time blots out whatever we do now through death and destruction; (2) no absolute or eternal measuring stick exists against which we can form and judge our lives; (3) our lives do not contribute or lead to any final goal. Her thoughts parallel an observation made by another existentialist, Simone de Beauvoir: "To declare that existence is absurd is to deny that it can ever be given a meaning; to say that it is ambiguous is to assert that its meaning is never fixed, that it must be constantly won."[9]

The crux of the controversy, then, among theists, pessimists, and humanists involves two questions: What must life be like in order for it to be meaningful? Is life, in fact, like this? Regarding the first question, we have seen that pessimists and theists agree on an answer, while humanists offer a different answer. Concerning the second question, theists affirm that life indeed fulfills the conditions necessary for meaningfulness, whereas pessimists register despair that life fails to fulfill those conditions. Humanists, however, deny both that those conditions are met and that it is desirable that they be met. For, it is claimed, such conditions reduce man to servility and impose upon his life a scheme which he neither chooses nor understands. Indeed, humanists insist that meaning and value can come to our lives only as a result of projects of our own choosing. But in saying this, the humanist opens himself to some important questions: What kinds of projects would make our lives meaningful? Would anything do, or only some things? Are these pursuits available to everyone, or only a few? Does it make a difference what our projects lead to, beyond their own completion?

Analyzing Questions about the Meaning of Life

When the ordinary person is asked the question, "What is the meaning of life?," his reaction may be one of hesitation or suspicion, followed by embarrassed laughter, silence, or a slightly vacant stare. How should we interpret these responses—as indicating that the question cannot be answered? As signifying that there is really no question to be asked? Or are these responses evidence of thoughts too deep and feelings too intense to be put into words? The readings by Hepburn, Nielsen, and Nagel help to answer these questions. These philosophers address problems relating to the analysis of question about the meaning of life.

Our earlier suggestion, that *answering* questions about the meaning of life is one thing, and *analyzing* them quite another, can be used to reinforce the point that if questions about the meaning of life are themselves unclear or

---

[9]Simone de Beauvoir, *The Ethics of Ambiguity* (New York: Philosophical Library, 1948), p. 129.

ambiguous, it will not be obvious how to answer them. A recognition of this fact provides the initial impulse for contemporary analytic inquiry into the meaning of life.

There can be no doubt that many of the key terms and idioms involved in doctrines of the meaning of life are in need of explanation. If, as one might suspect, the vocabulary available to philosophers—or indeed anybody who thinks and speaks about the meaning of life—is not sharply defined and clearly understood, then we need to ask: How shall we understand their claims? What kind of questions are we asking when we ask questions about the meaning of life? How are the ideas of 'meaning,' 'value,' 'purpose,' and 'importance' to be defined and understood? That this understanding consists—at least in large part—of knowing how these terms and concepts are *used,* and how they can continue to be used without incoherence or inconsistency, shows that analysis or conceptual clarification forms an integral part of the task of philosophizing about the meaning of life.

Analyses of questions about the meaning of life fall into three major groups: those which hold that such questions are cognitively meaningful; those which hold that such questions are not meaningful and reject them as worthless or unimportant nonsense; and those which hold that questions about the meaning of life are literally meaningless, but are revealing or important nonsense. Most contemporary analyses of questions about the meaning of life are of the first sort. Before we examine them, let us cite examples of the other two types of analyses.

A succinct expression of the second type is provided by the American philosopher Sidney Hook, who writes, "It would be easy to show, as all students in introductory courses in philosophy can show today, that it is these questions themselves ["Why is there Something, why is there not Nothing?" "Does man's existence or human life have a meaning?"], and the answers to them, that are meaningless."[10]

The third type, which considers questions about the meaning of life to be revealing or important nonsense, is derived from some remarks of the influential philosopher Ludwig Wittgenstein. Wittgenstein described the propositions of philosophy (including those of his own book *Tractatus Logico-Philosophicus*) as nonsensical, thereby distinguishing—at least by implication—between important and unimportant meaninglessness or nonsense. Wittgenstein also suggested that the problems of life are transcendental, that is, they lie outside the limits of intelligible discourse. "The solution of the problem of life," he writes, "is seen in the vanishing of the problem. (Is not this the reason why those who have found after a long period of doubt that the

---

[10] Sidney Hook, *Pragmatism and the Tragic Sense of Life* (New York: Basic Books, 1974), p. 44. Hook observes that if the term "meaning" is equivalent to "purpose," then an individual's life has a meaning if the individual can find some purpose *in* life.

sense of life became clear to them have then been unable to say what constituted that sense?)"[11]

Neither Hook's position nor that of Wittgenstein is widely held today. What has happened to make questions about the meaning of life seem intellectually respectable? It would be simplistic to assign this change to a mere shift in the intellectual climate. An important fact is that fatal criticisms have been leveled against the theories of meaning which made such strictures against questions of the meaning of life possible. In addition, recent philosophical analyses of questions of the meaning of life have made a strong case that these questions are intelligible, that at least they can be *given* a sense and thus do not come to nothing. This latter fact is convincingly illustrated in the selection by Kai Nielsen.

When we turn to those who are willing to try to state what questions of the meaning of life actually mean, we can divide them into two classes: those who seek to detach questions of the meaning of life from religious and metaphysical doctrines and affirmations, and those who do not. As we have already seen, Tolstoy and Schopenhauer furnish examples of the latter type. We shall not consider this type further.

Philosophers who seek to disconnect questions of the meaning of life from religious and metaphysical doctrines and beliefs typically proceed by arguing for the thesis that there is no necessary connection between religious or metaphysical claims and conclusions about the meaning of life. Three observations can be made to illustrate this thesis. First, consider the claim that if there is no God, then human existence can have no purpose and therefore no meaning. Critics such as Baier and Nielsen reject such a claim. They argue that since there can be purposes *in* life, life can have meaning even if there is no purpose *of* life, no purpose for life *as such*, as theism requires.

Second, consider the claim that life can have no meaning if death is complete annihilation. In connection with this claim, Edwards' discussion of Schopenhauer and Tolstoy is instructive. In Schopenhauer we encountered the question of whether life can have meaning if death is inevitable. Similarly, Tolstoy virtually identified questions about immortality with questions about meaning; to doubt claims about immortality is necessarily to doubt claims about life's meaning. The assumptions made by both Tolstoy and Schopenhauer are challenged by Edwards in such a way as to show how the connection between temporal infinity and value, or between finiteness and futility, can be broken.

Third, it might be claimed that one can always ask the questions "Is doing this *really* meaningful?" and "Is this *really* worthwhile?" As Nagel observes, asking such questions can lead to the quest for some larger context or "single controlling life scheme" which would justify *all* of one's aspirations and

---

[11]Ludwig Wittgenstein, *Tractatus Logico-Philosophicus*, trans. D.F. Pears and B. F. Mc-Guinness (London: Routledge and Kegan Paul, 1961), pp. 149-51.

activities. This is one explanation of the religious or metaphysical attempt to provide a self-justifying end or goal outside of life itself.

Nagel offers several replies to this kind of thinking. First, he observes that no such larger context or all-embracing purpose is needed in order to make taking aspirin or attending a concert one enjoys meaningful. He also argues that if an action is not justified unless the reason justifying the action is itself justified, an infinite regress of justifications results, making it impossible to provide reasons for doing anything at all. Nagel suggests that reasons available within life are all that is necessary to make it reasonable to do things.

In addition to the foregoing, there are many other themes found in the analytic essays. Let us turn first to three features of Ronald Hepburn's "Questions about the Meaning of Life." The first concerns his criticism of Antony Flew's paper on "Tolstoy and the Meaning of Life."[12] In this paper, Flew suggests that the question "Is life meaningful?" is not a request for facts. Living a meaningful life does not involve knowing *that* something is the case, but instead knowing *how* to live life "free from all sophisticated psychological disabilities." Hepburn's response to this claim consists, in part, of explaining how 'knowing how' is *related* to 'knowing that' and how each of these connects with questions about how to live.

A second important concern in Hepburn's essay is to argue that questions of the *meaning* of life should not be identified with questions of life's *worth*, though they are related. (You will recall that Camus alludes to this distinction when he asks if life can be worth living even though it is meaningless.) This distinction bears directly on Hepburn's question of whether a man's life could have or fail to have meaning without his *knowing* that it did or did not have meaning. As Hepburn points out, this question can be answered either way. We can answer yes if we equate 'having meaning' with 'contributing to valuable projects,' or we can answer no if 'giving meaning' to life is seen primarily as a task for the one whose life it is.

Third, Hepburn observes that the sense of 'meaning' which is found in questions of the meaning of life bears a close relation to the sense this word has when used in connection with language. For example, the words in a meaningful sentence cohere in a way that the events in a meaningless life do not. Exploring this analogy, Hepburn is led to consider the language of "timelessness" as it applies to the meaning of a sentence and the meaning of life.

The contribution by Kai Nielsen provides a sustained illustration of how philosophers who adopt the linguistic or analytic approach address themselves to, and help to clarify, important questions of human concern. Nielsen's central contention—one which we have met before—is that questions about

---

[12]Antony Flew, "Tolstoy and the Meaning of Life," *Ethics*, 73, 2 (January 1963), 110-18. A slightly revised version of this paper has been published under the title "What Does it Mean to Ask: 'What is the Meaning of Life?' " in Flew's *The Presumption of Atheism* (New York: Harper & Row, 1976).

the meaning of life are essentially questions about how to live. As such, they are not simply requests for facts; rather they call for individual *decision*. As we have noted before, this is a point of some controversy, for it raises the important question whether the meaning of life calls primarily for reflective human decision, or whether—as with theism—the meaning of life requires a *discovery* of some sort.

Nielsen also points out other interpretations of the question "What is the meaning of life?" One may be asking "Is anything worth seeking?" or "Does it matter what we do?" One may be asking a "limiting question" and giving expression to a personal predicament. These questions are clarified by Nielsen, and he suggests possible ways to answer them.

Thomas Nagel attempts to make explicit the sense in which life may be felt to be *absurd*. He offers an analysis of the idea of absurdity (which should be compared with Camus' reflections) and an explanation of various strategies to avoid absurdity. His article is especially illuminating in its examination of arguments in which one typically finds the sense of the absurd—for example, the argument that since nothing that we do now will matter a million years from now, "nothing matters." He notes similarities between the sense of the absurd and epistemological skepticism—fundamental doubt about the possibility of knowledge and justification—and he connects the attempts to escape them. Nagel concludes by asking us to consider whether the absurdity of human existence actually poses a *problem* to which a solution must be found.

We can generalize Nagel's question: Do doubts about the meaning of life constitute a problem which must be solved? Certainly it is too much to say that everybody has doubts about the meaning of life. But it is also no exaggeration to say that among reflective people, posing questions about the meaning of life is a widespread phenomenon. Of course, to say that there is a widespread propensity, at least among reflective persons, to ask questions about the meaning of life is one thing; it is another thing to explain this inclination; and it is yet another thing to try to justify answers to the questions that arise from this tendency. Thus we are brought full circle, for understanding questions about the meaning of life presupposes an understanding of what motivates those questions. In the readings that follow, you shall see how Tolstoy, Schopenhauer, and Stace put forward accounts of the sorts of considerations that result in questions about the meaning of life. These considerations are designed to suggest sources of the tendency to regard human existence or life in general as a problem to be solved. You may then consider the answers that are given by Baier, Camus, Taylor, Edwards, Hare, and Barnes. If it is possible to justify any of their answers, to determine their correctness, you should try to do so by reflecting upon their analyses and arguments, this reflection affording further opportunity for understanding questions of the meaning of life.

I

My Confession

Leo Tolstoy

Although I regarded authorship as a waste of time, I continued to write during those fifteen years. I had tasted of the seduction of authorship, of the seduction of enormous monetary remunerations and applauses for my insignificant labour, and so I submitted to it, as being a means for improving my material condition and for stifling in my soul all questions about the meaning of my life and life in general.

In my writings I advocated, what to me was the only truth, that it was necessary to live in such a way as to derive the greatest comfort for oneself and one's family.

Thus I proceeded to live, but five years ago something very strange began to happen with me: I was overcome by minutes at first of perplexity and then of an arrest of life, as though I did not know how to live or what to do, and I lost myself and was dejected. But that passed, and I continued to live as before. Then those minutes of perplexity were repeated oftener and oftener, and always in one and the same form. These arrests of life found their expression in ever the same questions: "Why? Well, and then?"

At first I thought that those were simply aimless, inappropriate questions. It seemed to me that that was all well known and that if I ever wanted to busy myself with their solution, it would not cost me much labour,—that now I had no time to attend to them, but that if I wanted to I should find the proper answers. But the questions began to repeat themselves oftener and oftener, answers were demanded more and more persistently, and, like dots that fall

From Leo Tolstoy, *My Confession*, trans. Leo Wiener (London: J. M. Dent & Sons, 1905); reprinted by permission of J. M. Dent & Sons Ltd.

on the same spot, these questions, without any answers, thickened into one black blotch.

There happened what happens with any person who falls ill with a mortal internal disease. At first there appear insignificant symptoms of indisposition, to which the patient pays no attention; then these symptoms are repeated more and more frequently and blend into one temporally indivisible suffering. The suffering keeps growing, and before the patient has had time to look around, he becomes conscious that what he took for an indisposition is the most significant thing in the world to him,—is death.

The same happened with me. I understood that it was not a passing indisposition, but something very important, and that, if the questions were going to repeat themselves, it would be necessary to find an answer for them. And I tried to answer them. The questions seemed to be so foolish, simple, and childish. But the moment I touched them and tried to solve them, I became convinced, in the first place, that they were not childish and foolish, but very important and profound questions in life, and, in the second, that, no matter how much I might try, I should not be able to answer them. Before attending to my Samára estate, to my son's education, or to the writing of a book, I ought to know why I should do that. So long as I did not know why, I could not do anything. I could not live. Amidst my thoughts of farming, which interested me very much during that time, there would suddenly pass through my head a question like this: "All right, you are going to have six thousand desyatínas of land in the Government of Samára, and three hundred horses,—and then?" And I completely lost my senses and did not know what to think farther. Or, when I thought of the education of my children, I said to myself: "Why?" Or, reflecting on the manner in which the masses might obtain their welfare, I suddenly said to myself: "What is that to me?" Or, thinking of the fame which my works would get me, I said to myself: "All right, you will be more famous than Gógol, Púshkin, Shakespeare, Molière, and all the writers in the world,—what of it?" And I was absolutely unable to make any reply. The questions were not waiting, and I had to answer them at once; if I did not answer them, I could not live.

I felt that what I was standing on had given way, that I had no foundation to stand on, that that which I lived by no longer existed, and that I had nothing to live by. . . .

All that happened with me when I was on every side surrounded by what is considered to be complete happiness. I had a good, loving, and beloved wife, good children, and a large estate, which grew and increased without any labour on my part. I was respected by my neighbours and friends, more than ever before, was praised by strangers, and, without any self-deception, could consider my name famous. With all that, I was not deranged or mentally unsound,—on the contrary, I was in full command of my mental and physical powers, such as I had rarely met with in people of my age: physically I could work in a field, mowing, without falling behind a peasant; mentally I could work from eight to ten hours in succession, without experiencing any consequences from the strain. And while in such condition I arrived at the conclusion that I could not live, and, fearing death, I had to use cunning against myself, in order that I might not take my life.

This mental condition expressed itself to me in this form: my life is a stupid, mean trick played on me by somebody. Although I did not recognize that "somebody" as having created me, the form of the conception that some one had played a mean, stupid trick on me by bringing me into the world was the most natural one that presented itself to me.

Involuntarily I imagined that there, somewhere, there was somebody who was now having fun as he looked down upon me and saw me, who had lived for thirty or forty years, learning, developing, growing in body and mind, now that I had become strengthened in mind and had reached that summit of life from which it lay all before me, standing as a complete fool on that summit and seeing clearly that there was nothing in life and never would be. And that was fun to him—

But whether there was or was not that somebody who made fun of me, did not make it easier for me. I could not ascribe any sensible meaning to a single act, or to my whole life. I was only surprised that I had not understood that from the start. All that had long ago been known to everybody. Sooner or later there would come diseases and death (they had come already) to my dear ones and to me, and there would be nothing left but stench and worms. All my affairs, no matter what they might be, would sooner or later be forgotten, and I myself should not exist. So why should I worry about all these things? How could a man fail to see that and live,—that was surprising! A person could live only so long as he was drunk; but the moment he sobered up, he could not help seeing that all that was only a deception, and a stupid deception at that! Really, there was nothing funny and ingenious about it, but only something cruel and stupid.

Long ago has been told the Eastern story about the traveller who in the steppe is overtaken by an infuriated beast. Trying to save himself from the animal, the traveller jumps into a waterless well, but at its bottom he sees a dragon who opens his jaws in order to swallow him. And the unfortunate man does not dare climb out, lest he perish from the infuriated beast, and does not dare jump down to the bottom of the well, lest he be devoured by the dragon, and so clutches the twig of a wild bush growing in a cleft of the well and holds on to it. His hands grow weak and he feels that soon he shall have to surrender to the peril which awaits him at either side; but he still holds on and sees two mice, one white, the other black, in even measure making a circle around the main trunk of the bush to which he is clinging, and nibbling at it on all sides.

Now, at any moment, the bush will break and tear off, and he will fall into the dragon's jaws. The traveller sees that and knows that he will inevitably perish; but while he is still clinging, he sees some drops of honey hanging on the leaves of the bush, and so reaches out for them with his tongue and licks the leaves. Just so I hold on to the branch of life, knowing that the dragon of death is waiting inevitably for me, ready to tear me to pieces, and I cannot understand why I have fallen on such suffering. And I try to lick that honey which used to give me pleasure; but now it no longer gives me joy, and the white and the black mouse day and night nibble at the branch to which I am holding on. I clearly see the dragon, and the honey is no longer sweet to me. I see only the inevitable dragon and the mice, and am unable to turn my glance away from them. That is not a fable, but a veritable, indisputable, comprehensible truth.

The former deception of the pleasures of life, which stifled the terror of the dragon, no longer deceives me. No matter how much one should say to me, "You cannot understand the meaning of life, do not think, live!" I am unable to do so, because I have been doing it too long before. Now I cannot help seeing day and night, which run and lead me up to death. I see that alone, because that alone is the truth. Everything else is a lie.

The two drops of honey that have longest turned my eyes away from the cruel truth, the love of family and of authorship, which I have called an art, are no longer sweet to me.

"My family—" I said to myself, "but my family, my wife and children, they are also human beings. They are in precisely the same condition that I am in: they must either live in the lie or see the terrible truth. Why should they live? Why should I love them, why guard, raise, and watch them? Is it for the same despair which is in me, or for dulness of perception? Since I love them, I cannot conceal the truth from them,—every step in cognition leads them up to this truth. And the truth is death."

"Art, poetry?" For a long time, under the influence of the success of human praise, I tried to persuade myself that that was a thing which could be done, even though death should come and destroy everything, my deeds, as well as my memory of them; but soon I came to see that that, too, was a deception. It was clear to me that art was an adornment of life, a decoy of life. But life lost all its attractiveness for me. How, then, could I entrap others? So long as I did not live my own life, and a strange life bore me on its waves; so long as I believed that life had some sense, although I was not able to express it,—the reflections of life of every description in poetry and in the arts afforded me pleasure, and I was delighted to look at life through this little mirror of art; but when I began to look for the meaning of life, when I experienced the necessity of living myself, that little mirror became either useless, superfluous, and ridiculous, or painful to me. I could no longer console myself with what I saw in the mirror, namely, that my situation was stupid and desperate. It was all right for me to rejoice so long as I believed in the depth of my soul that life had some sense. At that time the play of lights—of the comical, the tragical, the touching, the beautiful, the terrible in life—afforded me amusement. But when I knew that life was meaningless and terrible, the play in the little mirror could no longer amuse me. No sweetness of honey could be sweet to me, when I saw the dragon and the mice that were nibbling down my support. . . .

In my search after the question of life I experienced the same feeling which a man who has lost his way in the forest may experience.

He comes to a clearing, climbs a tree, and clearly sees an unlimited space before him; at the same time he sees that there are no houses there, and that there can be none; he goes back to the forest, into the darkness, and he sees darkness, and again there are no houses.

Thus I blundered in this forest of human knowledge, between the clearings of the mathematical and experimental sciences, which disclosed to me clear horizons, but such in the direction of which there could be no house, and between the darkness of the speculative sciences, where I sunk into a deeper darkness, the farther I proceeded, and I convinced myself at last that there was no way out and could not be.

By abandoning myself to the bright side of knowledge I saw that I only turned my eyes away from the question. No matter how enticing and clear the horizons were that were disclosed to me, no matter how enticing it was to bury myself in the infinitude of this knowledge, I comprehended that these sciences were the more clear, the less I needed them, the less they answered my question.

"Well, I know," I said to myself, "all which science wants so persistently to know, but there is no answer to the question about the meaning of my life." But in the speculative sphere I saw that, in spite of the fact that the aim of the knowledge was directed straight to the answer of my question, or because of that fact, there could be no other answer than what I was giving to myself: "What is the meaning of my life?"—"None." Or, "What will come of my life?"—"Nothing." Or, "Why does everything which exists exist, and why do I exist?"—"Because it exists."

Putting the question to the one side of human knowledge, I received an endless quantity of exact answers about what I did not ask: about the chemical composition of the stars, about the movement of the sun toward the constellation of Hercules, about the origin of species and of man, about the forms of infinitely small, imponderable particles of ether; but the answer in this sphere of knowledge to my question what the meaning of my life was, was always: "You are what you call your life; you are a temporal, accidental conglomeration of particles. The interrelation, the change of these particles, produces in you that which you call life. This congeries will last for some time; then the interaction of these particles will cease, and that which you call life and all your questions will come to an end. You are an accidentally cohering globule of something. The globule is fermenting. This fermentation the globule calls its life. The globule falls to pieces, and all fermentation and all questions will come to an end." Thus the clear side of knowledge answers, and it cannot say anything else, if only it strictly follows its principles.

With such an answer it appears that the answer is not a reply to the question. I want to know the meaning of my life, but the fact that it is a particle of the infinite not only gives it no meaning, but even destroys every possible meaning.

Those obscure transactions, which this side of the experimental, exact science has with speculation, when it says that the meaning of life consists in evolution and the coöperation with this evolution, because of their obscurity and inexactness cannot be regarded as answers.

The other side of knowledge, the speculative, so long as it sticks strictly to its fundamental principles in giving a direct answer to the question, everywhere and at all times has answered one and the same: "The world is something infinite and incomprehensible. Human life is an incomprehensible part of this incomprehensible *all*. . . ."

I lived for a long time in this madness, which, not in words, but in deeds, is particularly characteristic of us, the most liberal and learned of men. But, thanks either to my strange, physical love for the real working class, which made me understand it and see that it is not so stupid as we suppose, or to the sincerity of my conviction, which was that I could know nothing and that the best that I could do was to hang myself,—I felt that if I wanted to live and understand the meaning of life, I ought naturally to look for it, not among those who had lost the meaning of life and wanted to kill themselves, but among those billions departed and living men who had been carrying their own lives and ours upon their shoulders. And I looked around at the enormous masses of deceased and living men,—not learned and wealthy, but simple men,—and I saw something quite different. I saw that all these billions of men that lived or had lived, all, with rare exceptions, did not fit into my subdivisions,* and that I could not recognize them as not understanding the question, because they themselves put it and answered it with surprising clearness. Nor could I recognize them as Epicureans, because their lives were composed rather of privations and suffering than of enjoyment. Still less could I recognize them as senselessly living out their meaningless lives, because every act

---

*Tolstoy previously observed that each of his peers assumed one of four attitudes toward life: They lived in ignorance of the problem of life's meaning; ignored the problem and pursued whatever pleasures possible; acknowledged the meaninglessness of life and committed suicide; or, acknowledged the meaninglessness, but lived on aimlessly, usually lacking the fortitude to take their own lives. See Chapter Seven of *My Confession*. [Eds.]

of theirs and death itself was explained by them. They regarded it as the greatest evil to kill themselves. It appeared, then, that all humanity was in possession of a knowledge of the meaning of life, which I did not recognize and which I contemned. It turned out that rational knowledge did not give any meaning to life, excluded life, while the meaning which by billions of people, by all humanity, was ascribed to life was based on some despised, false knowledge.

The rational knowledge in the person of the learned and the wise denied the meaning of life, but the enormous masses of men, all humanity, recognized this meaning in an irrational knowledge. This irrational knowledge was faith, the same that I could not help but reject. That was God as one and three, the creation in six days, devils and angels, and all that which I could not accept so long as I had not lost my senses.

My situation was a terrible one. I knew that I should not find anything on the path of rational knowledge but the negation of life, and there, in faith, nothing but the negation of reason, which was still more impossible than the negation of life. From the rational knowledge it followed that life was an evil and men knew it,—it depended on men whether they should cease living, and yet they lived and continued to live, and I myself lived, though I had known long ago that life was meaningless and an evil. From faith it followed that, in order to understand life, I must renounce reason, for which alone a meaning was needed.

There resulted a contradiction, from which there were two ways out: either what I called rational was not so rational as I had thought; or that which to me appeared irrational was not so irrational as I had thought. And I began to verify the train of thoughts of my rational knowledge.

In verifying the train of thoughts of my rational knowledge, I found that it was quite correct. The deduction that life was nothing was inevitable; but I saw a mistake. The mistake was that I had not reasoned in conformity with the question put by me. The question was, "Why should I live?" that is, "What real, indestructible essence will come from my phantasmal, destructible life? What meaning has my finite existence in this infinite world?" And in order to answer this question, I studied life.

The solutions of all possible questions of life apparently could not satisfy me, because my question, no matter how simple it appeared in the beginning, included the necessity of explaining the finite through the infinite, and vice versa.

I asked, "What is the extra-temporal, extra-causal, extra-spatial meaning of life?" But I gave an answer to the question, "What is the temporal, causal, spatial meaning of my life?" The result was that after a long labour of mind I answered, "None."

In my reflections I constantly equated, nor could I do otherwise, the finite with the finite, the infinite with the infinite, and so from that resulted precisely what had to result: force was force, matter was matter, will was will, infinity was infinity, nothing was nothing,—and nothing else could come from it.

There happened something like what at times takes place in mathematics: you think you are solving an equation, when you have only an identity. The reasoning is correct, but you receive as a result the answer: $a = a$, or $x = x$, or $0 = 0$. The same happened with my reflection in respect to the question about the meaning of my life. The answers given by all science to that question are only identities.

Indeed, the strictly scientific knowledge, that knowledge which, as Descartes did, begins with a full doubt in everything, rejects all knowledge which has been taken on trust, and builds everything anew on the laws of reason and experience, cannot give any other answer to the question of life than what I received,—an indefinite answer. It only seemed to me at first that science gave me a positive answer,—Schopenhauer's answer: "Life has no meaning, it is an evil." But when I analyzed the matter, I saw that the answer was not a positive one, but that it was only my feeling which expressed it as such. The answer, strictly expressed, as it is expressed by the Brahmins, by Solomon, and by Schopenhauer, is only an indefinite answer, or an identity, $0 = 0$, life is nothing. Thus the philosophical knowledge does not negate anything, but only answers that the question cannot be solved by it, that for philosophy the solution remains insoluble.

When I saw that, I understood that it was not right for me to look for an answer to my question in rational knowledge, and that the answer given by rational knowledge was only an indication that the answer might be got if the question were differently put, but only when into the discussion of the question should be introduced the question of the relation of the finite to the infinite. I also understood that, no matter how irrational and monstrous the answers might be that faith gave, they had this advantage that they introduced into each answer the relation of the finite to the infinite, without which there could be no answer.

No matter how I may put the question, "How must I live?" the answer is, "According to God's law." "What real result will there be from my life?"— "Eternal torment or eternal bliss." "What is the meaning which is not destroyed by death?"—"The union with infinite God, paradise."

Thus, outside the rational knowledge, which had to me appeared as the only one, I was inevitably led to recognize that all living humanity had a certain other irrational knowledge, faith, which made it possible to live.

All the irrationality of faith remained the same for me, but I could not help recognizing that it alone gave to humanity answers to the questions of life, and, in consequence of them, the possibility of living.

The rational knowledge brought me to the recognition that life was meaningless,—my life stopped, and I wanted to destroy myself. When I looked around at people, at all humanity, I saw that people lived and asserted that they knew the meaning of life. I looked back at myself: I lived so long as I knew the meaning of life. As to other people, so even to me, did faith give the meaning of life and the possibility of living.

Looking again at the people of other countries, contemporaries of mine and those passed away, I saw again the same. Where life had been, there faith, ever since humanity had existed, had given the possibility of living, and the chief features of faith were everywhere one and the same.

No matter what answers faith may give, its every answer gives to the finite existence of man the sense of the infinite,—a sense which is not destroyed by suffering, privation, and death. Consequently in faith alone could we find the meaning and possibility of life. What, then, was faith? I understood that faith was not merely an evidence of things not seen, and so forth, not revelation (that is only the description of one of the symptoms of faith), not the relation of man to man (faith has to be defined, and then God, and not first God, and faith through him), not merely an agreement with what a man was told, as faith was generally understood,—that faith was the knowledge of the meaning of human life, in consequence of which man did not destroy himself, but lived. Faith is the power of life. If a man lives he believes in something. If he did not believe that he ought to live for some purpose, he would not live. If he does not see and understand the phantasm of the finite, he believes in that finite; if he understands the phantasm of the finite, he must believe in the infinite. Without faith one cannot live. . . .

In order that all humanity may be able to live, in order that they may continue living, giving a meaning to life, they, those billions, must have another, a real knowledge of faith, for not the fact that I, with Solomon and Schopenhauer, did not kill myself convinced me of the existence of faith, but that these billions had lived and had borne us, me and Solomon, on the waves of life.

Then I began to cultivate the acquaintance of the believers from among the poor, the simple and unlettered folk, of pilgrims, monks, dissenters, peasants. The doctrine of these people from among the masses was also the Christian doctrine that the quasi-believers of our circle professed. With the Christian truths were also mixed in very many superstitions, but there was this difference: the superstitions of our circle were quite unnecessary to them, had no connection with their lives, were only a kind of an Epicurean amusement, while the superstitions of the believers from among the labouring classes were to such an extent blended with their life that it would have been impossible to imagine it without these superstitions,—it was a necessary condition of that life. I began to examine closely the lives and beliefs of these people, and the more I examined them, the more did I become convinced that they had the real faith, that their faith was necessary for them, and that it alone gave them a meaning and possibility of life. In contradistinction to what I saw in our circle, where life without faith was possible, and where hardly one in a thousand professed to be a believer, among them there was hardly one in a thousand who was not a believer. In contradistinction to what I saw in our circle, where all life passed in idleness, amusements, and tedium of life, I saw that the whole life of these people was passed in hard work, and that they were satisfied with life. In contradistinction to the people of our circle, who struggled and murmured against fate because of their privations and their suffering, these people accepted diseases and sorrows without any perplexity or opposition, but with the calm and firm conviction that it was all for good. In contradistinction to the fact that the more intelligent we are, the less do we understand the meaning of life and the more do we see a kind of a bad joke in our suffering and death, these people live, suffer, and approach death, and suffer in peace and more often in joy. In contradistinction to the fact that a calm death, a death without terror or despair, is the greatest exception in our circle, a restless, insubmissive, joyless death is one of the greatest exceptions among the masses. And of such people, who are deprived of everything which for Solomon and for me constitutes the only good of life, and who withal experience the greatest happiness, there is an enormous number. I cast a broader glance about me. I examined the life of past and present vast masses of men, and I saw people who in like manner had understood the meaning of life, who had known how to live and die, not two, not three, not ten, but hundreds, thousands, millions. All of them, infinitely diversified as to habits, intellect, culture, situation, all equally and quite contrary to my ignorance knew the meaning of life and of death, worked calmly, bore privations and suffering, lived and died, seeing in that not vanity, but good.

I began to love those people. The more I penetrated into their life, the life of the men now living, and the life of men departed, of whom I had read and heard, the more did I love them, and the easier it became for me to live. Thus I lived for about two years, and within me took place a transformation, which had long been working within me, and the germ of which had always been in me. What happened with me was that the life of our circle,—of the rich and the learned,—not only disgusted me, but even lost all its meaning. All our acts, reflections, sciences, arts,—all that appeared to me in a new light. I saw that all that was mere pampering of the appetites, and that no meaning could be found in it; but the life of all the working masses, of all humanity, which created life, presented itself to me in its real significance. I saw that that was life itself and that the meaning given to this life was truth, and I accepted it.

II

On the Suffering of the World

Arthur Schopenhauer

1

If the immediate and direct purpose of our life is not suffering then our existence is the most ill-adapted to its purpose in the world: for it is absurd to suppose that the endless affliction of which the world is everywhere full, and which arises out of the need and distress pertaining essentially to life, should be purposeless and purely accidental. Each individual misfortune, to be sure, seems an exceptional occurrence; but misfortune in general is the rule.

2

Just as a stream flows smoothly on as long as it encounters no obstruction, so the nature of man and animal is such that we never really notice or become conscious of what is agreeable to our will; if we are to notice something, our will has to have been thwarted, has to have experienced a shock of some kind. On the other hand, all that opposes, frustrates and resists our will, that is to say all that is unpleasant and painful, impresses itself upon us instantly, directly and with great clarity. Just as we are conscious not of the healthiness of our whole body but only of the little place where the shoe pinches, so we think not of the totality of our successful activities but of some insignificant trifle or other which continues to vex us. On this fact is founded what I have often before drawn attention to: the negativity of well-being and happiness, in antithesis to the positivity of pain.

I therefore know of no greater absurdity than that absurdity which characterizes almost all metaphysical systems: that of explaining evil as something negative. For evil is precisely that which is positive, that which makes itself palpable; and good, on the other hand, i.e. all happiness and all gratification, is that which is negative, the mere abolition of a desire and extinction of a pain.

This is also consistent with the fact that as a rule we find pleasure much less pleasurable, pain much more painful than we expected.

A quick test of the assertion that enjoyment outweighs pain in this world, or that they are at any rate balanced, would be to compare the feelings of an animal engaged in eating another with those of the animal being eaten.

3

The most effective consolation in every misfortune and every affliction is to observe others who are more unfortunate than we: and everyone can do this. But what does that say for the condition of the whole?

History shows us the life of nations and finds nothing to narrate but wars and tumults; the peaceful years appear only as occasional brief pauses and interludes. In just the same way the life of the individual is a constant struggle, and not merely a metaphorical one against want or boredom, but also an actual struggle against other people. He discovers adversaries everywhere, lives in continual conflict and dies with sword in hand.

4

Not the least of the torments which plague our existence is the constant pressure of *time*, which never lets us so much as draw breath but pursues us all like a taskmaster with a whip. It ceases to persecute only him it has delivered over to boredom.

5

And yet, just as our body would burst asunder if the pressure of the atmosphere were removed from it, so would the arrogance of men expand, if not to the point of bursting then to that of the most unbridled folly, indeed madness, if the pressure of want, toil, calamity and frustration were removed from their life. One can even say that we *require* at all times a certain quantity of care or sorrow or want, as a ship requires ballast, in order to keep on a straight course.

Work, worry, toil and trouble are indeed the lot of almost all men their whole life long. And yet if every desire were satisfied as soon as it arose how would men occupy their lives, how would they pass the time? Imagine this race transported to a Utopia where everything grows of its own accord and turkeys fly around ready-roasted, where lovers find one another without any delay and keep one another without any difficulty: in such a place some men would die of boredom or hang themselves, some would fight and kill one another, and thus they would create for themselves more suffering than nature inflicts on them as it is. Thus for a race such as this no stage, no form of existence is suitable other than the one it already possesses.

6

Since, as we recalled above, pleasure and well-being is negative and suffering positive, the happiness of a given life is not to be measured according to the joys and pleasures it contains but according to the absence of the positive element, the absence of suffering. This being so, however, the lot of the animals appears more endurable than that of man. Let us look at both a little more closely.

However varied the forms may be which human happiness and misery assume, inciting man to seek the one and flee from the other, the material basis of them all is physical pleasure or physical pain. This basis is very narrow: it consists of health, food, protection from wet and cold, and sexual gratification; or the lack of these things. Man has, consequently, no larger share of real physical pleasure than the animals have, except perhaps to the extent that his more highly charged nervous system intensifies every sensation of pleasure —as it also does every sensation of pain. Yet how much stronger are the emotions aroused in him than those aroused in the animals! how incomparably more profound and vehement are his passions!—and all to achieve exactly the same result in the end: health, food, covering, etc.

This arises first and foremost because with him everything is powerfully intensified by thinking about absent and future things, and this is in fact the origin of care, fear and hope, which, once they have been aroused, make a far stronger impression on men than do actual present pleasures or sufferings, to which the animal is limited. For, since it lacks the faculty of reflection, joys and sorrows cannot accumulate in the animal as they do in man through memory and anticipation. With the animal, present suffering, even if repeated countless times, remains what it was the first time: it cannot sum itself up. Hence the enviable composure and unconcern which characterizes the animal. With man, on the other hand, there evolves out of those elements of pleasure and suffering which he has in common with the animal an intensification of his sensations of happiness and misery which can lead to momentary transports which may sometimes even prove fatal, or to suicidal despair. More closely considered, what happens is this: he deliberately intensifies his needs, which are originally scarcely harder to satisfy than those of the animal, so as to intensify his pleasure: hence luxury, confectionery, tobacco, opium, alcoholic drinks, finery and all that pertains to them. To these is then added, also as a result of reflection, a source of pleasure, and consequently of suffering, available to him alone and one which preoccupies him beyond all measure, indeed more than all the rest put together: ambition and the sense of honour and shame—in plain words, what he thinks others think of him. This, in a thousand, often curious shapes then becomes the goal of all those endeavours of his which go beyond physical pleasure or pain. He excels the animal in his capacity for enjoying intellectual pleasures, to be sure, and these are available to him in many degrees, from the simplest jesting and conversation up to the highest achievements of the mind; but as a counterweight to this, on the side of suffering stands boredom, which is unknown to the animals at least in the state of nature and is only very slightly perceptible in the very cleverest domesticated ones, while to man it has become a veritable scourge. Want and boredom are indeed the twin poles of human life. Finally it remains to be mentioned that with man sexual gratification is tied to a very obstinate selectivity which is sometimes intensified into a more or less passionate love. Thus sexuality becomes for man a source of brief pleasure and protracted suffering.

It is indeed remarkable how, through the mere addition of thought, which the animal lacks, there should have been erected on the same narrow basis of pain and pleasure that the animal possesses so vast and lofty a structure of human happiness and misery, and man should be subjected to such vehement emotions, passions and convulsions that their impress can be read in enduring lines on his face; while all the time and in reality he is concerned only with the very same things which the animal too attains, and attains with an incomparably smaller expenditure of emotion. Through all this, however, the measure of suffering increases in man far more than the enjoyment, and it is very greatly enhanced specifically by the fact that he actually *knows* of death, while the animal only instinctively flees it without actually knowing of it and therefore without ever really having it in view, which man does all the time.

The animals are much more content with mere existence than we are; the plants are wholly so; and man is so according to how dull and insensitive he is.

The animal's life consequently contains less suffering but also less pleasure than the human's, the direct reason being that on the one hand it is free from care and anxiety and the torments that attend them, but on the other is without hope and therefore has no share in that anticipation of a happy future which, together with the enchanting products of the imagination which accompany it, is the source of most of our greatest joys and pleasures. The animal lacks both anxiety and hope because its consciousness is restricted to what is clearly evident and thus to the present moment: the animal is the present incarnate. But precisely because this is so it appears in one respect to be truly sagacious compared with us, namely in its peaceful, untroubled enjoyment of the present: its obvious composure often puts to shame our own frequently restless and discontented condition.

7

If the above discussion has demonstrated that the reason man's life is more full of suffering than the animal's is his greater capacity for knowledge, we can now trace this back to a more general law and thus attain to a much more comprehensive view.

Knowledge is in itself always painless. Pain affects only the will and consists in an obstruction, impediment or frustration of it: nonetheless, this frustration of the will, if it is to be felt as pain, must be accompanied by knowledge. That is why even physical pain is conditioned by the nerves and their connexion with the brain, so that an injury to a limb is not felt if the nerves leading from the limb to the brain are severed or the brain itself is devitalized by chloroform. That spiritual pain is conditional upon knowledge goes without saying, and it is easy to see that it will increase with the degree of knowledge. We can thus express the whole relationship figuratively by saying that the will is the string, its frustration or impediment the vibration of the string, knowledge the sounding-board, and pain the sound.

Now this means that not only inorganic matter but the plant too is incapable of feeling pain, however many frustrations its will may undergo. On the other hand, every animal, even an *infusorium*, suffers pain, because knowledge, however imperfect, is the true characteristic of animality. At each higher stage of animal life there is a corresponding increase in pain. In the lowest animals it is extremely slight, but even in the highest it nowhere approaches the pain which man is capable of feeling, since even the highest animals lack thought and concepts. And it is right that this capacity for pain should reach its zenith only where, by virtue of the existence of reason, there also exists the possibility of denial of the will: for otherwise it would be nothing but aimless cruelty.

8

In our early youth we sit before the life that lies ahead of us like children sitting before the curtain in a theatre, in happy and tense anticipation of whatever is going to appear. Luckily we do not know what really will appear. For to him who does know, children can sometimes seem like innocent delinquents, sentenced not to death but to life, who have not yet discovered what their punishment will consist of. Nonetheless, everyone desires to achieve old age, that is to say a condition in which one can say: 'Today it is bad, and day by day it will get worse—until at last the worst of all arrives.'

9

If you imagine, in so far as it is approximately possible, the sum total of distress, pain and suffering of every kind which the sun shines upon in its course, you will have to admit it would have been much better if the sun had been able to call up the phenomenon of life as little on the earth as on the moon; and if, here as there, the surface were still in a crystalline condition.

You can also look upon our life as an episode unprofitably disturbing the blessed calm of nothingness. In any case, even he who has found life tolerably bearable will, the longer he lives, feel the more clearly that on the whole it is a disappointment, nay a cheat.[1] If two men who were friends in youth meet in old age after the lapse of an entire generation, the principal feeling the sight of one another, linked as it is with recollections of earlier years, will arouse in both will be one of total disappointment with the whole of life, which once lay so fair before them in the rosy dawn of youth, promised so much and performed so little. This feeling will dominate so decidedly over every other that they will not even think it necessary to speak of it but will silently assume it as the basis of their conversation.

If the act of procreation were neither the outcome of a desire nor accompanied by feelings of pleasure, but a matter to be decided on the basis of purely rational considerations, is it likely the human race would still exist? Would each of us not rather have felt so much pity for the coming generation as to prefer to spare it the burden of existence, or at least not wish to take it upon himself to impose that burden upon it in cold blood?

For the world is Hell, and men are on the one hand the tormented souls and on the other the devils in it.

Brahma is supposed to have created the world by a kind of fall into sin, or by an error, and has to atone for this sin or error by remaining in it himself until

---

[1] The last four words are in English in the original.

he has redeemed himself out of it. Very good! In *Buddhism* the world arises as a consequence of an inexplicable clouding of the heavenly clarity of the blessed state of Nirvana after a long period of quietude. Its origin is thus a kind of fatality which is fundamentally to be understood in a moral sense, notwithstanding the case has an exact analogy in the physical world in the origin of the sun in an inexplicable primeval streak of mist. Subsequently, however, as a consequence of moral misdeeds it gradually deteriorates physically too, until it has assumed its present sad condition. Excellent! To the *Greeks* the world and the gods were the work of an unfathomable necessity: that will do as a provisional explanation. *Ormuzd* is continually at war with *Ahriman:* that is worth considering.[2] But that a god like *Jehovah* should create this world of want and misery *animi causa*[3] and *de gaieté de coeur* and then go so far as to applaud himself for it, saying it is all very good: that is quite unacceptable.

In general, however, two things cry out against any such view of the world as the successful work of an infinitely wise, infinitely good and at the same time infinitely powerful being: the misery of which it is full and the obvious imperfection of its most highly developed phenomenon, man, who is indeed a grotesque caricature. This is a dissonance that cannot be resolved. On the contrary, it is precisely these instances which support what we have been saying and which provide evidence for our conception of the world as the product of our own sins and therefore as something that had better not have been. Under the former conception they become a bitter indictment of the Creator and supply material for cynicisms, while under our conception they appear as an indictment of our own nature and will, and one calculated to teach us humility. For they lead us to the insight that, like the children of libertine fathers, we come into the world already encumbered with guilt and that it is only because we have continually to atone for this guilt that our existence is so wretched and its end is death. Nothing is more certain than that, generally speaking, it is the grievous *sin of the world* which gives rise to the manifold and great *suffering of the world;* whereby is meant not any physical-empirical connexion but a metaphysical one. The story of the Fall is consequently the only thing which reconciles me to the Old Testament; I even regard it as the sole metaphysical truth contained in that book, even though it does appear clothed in allegory. For our existence resembles nothing so much as the consequence of a misdeed, punishment for a forbidden desire.

As a reliable compass for orientating yourself in life nothing is more useful than to accustom yourself to regarding this world as a place of atonement, a sort of penal colony. When you have done this you will order your expectations of life according to the nature of things and no longer regard the calamities, sufferings, torments and miseries of life as something irregular and

[2]Brahma is the principal deity of Hinduism. Ormuzd is the good God, Ahriman the bad God of Zoroastrianism, the ancient religion of Persia.
[3]Capriciously, voluntarily.

not to be expected but will find them entirely in order, well knowing that each of us is here being punished for his existence and each in his own particular way. This outlook will enable us to view the so-called imperfections of the majority of men, i.e. their moral and intellectual shortcomings and the facial appearance resulting therefrom, without surprise and certainly without indignation: for we shall always bear in mind where we are and consequently regard every man first and foremost as a being who exists only as a consequence of his culpability and whose life is an expiation of the crime of being born.

The conviction that the world, and therefore man too, is something which really ought not to exist is in fact calculated to instil in us indulgence towards one another: for what can be expected of beings placed in such a situation as we are? From this point of view one might indeed consider that the appropriate form of address between man and man ought to be, not *monsieur, sir,* but *fellow sufferer, compagnon de misères.* However strange this may sound it corresponds to the nature of the case, makes us see other men in a true light and reminds us of what are the most necessary of all things: tolerance, patience, forbearance and charity, which each of us needs and which each of us therefore owes.

On the Vanity of Existence

Arthur Schopenhauer

1

The vanity of existence is revealed in the whole form existence assumes: in the infiniteness of time and space contrasted with the finiteness of the individual in both; in the fleeting present as the sole form in which actuality exists; in the contingency and relativity of all things; in continual becoming without being; in continual desire without satisfaction; in the continual frustration of striving of which life consists. *Time* and that *perishability* of all things existing in time that time itself brings about is simply the form under which the will to live, which as thing in itself is imperishable, reveals to itself the vanity of its striving. Time is that by virtue of which everything becomes nothingness in our hands and loses all real value.

2

That which *has been* no longer *is;* it as little exists as does that which has *never* been. But everything that *is* in the next moment *has been.* Thus the most insignificant present has over the most significant past the advantage of *actuality,* which means that the former bears to the latter the relation of something to nothing.

To our amazement we suddenly exist, after having for countless millennia not existed; in a short while we will again not exist, also for countless millennia. That cannot be right, says the heart: and even upon the crudest intelligence there must, when it considers such an idea, dawn a presentiment of the ideality of time. This however, together with that of space, is the key to all true metaphysics, because it makes room for a quite different order of things than that of nature. That is why Kant is so great.

Every moment of our life belongs to the present only for a moment; then it belongs for ever to the past. Every evening we are poorer by a day. We would perhaps grow frantic at the sight of this ebbing away of our short span of time were we not secretly conscious in the profoundest depths of our being that we share in the inexhaustible well of eternity, out of which we can for ever draw new life and renewed time.

You could, to be sure, base on considerations of this kind a theory that the greatest *wisdom* consists in enjoying the present and making this enjoyment the goal of life, because the present is all that is real and everything else merely imaginary. But you could just as well call this mode of life the greatest *folly:* for that which in a moment ceases to exist, which vanishes as completely as a dream, cannot be worth any serious effort.

3

Our existence has no foundation on which to rest except the transient present. Thus its form is essentially unceasing *motion,* without any possibility of that repose which we continually strive after. It resembles the course of a man running down a mountain who would fall over if he tried to stop and can stay on his feet only by running on; or a pole balanced on the tip of the finger; or a planet which would fall into its sun if it ever ceased to plunge irresistibly forward. Thus existence is typified by unrest.

In such a world, where no stability of any kind, no enduring state is possible, where everything is involved in restless change and confusion and keeps itself on its tightrope only by continually striding forward—in such a world, happiness is not so much as to be thought of. It cannot dwell where nothing occurs but Plato's 'continual becoming and never being'. In the first place, no man is happy but strives his whole life long after a supposed happiness which he seldom attains, and even if he does it is only to be disappointed with it; as a rule, however, he finally enters harbour shipwrecked and dismasted. In the second place, however, it is all one whether he has been happy or not in a life which has consisted merely of a succession of transient present moments and is now at an end.

4

The scenes of our life resemble pictures in rough mosaic; they are ineffective from close up, and have to be viewed from a distance if they are to seem beautiful. That is why to attain something desired is to discover how vain it is; and why, though we live all our lives in expectation of better things, we often at the same time long regretfully for what is past. The present, on the other hand, is regarded as something quite temporary and serving only as the road to our goal. That is why most men discover when they look back on their life that they have the whole time been living *ad interim,* and are surprised to see that which they let go by so unregarded and unenjoyed was precisely their life, was precisely that in expectation of which they lived.

5

Life presents itself first and foremost as a task: the task of maintaining itself, *de gagner sa vie.* If this task is accomplished, what has been gained is a burden, and there then appears a second task: that of doing something with it so as to ward off boredom, which hovers over every secure life like a bird of prey. Thus the first task is to gain something and the second to become unconscious of what has been gained, which is otherwise a burden.

That human life must be some kind of mistake is sufficiently proved by the simple observation that man is a compound of needs which are hard to satisfy; that their satisfaction achieves nothing but a painless condition in which he is only given over to boredom; and that boredom is a direct proof that existence is in itself valueless, for boredom is nothing other than the sensation of the emptiness of existence. For if life, in the desire for which our essence and existence consists, possessed in itself a positive value and real content, there would be no such thing as boredom: mere existence would fulfil and satisfy us. As things are, we take no pleasure in existence except when we are striving after something—in which case distance and difficulties make our goal look as if it would satisfy us (an illusion which fades when we reach it)—or when engaged in purely intellectual activity, in which case we are really stepping out of life so as to regard it from outside, like spectators at a play. Even sensual pleasure itself consists in a continual striving and ceases as soon as its goal is reached. Whenever we are not involved in one or other of these things but directed back to existence itself we are overtaken by its worthlessness and vanity and this is the sensation called boredom.

6

That the most perfect manifestation of the will to live represented by the human organism, with its incomparably ingenious and complicated machinery, must crumble to dust and its whole essence and all its striving be palpably given over at last to annihilation—this is nature's unambiguous declaration that all the striving of this will is essentially vain. If it were something possessing value in itself, something which ought unconditionally to exist, it would not have non-being as its goal.

Yet what a difference there is between our beginning and our end! We begin in the madness of carnal desire and the transport of voluptuousness, we end in the dissolution of all our parts and the musty stench of corpses. And the road from the one to the other too goes, in regard to our well-being and enjoyment of life, steadily downhill: happily dreaming childhood, exultant youth, toil-filled years of manhood, infirm and often wretched old age, the torment of the last illness and finally the throes of death—does it not look as if existence were an error the consequences of which gradually grow more and more manifest?

We shall do best to think of life as a *desengaño*, as a process of disillusionment: since this is, clearly enough, what everything that happens to us is calculated to produce.

III

Man Against Darkness

Walter T. Stace

The Catholic bishops of America once issued a statement in which they said that the chaotic and bewildered state of the modern world is due to man's loss of faith, his abandonment of God and religion. I agree with this statement though I do not accept the religious beliefs of most bishops. It is no doubt an oversimplification to speak of *the* cause of so complex a state of affairs as the tortured condition of the world today. Its causes are doubtless multitudinous. Yet allowing for some element of oversimplification, I say that the bishops' assertion is substantially true.

M. Jean-Paul Sartre, the French existentialist philosopher, labels himself an atheist. Yet his views seem to me plainly to support the statement of the bishops. So long as there was believed to be a God in the sky, he says, men could regard him as the source of their moral ideals. The universe, created and governed by a fatherly God, was a friendly habitation for man. We could be sure that, however great the evil in the world, good in the end would triumph and the forces of evil would be routed. With the disappearance of God from the sky all this has changed. Since the world is not ruled by a spiritual being, but rather by blind forces, there cannot be any ideals, moral or otherwise, in the universe outside us. Our ideals, therefore, must proceed only from our own minds; they are our own inventions. Thus the world which surrounds us is nothing but an immense spiritual emptiness. It is a dead universe. We do not live in a universe which is on the side of our values. It is completely indifferent to them.

Years ago Mr. Bertrand Russell, in his essay "A Free Man's Worship," said much the same thing.

> Such in outline, but even more purposeless, more void of meaning, is the world which Science presents for our belief. Amid such a world, if anywhere, our ideals henceforward must find a home. . . . Blind to good and evil, reckless of destruction, omnipotent matter rolls on its relentless way; for man, condemned today to lose his dearest, tomorrow himself to pass through the gate of darkness, it remains only to cherish, ere yet the blow falls, the lofty thoughts that ennoble his little day; . . . to worship at the shrine his own hands have built; . . . to sustain alone, a weary but unyielding Atlas, the world that his own ideals have fashioned despite the trampling march of unconscious power.

It is true that Mr. Russell's personal attitude to the disappearance of religion is quite different from either that of M. Sartre or the bishops or myself. The bishops think it a calamity. So do I. M. Sartre finds it "very distressing." And he berates as shallow the attitude of those who think that without God the world can go on just the same as before, as if nothing had happened. This creates for mankind, he thinks, a terrible crisis. And in this I agree with him. Mr. Russell, on the other hand, seems to believe that religion has done more harm than good in the world, and that its disappearance will be a blessing. But his picture of the world, and of the modern mind, is the same as that of M. Sartre. He stresses the *purposelessness* of the universe, the facts that man's ideals are his own creations, that the universe outside him in no way supports them, that man is alone and friendless in the world.

Mr. Russell notes that it is science which has produced this situation. There is no doubt that this is correct. But the way in which it has come about is not generally understood. There is a popular belief that some particular scientific discoveries or theories, such as the Darwinian theory of evolution, or the views of geologists about the age of the earth, or a series of such discoveries, have done the damage. It would be foolish to deny that these discoveries have had a great effect in undermining religious dogmas. But this account does not at all go to the root of the matter. Religion can probably outlive any scientific discoveries which could be made. It can accommodate itself to them. The root cause of the decay of faith has not been any particular discovery of science, but rather the general spirit of science and certain basic assumptions upon which modern science, from the seventeenth century onwards, has proceeded.

It was Galileo and Newton—notwithstanding that Newton himself was a deeply religious man—who destroyed the old comfortable picture of a friendly universe governed by spiritual values. And this was effected, not by Newton's discovery of the law of gravitation nor by any of Galileo's brilliant investigations, but by the general picture of the world which these men and others of their time made the basis of the science, not only of their own day,

but of all succeeding generations down to the present. That is why the century immediately following Newton, the eighteenth century, was notoriously an age of religious skepticism. Skepticism did not have to wait for the discoveries of Darwin and the geologists in the nineteenth century. It flooded the world immediately after the age of the rise of science. Neither the Copernican hypothesis nor any of Newton's or Galileo's particular discoveries were the real causes. Religious faith might well have accommodated itself to the new astronomy. The real turning point between the medieval age of faith and the modern age of unfaith came when the scientists of the seventeenth century turned their backs upon what used to be called "final causes." The final cause of a thing or event meant the purpose which it was supposed to serve in the universe, its cosmic purpose. What lay back of this was the presupposition that there is a cosmic order or plan and that everything which exists could in the last analysis be explained in terms of its place in this cosmic plan, that is, in terms of its purpose.

Plato and Aristotle believed this, and so did the whole medieval Christian world. For instance, if it were true that the sun and the moon were created and exist for the purpose of giving light to man, then this fact would explain why the sun and the moon exist. We might not be able to discover the purpose of everything, but everything must have a purpose. Belief in final causes thus amounted to a belief that the world is governed by purposes, presumably the purposes of some overruling mind. This belief was not the invention of Christianity. It was basic to the whole of Western civilization, whether in the ancient pagan world or in Christendom, from the time of Socrates to the rise of science in the seventeenth century.

The founders of modern science—for instance, Galileo, Kepler, and Newton—were mostly pious men who did not doubt God's purposes. Nevertheless they took the revolutionary step of consciously and deliberately expelling the idea of purpose as controlling nature from their new science of nature. They did this on the ground that inquiry into purposes is useless for what science aims at: namely, the prediction and control of events. To predict an eclipse, what you have to know is not its purpose but its causes. Hence science from the seventeenth century onwards became exclusively an inquiry into causes. The conception of purpose in the world was ignored and frowned on. This, though silent and almost unnoticed, was the greatest revolution in human history, far outweighing in importance any of the political revolutions whose thunder has reverberated through the world.

For it came about in this way that for the past three hundred years there has been growing up in men's minds, dominated as they are by science, a new imaginative picture of the world. The world, according to this new picture, is purposeless, senseless, meaningless. Nature is nothing but matter in motion. The motions of matter are governed, not by any purpose, but by blind forces and laws. Nature in this view, says Whitehead—to whose writings I am indebted in this part of my essay—is "merely the hurrying of material, endlessly, meaninglessly." You can draw a sharp line across the history of Europe dividing it into two epochs of very unequal length. The line passes through the lifetime of Galileo. European man before Galileo—whether ancient pagan or more recent Christian—thought of the world as controlled by plan and purpose. After Galileo European man thinks of it as utterly purposeless. This is the great revolution of which I spoke.

It is this which has killed religion. Religion could survive the discoveries that the sun, not the earth, is the center; that men are descended from simian ancestors; that the earth is hundreds of millions of years old. These discoveries may render out of date some of the details of older theological dogmas, may force their restatement in new intellectual frameworks. But they do not touch the essence of the religious vision itself, which is the faith that there is plan and purpose in the world, that the world is a moral order, that in the end all things are for the best. This faith may express itself through many different intellectual dogmas, those of Christianity, of Hinduism, of Islam. All and any of these intellectual dogmas may be destroyed without destroying the essential religious spirit. But that spirit cannot survive destruction of belief in a plan and purpose of the world, for that is the very heart of it. Religion can get on with any sort of astronomy, geology, biology, physics. But it cannot get on with a purposeless and meaningless universe. If the scheme of things is purposeless and meaningless, then the life of man is purposeless and meaningless too. Everything is futile, all effort is in the end worthless. A man may, of course, still pursue disconnected ends, money, fame, art, science, and may gain pleasure from them. But his life is hollow at the center. Hence the dissatisfied, disillusioned, restless, spirit of modern man.

The picture of a meaningless world, and a meaningless human life is, I think, the basic theme of much modern art and literature. Certainly it is the basic theme of modern philosophy. According to the most characteristic philosophies of the modern period from Hume in the eighteenth century to the so-called positivists of today, the world is just what it is, and that is the end of all inquiry. There is no *reason* for its being what it is. Everything might just as well have been quite different, and there would have been no reason for that either. When you have stated what things are, what things the world contains, there is nothing more which could be said, even by an omniscient being. To ask any question about *why* things are thus, or what purpose their being so serves, is to ask a senseless question, because they serve no purpose at all. For instance, there is for modern philosophy no such thing as the ancient problem of evil. For this once famous question presupposes that pain and misery, though they seem so inexplicable and irrational to us, must ultimately subserve some rational purpose, must have their places in the cosmic plan. But this is nonsense. There is no such overruling rationality in the universe. Belief in the ultimate irrationality of everything is the quintessence of what is called the modern mind.

It is true that, parallel with these philosophies which are typical of the modern mind, preaching the meaninglessness of the world, there has run a line of idealistic philosophies whose contention is that the world is after all spiritual in nature and that moral ideals and values are inherent in its structure. But most of these idealisms were simply philosophical expressions of romanticism, which was itself no more than an unsuccessful counterattack of the religious against the scientific view of things. They perished, along with romanticism in literature and art, about the beginning of the present century, though of course they still have a few adherents. At the bottom these idealistic systems of thought were rationalizations of man's wishful thinking. They were born of the refusal of men to admit the cosmic darkness. They were comforting illusions within the warm glow of which the more tender-minded intellectuals sought to shelter themselves from the icy winds of the universe. They lasted a little while. But they are shattered now, and we return once more to the vision of a purposeless world.

Along with the ruin of the religious vision there went the ruin of moral principles and indeed of all values. If there is a cosmic purpose, if there is in the nature of things a drive towards goodness, then our moral systems will derive their validity from this. But if our moral rules do not proceed from something outside us in the nature of the universe—whether we say it is God or simply the universe itself—then they must be our own inventions. Thus it came to be believed that moral rules must be merely an expression of our own likes and dislikes. But likes and dislikes are notoriously variable. What pleases one man, people, or culture displeases another. Therefore morals are wholly relative. This obvious conclusion from the idea of a purposeless world made its appearance in Europe immediately after the rise of science, for instance in the philosophy of Hobbes. Hobbes saw at once that if there is no purpose in the world there are no values either. "Good and evil," he writes, "are names that signify our appetites and aversions; which in different tempers, customs, and doctrines of men are different. . . . Every man calleth that which pleaseth him, good; and that which displeaseth him, evil."

This doctrine of the relativity of morals, though it has recently received an impetus from the studies of anthropologists, was thus really implicit in the whole scientific mentality. It is disastrous for morals because it destroys their entire traditional foundation. That is why philosophers who see the danger signals, from the time at least of Kant, have been trying to give to morals a new foundation, that is, a secular or non-religious foundation. This attempt may very well be intellectually successful. Such a foundation, independent of the religious view of the world, might well be found. But the question is whether it can ever be a *practical* success, that is, whether apart from its logical validity and its influence with intellectuals, it can ever replace among the masses of men the lost religious foundation. On that question hangs perhaps the future of civilization. But meanwhile disaster is overtaking us.

The widespread belief in "ethical relativity" among philosophers, psychologists, ethnologists, and sociologists is the theoretical counterpart of the repudiation of principle which we see all around us, especially in international affairs, the field in which morals have always had the weakest foothold. No one any longer effectively believes in moral principles except as the private prejudices either of individual men or of nations or cultures. This is the inevitable consequence of the doctrine of ethical relativity, which in turn is the inevitable consequence of believing in a purposeless world.

Another characteristic of our spiritual state is loss of belief in the freedom of the will. This also is a fruit of the scientific spirit, though not of any particular scientific discovery. Science has been built up on the basis of determinism, which is the belief that every event is completely determined by a chain of causes and is therefore theoretically predictable beforehand. It is true that recent physics seems to challenge this. But so far as its practical consequences are concerned, the damage has long ago been done. A man's actions, it was argued, are as much events in the natural world as is an eclipse of the sun. It follows that men's actions are as theoretically predictable as an eclipse. But if it is certain now that John Smith will murder Joseph Jones at 2:15 P.M. on January 1, 2000 A.D., what possible meaning can it have to say that when that time comes John Smith will be *free* to choose whether he will commit the murder or not? And if he is not free, how can he be held responsible?

It is true that the whole of this argument can be shown by a competent philosopher to be a tissue of fallacies—or at least I claim that it can. But the point is that the analysis required to show this is much too subtle to be understood by the average entirely unphilosophical man. Because of this, the argument against free will is generally swallowed whole by the unphilosophical. Hence the thought that man is not free, that he is the helpless plaything of forces over which he has no control, has deeply penetrated the modern mind. We hear of economic determinism, cultural determinism, historical determinism. We are not responsible for what we do because our glands control us, or because we are the products of environment or heredity. Not moral self-control, but the doctor, the psychiatrist, the educationist, must save us from doing evil. Pills and injections in the future are to do what Christ and the prophets have failed to do. Of course I do not mean to deny that doctors and educationists can and must help. And I do not mean in any way to belittle their efforts. But I do wish to draw attention to the weakening of moral controls, the greater or less repudiation of personal responsibility which, in the popular thinking of the day, result from these tendencies of thought.

What, then, is to be done? Where are we to look for salvation from the evils of our time? All the remedies I have seen suggested so far are, in my opinion, useless. Let us look at some of them.

Philosophers and intellectuals generally can, I believe, genuinely do something to help. But it is extremely little. What philosophers can do is to show that neither the relativity of morals nor the denial of free will really follows from the grounds which have been supposed to support them. They can also try to discover a genuine secular basis for morals to replace the religious basis which has disappeared. Some of us are trying to do these things. But in the first place philosophers unfortunately are not agreed about these matters, and their disputes are utterly confusing to the non-philosophers. And in the second place their influence is practically negligible because their analyses necessarily take place at a level on which the masses are totally unable to follow them.

The bishops, of course, propose as remedy a return to belief in God and in the doctrines of the Christian religion. Others think that a new religion is what is needed. Those who make these proposals fail to realize that the crisis in man's spiritual condition is something unique in history for which there is no sort of analogy in the past. They are thinking perhaps of the collapse of the ancient Greek and Roman religions. The vacuum then created was easily filled by Christianity, and it might have been filled by Mithraism if Christianity had not appeared. By analogy they think that Christianity might now be replaced by a new religion, or even that Christianity itself, if revivified, might bring back health to men's lives.

But I believe that there is no analogy at all between our present state and that of the European peoples at the time of the fall of paganism. Men had at that time lost their belief only in particular dogmas, particular embodiments of the religious view of the world. It had no doubt become incredible that Zeus and the other gods were living on the top of Mount Olympus. You could go to the top and find no trace of them. But the imaginative picture of a world governed by purpose, a world driving towards the good—which is the inner spirit of religion—had at that time received no serious shock. It had merely to re-embody itself in new dogmas, those of Christianity or some other religion. Religion itself was not dead in the world, only a particular form of it.

But now the situation is quite different. It is not merely that particular dogmas, like that of the virgin birth, are unacceptable to the modern mind. That is true, but it constitutes a very superficial diagnosis of the present situation of religion. Modern skepticism is of a wholly different order from that of the intellectuals of the ancient world. It has attacked and destroyed not merely the outward forms of the religious spirit, its particularized dogmas, but the very essence of that spirit itself, belief in a meaningful and purposeful world. For the founding of a new religion a new Jesus Christ or Buddha would have to appear, in itself a most unlikely event and one for which in any case we cannot afford to sit and wait. But even if a new prophet and a new religion did appear, we may predict that they would fail in the modern world. No one for long would believe in them, for modern men have lost the vision, basic to all religion, of an ordered plan and purpose of the world. They have before their minds the picture of a purposeless universe, and such a world-picture must be fatal to any religion at all, not merely to Christianity.

We must not be misled by occasional appearances of a revival of the religious spirit. Men, we are told, in their disgust and disillusionment at the emptiness of their lives, are turning once more to religion, or are searching for a new message. It may be so. We must expect such wistful yearnings of the spirit. We must expect men to wish back again the light that is gone, and to try to bring it back. But however they may wish and try, the light will not shine again—not at least in the civilization to which we belong.

Another remedy commonly proposed is that we should turn to science itself, or the scientific spirit, for our salvation. Mr. Russell and Professor Dewey both made this proposal, though in somewhat different ways. Professor Dewey seemed to believe that discoveries in sociology, the application of scientific method to social and political problems, will rescue us. This seems to me to be utterly naive. It is not likely that science, which is basically the cause of our spiritual troubles, is likely also to produce the cure for them. Also it lies in the nature of science that, though it can teach us the best means for achieving our ends, it can never tell us what ends to pursue. It cannot give us any ideals. And our trouble is about ideals and ends, not about the means for reaching them.

No civilization can live without ideals, or to put it in another way, without a firm faith in moral ideas. Our ideals and moral ideas have in the past been rooted in religion. But the religious basis of our ideals has been undermined, and the superstructure of ideals is plainly tottering. None of the commonly suggested remedies on examination seems likely to succeed. It would therefore look as if the early death of our civilization were inevitable.

Of course we know that it is perfectly possible for individual men, very highly educated men, philosophers, scientists, intellectuals in general, to live moral lives without any religious convictions. But the question is whether a whole civilization, a whole family of peoples, composed almost entirely of relatively uneducated men and women, can do this. It follows, of course, that if we could make the vast majority of men as highly educated as the very few are now, we might save the situation. And we are already moving slowly in that direction through the techniques of mass education. But the critical question seems to concern the time-lag. Perhaps in a hundred years most of the population will, at the present rate, be sufficiently highly educated and civilized to combine high ideals with an absence of religion. But long before we reach any such stage, the collapse of our civilization may have come about. How are we to live through the intervening period?

I am sure that the first thing we have to do is to face the truth, however bleak it may be, and then next we have to learn to live with it. Let me say a word about each of these two points. What I am urging as regards the first is complete honesty. Those who wish to resurrect Christian dogmas are not, of course, consciously dishonest. But they have that kind of unconscious dishonesty which consists in lulling oneself with opiates and dreams. Those who talk of a new religion are merely hoping for a new opiate. Both alike refuse to face the truth that there is, in the universe outside man, no spirituality, no regard for values, no friend in the sky, no help or comfort for man of any sort. To be perfectly honest in the admission of this fact, not to seek shelter in new or old illusions, not to indulge in wishful dreams about this matter, this is the first thing we shall have to do.

I do not urge this course out of any special regard for the sanctity of truth in the abstract. It is not self-evident to me that truth is the supreme value to which all else must be sacrificed. Might not the discoverer of a truth which would be fatal to mankind be justified in suppressing it, even in teaching men a falsehood? Is truth more valuable than goodness and beauty and happiness? To think so is to invent yet another absolute, another religious delusion in which Truth with a capital T is substituted for God. The reason why we must now boldly and honestly face the truth that the universe is non-spiritual and indifferent to goodness, beauty, happiness, or truth is not that it would be wicked to suppress it, but simply that it is too late to do so, so that in the end we cannot do anything else but face it. Yet we stand on the brink, dreading the icy plunge. We need courage. We need honesty.

Now about the other point, the necessity of learning to live with the truth. This means learning to live virtuously and happily, or at least contentedly, without illusions. And this is going to be extremely difficult because what we have now begun dimly to perceive is that human life in the past, or at least human happiness, has almost wholly depended upon illusions. It has been said that man lives by truth, and that the truth will make us free. Nearly the opposite seems to me to be the case. Mankind has managed to live only by means of lies, and the truth may very well destroy us. If one were a Bergsonian one might believe that nature deliberately puts illusions into our souls in order to induce us to go on living.

The illusions by which men have lived seem to be of two kinds. First, there is what one may perhaps call the Great Illusion—I mean the religious illusion that the universe is moral and good, that it follows a wise and noble plan, that it is gradually generating some supreme value, that goodness is bound to triumph in it. Secondly, there is a whole host of minor illusions on which human happiness nourishes itself. How much of human happiness notoriously comes from the illusions of the lover about his beloved? Then again we work and strive because of the illusions connected with fame, glory, power, or money. Banners of all kinds, flags, emblems, insignia, ceremonials, and rituals are invariably symbols of some illusion or other. The British Empire, the connection between mother country and dominions, used to be partly kept going by illusions surrounding the notion of kingship. Or think of the vast amount of human happiness which is derived from the illusion of supposing that if some nonsense syllable, such as "sir" or "count" or "lord" is pronounced in conjunction with our names, we belong to a superior order of people.

There is plenty of evidence that human happiness is almost wholly based upon illusions of one kind or another. But the scientific spirit, or the spirit of truth, is the enemy of illusions and therefore the enemy of human happiness. That is why it is going to be so difficult to live with the truth. There is no reason why we should have to give up the host of minor illusions which render life supportable. There is no reason why the lover should be scientific about the loved one. Even the illusions of fame and glory may persist. But without the Great Illusion, the illusion of a good, kindly, and purposeful universe, we shall *have* to learn to live. And to ask this is really no more than to ask that we become genuinely civilized beings and not merely sham civilized beings.

I can best explain the difference by a reminiscence. I remember a fellow student in my college days, an ardent Christian, who told me that if he did not believe in a future life, in heaven and hell, he would rape, murder, steal and be a drunkard. That is what I call being a sham civilized being. On the other hand, not only could a Huxley, a John Stuart Mill, a David Hume, live great and fine lives without any religion, but a great many others of us, quite obscure persons, can at least live decent lives without it. To be genuinely civilized means to be able to walk straightly and to live honorably without the props and crutches of one or another of the childish dreams which have so far supported men. That such a life is likely to be ecstatically happy I will not claim. But that it can be lived in quiet content, accepting resignedly what cannot be helped, not expecting the impossible, and being thankful for small mercies, this I would maintain. That it will be difficult for men in general to learn this lesson I do not deny. But that it will be impossible I would not admit since so many have learned it already.

Man has not yet grown up. He is not adult. Like a child he cries for the moon and lives in a world of fantasies. And the race as a whole has perhaps reached the great crisis of its life. Can it grow up as a race in the same sense as individual men grow up? Can man put away childish things and adolescent dreams? Can he grasp the real world as it actually is, stark and bleak, without its romantic or religious halo, and still retain his ideals, striving for great ends and noble achievements? If he can, all may yet be well. If he cannot, he will probably sink back into the savagery and brutality from which he came, taking a humble place once more among the lower animals.

IV

The Meaning of Life

Kurt Baier

Tolstoy, in his autobiographical work, "A Confession", reports how, when he was fifty and at the height of his literary success, he came to be obsessed by the fear that life was meaningless.

"At first I experienced moments of perplexity and arrest of life, as though I did not know what to do or how to live; and I felt lost and became dejected. But this passed, and I went on living as before. Then these moments of perplexity began to recur oftener and oftener, and always in the same form. They were always expressed by the questions: What is it for? What does it lead to? At first it seemed to me that these were aimless and irrelevant questions. I thought that it was all well known, and that if I should ever wish to deal with the solution it would not cost me much effort; just at present I had no time for it, but when I wanted to, I should be able to find the answer. The questions however began to repeat themselves frequently, and to demand replies more and more insistently and like drops of ink always falling on one place they ran together into one black blot." [1]

A Christian living in the Middle Ages would not have felt any serious doubts about Tolstoy's questions. To him it would have seemed quite certain that life had a meaning and quite clear what it was. The medieval Christian world picture assigned to man a highly significant, indeed the central part in the grand scheme of things. The universe was made for the express purpose of

From Kurt Baier, *The Meaning of Life,* The Inaugural Lecture at Canberra University College (1957), pp. 3-4, 18-29; reprinted by permission of the author and the Registrar, The School of General Studies, The Australian National University.

[1]Count Leo Tolstoy, "A Confession", reprinted in *A Confession, The Gospel in Brief, and What I Believe*, No. 229, The World's Classics (London: Geoffrey Cumberlege, 1940).

providing a stage on which to enact a drama starring Man in the title role.

To be exact, the world was created by God in the year 4004 B.C. Man was the last and the crown of this creation, made in the likeness of God, placed in the Garden of Eden on earth, the fixed centre of the universe, round which revolved the nine heavens of the sun, the moon, the planets and the fixed stars, producing as they revolved in their orbits the heavenly harmony of the spheres. And this gigantic universe was created for the enjoyment of man, who was originally put in control of it. Pain and death were unknown in paradise. But this state of bliss was not to last. Adam and Eve ate of the forbidden tree of knowledge, and life on this earth turned into a death-march through a vale of tears. Then, with the birth of Jesus, new hope came into the world. After He had died on the cross, it became at least possible to wash away with the purifying water of baptism some of the effects of Original Sin and to achieve salvation. That is to say, on condition of obedience to the law of God, man could now enter heaven and regain the state of everlasting, deathless bliss, from which he had been excluded because of the sin of Adam and Eve.

To the medieval Christian the meaning of human life was therefore perfectly clear. The stretch on earth is only a short interlude, a temporary incarceration of the soul in the prison of the body, a brief trial and test, fated to end in death, the release from pain and suffering. What really matters, is the life after the death of the body. One's existence acquires meaning not by gaining what this life can offer but by saving one's immortal soul from death and eternal torture, by gaining eternal life and everlasting bliss.

The scientific world picture which has found ever more general acceptance from the beginning of the modern era onwards is in profound conflict with all this. At first, the Christian conception of the world was discovered to be erroneous in various important details. The Copernican theory showed up the earth as merely one of several planets revolving round the sun, and the sun itself was later seen to be merely one of many fixed stars each of which is itself the nucleus of a solar system similar to our own. Man, instead of occupying the centre of creation, proved to be merely the inhabitant of a celestial body no different from millions of others. Furthermore, geological investigations revealed that the universe was not created a few thousand years ago, but was probably millions of years old.

Disagreements over details of the world picture, however, are only superficial aspects of a much deeper conflict. The appropriateness of the whole Christian outlook is at issue. For Christianity, the world must be regarded as the "creation" of a kind of Superman, a person possessing all the human excellences to an infinite degree and none of the human weaknesses, Who has made man in His image, a feeble, mortal, foolish copy of Himself. In creating the universe, God acts as a sort of playwright-cum-legislator-cum-judge-cum-executioner. In the capacity of playwright, He creates the historical world process, including man. He erects the stage and writes, in outline, the plot. He creates the *dramatis personae* and watches over them with the eye partly of a father, partly of the law. While on stage, the actors are free to extemporise, but if they infringe the divine commandments, they are later dealt with by their creator in His capacity of judge and executioner.

Within such a framework, the Christian attitudes towards the world are natural and sound: it is natural and sound to think that all is arranged for the best even if appearances belie it; to resign oneself cheerfully to one's lot; to be filled with awe and veneration in regard to anything and everything that happens; to want to fall on one's knees and worship and praise the Lord. These are wholly fitting attitudes within the framework of the world view just outlined. And this world view must have seemed wholly sound and acceptable because it offered the best explanation which was then available of all the observed phenomena of nature.

As the natural sciences developed, however, more and more things in the universe came to be explained without the assumption of a supernatural creator. Science, moreover, could explain them better, that is, more accurately and more reliably. The Christian hypothesis of a supernatural maker, whatever other needs it was capable of satisfying, was at any rate no longer indispensable for the purpose of explaining the existence or occurrence of anything. In fact, scientific explanations do not seem to leave any room for this hypothesis. The scientific approach demands that we look for a natural explanation of anything and everything. The scientific way of looking at and explaining things has yielded an immensely greater measure of understanding of, and control over, the universe than any other way. And when one looks at the world in this scientific way, there seems to be no room for a personal relationship between human beings and a supernatural perfect being ruling and guiding men. Hence many scientists and educated men have come to feel that the Christian attitudes towards the world and human existence are inappropriate. They have become convinced that the universe and human existence in it are without a purpose and therefore devoid of meaning. . . .[2]

The Purpose of Man's Existence

Our conclusion in the previous section has been that science is in principle able to give complete and real explanations of every occurrence and thing in the universe. This has two important corollaries: (i) Acceptance of the scientific world picture cannot be *one's reason for* the belief that the universe is unintelligible and therefore meaningless, though coming to accept it, after having been taught the Christian world picture, may well have been, in the

[2]See e.g. Edwyn Bevan, *Christianity*, pp. 211-227. See also H. J. Paton, *The Modern Predicament* (London: George Allen and Unwin Ltd., 1955) pp. 103-116, 374.

case of many individuals, *the only or the main cause* of their belief that the universe and human existence are meaningless. (ii) It is not in accordance with reason to reject this pessimistic belief on the grounds that scientific explanations are only provisional and incomplete and must be supplemented by religious ones.

In fact, it might be argued that the more clearly we understand the explanations given by science, the more we are driven to the conclusion that human life has no purpose and therefore no meaning. The science of astronomy teaches us that our earth was not specially created about 6,000 years ago, but evolved out of hot nebulae which previously had whirled aimlessly through space for countless ages. As they cooled, the sun and the planets formed. On one of these planets at a certain time the circumstances were propitious and life developed. But conditions will not remain favourable to life. When our solar system grows old, the sun will cool, our planet will be covered with ice, and all living creatures will eventually perish. Another theory has it that the sun will explode and that the heat generated will be so great that all organic life on earth will be destroyed. That is the comparatively short history and prospect of life on earth. Altogether it amounts to very little when compared with the endless history of the inanimate universe.

Biology teaches us that the species man was not specially created but is merely, in a long chain of evolutionary changes of forms of life, the last link, made in the likeness not of God but of nothing so much as an ape. The rest of the universe, whether animate or inanimate, instead of serving the ends of man, is at best indifferent, at worst savagely hostile. Evolution to whose operation the emergence of man is due is a ceaseless battle among members of different species, one species being gobbled up by another, only the fittest surviving. Far from being the gentlest and most highly moral, man is simply the creature best fitted to survive, the most efficient if not the most rapacious and insatiable killer. And in this unplanned, fortuitous, monstrous, savage world man is madly trying to snatch a few brief moments of joy, in the short intervals during which he is free from pain, sickness, persecution, war or famine until, finally, his life is snuffed out in death. Science has helped us to know and understand this world, but what purpose or meaning can it find in it?

Complaints such as these do not mean quite the same to everybody, but one thing, I think, they mean to most people: science shows life to be meaningless, because life is without purpose. The medieval world picture provided life with a purpose, hence medieval Christians could believe that life had a meaning. The scientific account of the world takes away life's purpose and with it its meaning.

There are, however, two quite different senses of "purpose". Which one is meant? Has science deprived human life of purpose in both senses? And if not, is it a harmless sense, in which human existence has been robbed of purpose? Could human existence still have meaning if it did not have a purpose in that sense?

What are the two senses? In the first and basic sense, purpose is normally attributed only to persons or their behaviour as in "Did you have a purpose in leaving the ignition on?" In the second sense, purpose is normally attributed only to things, as in "What is the purpose of that gadget you installed in the workshop?" The two uses are intimately connected. We cannot attribute a purpose to a thing without implying that someone did something, in the doing of which he had some purpose, namely, to bring about the thing with the purpose. Of course, *his* purpose is not identical with *its* purpose. In hiring labourers and engineers and buying materials and a site for a factory and the like, the entrepreneur's purpose, let us say, is to manufacture cars, but the purpose of cars is to serve as a means of transportation.

There are many things that a man may do, such as buying and selling, hiring labourers, ploughing, felling trees, and the like, which it is foolish, pointless, silly, perhaps crazy, to do if one has no purpose in doing them. A man who does these things without a purpose is engaging in inane, futile pursuits. Lives crammed full with such activities devoid of purpose are pointless, futile, worthless. Such lives may indeed be dismissed as meaningless. But it should also be perfectly clear that acceptance of the scientific world picture does not force us to regard our lives as being without a purpose in this sense. Science has not only not robbed us of any purpose which we had before, but it has furnished us with enormously greater power to achieve these purposes. Instead of praying for rain or a good harvest or offspring, we now use ice pellets, artificial manure, or artificial insemination.

By contrast, having or not having a purpose, in the other sense, is value neutral. We do not think more or less highly of a thing for having or not having a purpose. "Having a purpose", in this sense, confers no kudos, "being purposeless" carries no stigma. A row of trees growing near a farm may or may not have a purpose: it may or may not be a windbreak, may or may not have been planted or deliberately left standing there in order to prevent the wind from sweeping across the fields. We do not in any way disparage the trees if we say they have no purpose, but have just grown that way. They are as beuatiful, made of as good wood, as valuable, as if they had a purpose. And, of course, they break the wind just as well. The same is true of living creatures. We do not disparage a dog when we say that it has no purpose, is not a sheep dog or a watch dog or a rabbiting dog, but just a dog that hangs around the house and is fed by us.

Man is in a different category, however. To attribute to a human being a purpose in that sense is not neutral, let alone complimentary: it is offensive. It is degrading for a man to be regarded as merely serving a purpose. If, at a garden party, I ask a man in livery, "What is your purpose?" I am insulting him. I might as well have asked, "What are you *for?*" Such questions reduce him to the level of a gadget, a domestic animal, or perhaps a slave. I imply that *we* allot to *him* the tasks, the goals, the aims which he is to pursue; that *his* wishes and desires and aspirations and purposes are to count for little or nothing. We are treating him, in Kant's phrase, merely as a means to our ends, not as an end in himself.

The Christian and the scientific world pictures do indeed differ fundamentally on this point. The latter robs man of a purpose in this sense. It sees him as a being with no purpose allotted to him by anyone but himself. It robs him of any goal, purpose, or destiny appointed for him by any outside agency. The Christian world picture, on the other hand, sees man as a creature, a divine artefact, something halfway between a robot (manufactured) and an animal (alive), a homunculus, or perhaps Frankenstein, made in God's laboratory, with a purpose or task assigned him by his Maker.

However, lack of purpose in this sense does not in any way detract from the meaningfulness of life. I suspect that many who reject the scientific outlook because it involves the loss of purpose of life, and therefore meaning, are guilty of a confusion between the two senses of "purpose" just distinguished. They confusedly think that if the scientific world picture is true, then their lives must be futile because that picture implies that man has no purpose given him from without. But this is muddled thinking, for, as has already been shown, pointlessness is implied only by purposelessness in the other sense, which is not at all implied by the scientific picture of the world. These people mistakenly conclude that there can be no purpose *in* life because there is no purpose *of* life; that *men* cannot themselves adopt and achieve purposes because *man*, unlike a robot or a watchdog, is not a creature with a purpose.[3]

However, not all people taking this view are guilty of the above confusion. Some really hanker after a purpose of life in this sense. To some people the greatest attraction of the medieval world picture is the belief in an omnipotent, omniscient, and all-good Father, the view of themselves as His children who worship Him, of their proper attitude to what befalls them as submission, humility, resignation in His will, and what is often described as the "creaturely feeling".[4] All these are attitudes and feelings appropriate to a being that stands to another in the same sort of relation, though of course on a higher plane, in which a helpless child stands to his progenitor. Many regard the scientific picture of the world as cold, unsympathetic, unhomely, frightening, because it does not provide for any appropriate object of this creaturely attitude. There is nothing and no one in the world, as science depicts it, in

[3]See e.g. "Is Life Worth Living?" B.B.C. Talk by the Rev. John Sutherland Bonnell in *Asking Them Questions*, Third Series, ed. by R. S. Wright (London: Geoffrey Cumberlege, 1950).

[4]See e.g. Rudolf Otto, *The Idea of the Holy*, pp. 9-11. See also C.A. Campbell, *On Selfhood and Godhood* (London: George Allen & Unwin Ltd., 1957) p. 246, and H. J. Paton, *The Modern Predicament*, pp. 69-71.

which we can have faith or trust, on whose guidance we can rely, to whom we can turn for consolation, whom we can worship or submit to—except other human beings. This may be felt as a keen disappointment, because it shows that the meaning of life cannot lie in submission to His will, in acceptance of whatever may come, and in worship. But it does not imply that life can have *no* meaning. It merely implies that it must have a different meaning from that which it was thought to have. Just as it is a great shock for a child to find that he must stand on his own feet, that his father and mother no longer provide for him, so a person who has lost his faith in God must reconcile himself to the idea that he has to stand on his own feet, alone in the world except for whatever friends he may succeed in making.

But is not this to miss the point of the Christian teaching? Surely, Christianity can tell us the meaning of life because it tells us the grand and noble end for which God has created the universe and man. No human life, however pointless it may seem, is meaningless because in being part of God's plan, every life is assured of significance.

This point is well taken. It brings to light a distinction of some importance: we call a person's life meaningful not only if it is worthwhile, but also if he has helped in the realization of some plan or purpose transcending his own concerns. A person who knows he must soon die a painful death, can give significance to the remainder of his doomed life by, say, allowing certain experiments to be performed on him which will be useful in the fight against cancer. In a similar way, only on a much more elevated plane, every man, however humble or plagued by suffering, is guaranteed significance by the knowledge that he is participating in God's purpose.

What then, on the Christian view, is the grand and noble end for which God has created the world and man in it? We can immediately dismiss that still popular opinion that the smallness of our intellect prevents us from stating meaningfully God's design in all its imposing grandeur.[5] This view cannot possibly be a satisfactory answer to our question about the purpose of life. It is, rather, a confession of the impossibility of giving one. If anyone thinks that this "answer" can remove the sting from the impression of meaninglessness and insignificance in our lives, he cannot have been stung very hard.

[5]For a discussion of this issue see the eighteenth century controversy between Deists and Theists, for instance, in Sir Leslie Stephen's *History of English Thought in the Eighteenth Century* (London: Smith, Elder & Co., 1902) pp. 112-119 and pp. 134-163. See also the attacks by Toland and Tindal on "the mysterious" in *Christianity not Mysterious* and *Christianity as Old as the Creation, or the Gospel a Republication of the Religion of Nature,* resp., parts of which are reprinted in Henry Bettenson's *Doctrines of the Christian Church,* pp. 426-431. For modern views maintaining that mysteriousness is an essential element in religion, see Rudolf Otto, *The Idea of the Holy,* esp. pp. 25-40, and most recently M. B. Foster, *Mystery and Philosophy* (London: S.C.M. Press, 1957) esp. Chs. IV. and VI. For the view that statements about God must be nonsensical or absurd, see e.g. H. J. Paton, op. cit. pp. 119-120, 367-369. See also "Theology and Falsification" in *New Essays in Philosophical Theology,* ed. by A. Flew and A. MacIntyre (London: S.C.M. Press, 1955) pp. 96-131; also N. McPherson, "Religion as the Inexpressible", ibid, esp. pp. 137-143.

If, then, we turn to those who are willing to state God's purpose in so many words, we encounter two insuperable difficulties. The first is to find a purpose grand and noble enough to explain and justify the great amount of undeserved suffering in this world. We are inevitably filled by a sense of bathos when we read statements such as this: ". . . history is the scene of a divine purpose, in which the whole of history is included, and Jesus of Nazareth is the centre of that purpose, both as revelation and as achievement, as the fulfillment of all that was past, and the promise of all that was to come . . . If God is God, and if He made all these things, why did He do it? . . . God created a universe, bounded by the categories of time, space, matter, and causality, because He desired to enjoy for ever the society of a fellowship of finite and redeemed spirits which have made to His love the response of free and voluntary love and service."[6] Surely this cannot be right? Could a God be called omniscient, omnipotent, *and* all-good who, for the sake of satisfying his desire to be loved and served, imposes (or has to impose) on his creatures the amount of undeserved suffering we find in the world?

There is, however, a much more serious difficulty still: God's purpose in making the universe must be stated in terms of a dramatic story many of whose key incidents symbolize religious conceptions and practices which we no longer find morally acceptable: the imposition of a taboo on the fruits of a certain tree, the sin and guilt incurred by Adam and Eve by violating the taboo, the wrath of God,[7] the curse of Adam and Eve and all their progeny, the expulsion from Paradise, the Atonement by Christ's bloody sacrifice on the cross which makes available by way of the sacraments God's Grace by which alone men can be saved (thereby, incidentally, establishing the valuable power of priests to forgive sins and thus alone make possible a man's entry to heaven[8]), Judgment Day on which the sheep are separated from the goats and the latter condemned to eternal torment in hell-fire.

Obviously it is much more difficult to formulate a purpose for creating the universe and man that will justify the enormous amount of undeserved suffering which we find around us, if that story has to be fitted in as well. For now we have to explain not only why an omnipotent, omniscient, and all-good God should create such a universe and such a man, but also why, foreseeing every move of the feeble, weak-willed, ignorant, and covetous creature to be created, He should nevertheless have created him and, having done so,

---

[6]Stephen Neill, *Christian Faith To-day* (London: Penguin Books, 1955) pp. 240-241.

[7]It is difficult to feel the magnitude of this first sin unless one takes seriously the words "Behold, the man has eaten of the fruit of the tree of knowledge of good and evil, and is become as one of us; and now, may he not put forth his hand, and take also of the tree of life, and eat, and live for ever?" Genesis iii, 22.

[8]See in this connection the pastoral letter of 2nd February, 1905, by Johannes Katschtaler, Prince Bishop of Salzburg on the honour due to priests, contained in *Quellen zur Geschichte des Papsttums,* by Mirbt pp. 497-9, translated and reprinted in *The Protestant Tradition,* by J. S. Whale (Cambridge: University Press, 1955) pp. 259-262.

should be incensed and outraged by man's sin, and why He should deem it necessary to sacrifice His own son on the cross to atone for this sin which was, after all, only a disobedience of one of his commands, and why this atonement and consequent redemption could not have been followed by man's return to Paradise—particularly of those innocent children who had not yet sinned— and why, on Judgment Day, this merciful God should condemn some to eternal torment.[9] It is not surprising that in the face of these and other difficulties, we find, again and again, a return to the first view: that God's purpose cannot meaningfully be stated.

It will perhaps be objected that no Christian to-day believes in the dramatic history of the world as I have presented it. But this is not so. It is the official doctrine of the Roman Catholic, the Greek Orthodox, and a large section of the Anglican Church.[10] Nor does Protestantism substantially alter this picture. In fact, by insisting on "Justification by Faith Alone" and by rejecting the ritualistic, magical character of the medieval Catholic interpretation of certain elements in the Christian religion, such as indulgences, the sacraments, and prayer, while at the same time insisting on the necessity of grace, Protestantism undermined the moral element in medieval Christianity expressed in the Catholics' emphasis on personal merit.[11] Protestantism, by harking back to St. Augustine, who clearly realized the incompatibility of grace and personal merit,[12] opened the way for Calvin's doctrine of Predestination (the intellectual parent of that form of rigid determinism which is usually blamed on science) and Salvation or Condemnation from all eternity.[13] Since Roman Catholics, Lutherans, Calvinists, Presbyterians and Baptists officially subscribe to the views just outlined, one can justifiably claim that the overwhelming majority of professing Christians hold or ought to hold them.

It might still be objected that the best and most modern views are wholly different. I have not the necessary knowledge to pronounce on the accuracy of this claim. It may well be true that the best and most modern views are such as Professor Braithwaite's who maintains that Christianity is, roughly speaking, "morality plus stories", where the stories are intended merely to make the strict moral teaching both more easily understandable and more palatable.[14]

[9]How impossible it is to make sense of this story has been demonstrated beyond any doubt by Tolstoy in his famous "Conclusion of A Criticism of Dogmatic Theology", reprinted in *A Confession, The Gospel in Brief, and What I Believe.*

[10]See "The Nicene Creed", "The Tridentine Profession of Faith", "The Syllabus of Errors", reprinted in *Documents of the Christian Church*, pp. 34, 373 and 380 resp.

[11]See e.g. J. S. Whale, *The Protestant Tradition*, Ch. IV., esp. pp. 48-56.

[12]See ibid., pp. 61 ff.

[13]See "The Confession of Augsburg" esp. Articles II., IV., XVIII., XIX., XX.; "Christianae Religionis Institutio", "The Westminster Confession of Faith", esp. Articles III., VI., IX., X., XI., XVI., XVII.; "The Baptist Confession of Faith", esp. Articles III., XXI., XXIII., reprinted in *Documents of the Christian Church*, pp. 294 ff., 298 ff., 344 ff., 349 ff.

[14]See e.g. his *An Empiricist's View of the Nature of Religious Belief* (Eddington Memorial Lecture).

Or it may be that one or the other of the modern views on the nature and importance of the dramatic story told in the sacred Scriptures is the best. My reply is that, even if it is true, it does not prove what I wish to disprove, that one can extract a sensible answer to our question, "What is the meaning of life?" from the kind of story subscribed to by the overwhelming majority of Christians, who would, moreover, reject any such modernist interpretation at least as indignantly as the scientific account. Moreover, though such views can perhaps avoid some of the worst absurdities of the traditional story, they are hardly in a much better position to state the purpose for which God has created the universe and man in it, because they cannot overcome the difficulty of finding a purpose grand and noble enough to justify the enormous amount of undeserved suffering in the world.

Let us, however, for argument's sake, waive all these objections. There remains one fundamental hurdle which no form of Christianity can overcome: the fact that it demands of man a morally repugnant attitude towards the universe. It is now very widely held[15] that the basic element of the Christian religion is an attitude of worship towards a being supremely worthy of being worshipped and that it is religious feelings and experiences which apprise their owner of such a being and which inspire in him the knowledge or the feeling of complete dependence, awe, worship, mystery, and self-abasement. There is, in other words, a bi-polarity (the famous "I-Thou relationship") in which the object, "the wholly-other", is exalted whereas the subject is abased to the limit. Rudolf Otto has called this the "creature-feeling"[16] and he quotes as an expression of it, Abraham's words when venturing to plead for the men of Sodom: "Behold now, I have taken upon me to speak unto the Lord, which am but dust and ashes". (Gen. XVIII.27). Christianity thus demands of men an attitude inconsistent with one of the presuppositions of morality: that man is not wholly dependent on something else, that man has free will, that man is in principle capable of responsibility. We have seen that the concept of grace is the Christian attempt to reconcile the claim of total dependence and the claim of individual responsibility (partial independence), and it is obvious that such attempts must fail. We may dismiss certain doctrines, such as the doctrine of original sin or the doctrine of eternal hellfire or the doctrine that there can be no salvation outside the Church as extravagant and peripheral, but we cannot reject the doctrine of total dependence without rejecting the characteristically Christian attitude as such.

[15]See e.g. the two series of Gifford Lectures most recently published: *The Modern Predicament* by H. J. Paton (London: George Allen & Unwin Ltd., 1955) pp. 69 ff., and *On Selfhood and Godhood* by C. A. Campbell (London: George Allen & Unwin Ltd., 1957) pp. 231-250.
[16]Rudolf Otto, *The Idea of the Holy*, p. 9.

The Meaning of Life

Perhaps some of you will have felt that I have been shirking the real problem. To many people the crux of the matter seems as follows. How can there be any meaning in our life if it ends in death? What meaning can there be in it that our inevitable death does not destroy? How can our existence be meaningful if there is no after-life in which perfect justice is meted out? How can life have any meaning if all it holds out to us are a few miserable earthly pleasures and even these to be enjoyed only rarely and for such a piteously short time?

I believe this is the point which exercises most people most deeply. Kirilov, in Dostoevsky's novel, *The Possessed*, claims, just before committing suicide, that as soon as we realize that there is no God, we cannot live any longer, we must put an end to our lives. One of the reasons which he gives is that when we discover that there is no paradise, we have nothing to live for.

". . . there was a day on earth, and in the middle of the earth were three crosses. One on the cross had such faith that He said to another, 'To-day thou shalt be with me in paradise'. The day came to an end, both died, and they went, but they found neither paradise nor resurrection. The saying did not come true. Listen: that man was the highest of all on earth . . . There has never been any one like Him before or since, and never will be . . . And if that is so, if the laws of Nature did not spare even *Him,* and made even Him live in the midst of lies and die for a lie, then the whole planet is a lie and is based on a lie and a stupid mockery. So the very laws of the planet are a lie and a farce of the devil. What, then, is there to live for?"[17] And Tolstoy, too, was nearly driven to suicide when he came to doubt the existence of God and an after-life.[18] And this is true of many.

What, then, is it that inclines us to think that if life is to have a meaning, there would have to be an after-life? It is this. The Christian world view contains the following three propositions. The first is that since the Fall, God's curse of Adam and Eve, and the expulsion from Paradise, life on earth for mankind has not been worth while, but a vale of tears, one long chain of misery, suffering, unhappiness, and injustice. The second is that a perfect after-life is awaiting us after the death of the body. The third is that we can enter this perfect life only on certain conditions, among which is also the condition of enduring our earthly existence to its bitter end. In this way, our earthly existence which, in itself, would not (at least for many people if not all)

---

[17]Fyodor Dostoyevsky, *The Devils* (London: The Penguin Classics, 1953) pp. 613-614.

[18]Leo Tolstoy, *A Confession, The Gospel in Brief, and What I Believe,* The World's Classics, p. 24.

be worth living, acquires meaning and significance: only if we endure it, can we gain admission to the realm of the blessed.

It might be doubted whether this view is still held to-day. However, there can be no doubt that even to-day we all imbibe a good deal of this view with our earliest education. In sermons, the contrast between the perfect life of the blessed and our life of sorrow and drudgery is frequently driven home and we hear it again and again that Christianity has a message of hope and consolation for all those "who are weary and heavy laden".[19]

It is not surprising, then, that when the implications of the scientific world picture begin to sink in, when we come to have doubts about the existence of God and another life, we are bitterly disappointed. For if there is no afterlife, then all we are left is our earthly life which we have come to regard as a necessary evil, the painful fee of admission to the land of eternal bliss. But if there is no eternal bliss to come and if this hell on earth is all, why hang on till the horrible end?

Our disappointment therefore arises out of these two propositions, that the earthly life is not worth living, and that there is another perfect life of eternal happiness and joy which we may enter upon if we satisfy certain conditions. We can regard our lives as meaningful, if we believe both. We cannot regard them as meaningful if we believe merely the first and not the second. It seems to me inevitable that people who are taught something of the history of science, will have serious doubts about the second. If they cannot overcome these, as many will be unable to do, then they must either accept the sad view that their life is meaningless or they must abandon the first proposition: that this earthly life is not worth living. They must find the meaning of their life in this earthly existence. But is this possible?

A moment's examination will show us that the Christian evaluation of our earthly life as worthless, which we accept in our moments of pessimism and dissatisfaction, is not one that we normally accept. Consider only the question of murder and suicide. On the Christian view, other things being equal, the most kindly thing to do would be for every one of us to kill as many of our friends and dear ones as still have the misfortune to be alive, and then to commit suicide without delay, for every moment spent in this life is wasted. On the Christian view, God has not made it that easy for us. He has forbidden us to hasten others or ourselves into the next life. Our bodies are his private property and must be allowed to wear themselves out in the way decided by Him, however painful and horrible that may be. We are, as it were, driving a burning car. There is only one way out, to jump clear and let it hurtle to destruction. But the owner of the car has forbidden it on pain of eternal tortures worse than burning. And so we do better to burn to death inside.

On this view, murder is a less serious wrong than suicide. For murder can always be confessed and repented and therefore forgiven, suicide cannot—

[19]See for instance J. S. Whale, *Christian Doctrine*, pp. 171, 176-178, &c. See also Stephen Neill, *Christian Faith To-day*, p. 241.

unless we allow the ingenious way out chosen by the heroine of Graham Greene's play, The Living Room, who swallows a slow but deadly poison and, while awaiting its taking effect, repents having taken it. Murder, on the other hand, is not so serious because, in the first place, it need not rob the victim of anything but the last lap of his march in the vale of tears, and, in the second place, it can always be forgiven. Hamlet, it will be remembered, refrains from killing his uncle during the latter's prayers because, as a true Christian, he believes that killing his uncle at that point, when the latter has purified his soul by repentance, would merely be doing him a good turn, for murder at such a time would simply despatch him to undeserved and everlasting happiness.

These views strike us as odd, to say the least. They are the logical consequence of the official medieval evaluation of this our earthly existence. If this life is not worth living, then taking it is not robbing the person concerned of much. The only thing wrong with it is the damage to God's property, which is the same both in the case of murder and suicide. We do not take this view at all. Our view, on the contrary, is that murder is the most serious wrong because it consists in taking away from some one else against his will his most precious possession, his life. For this reason, when a person suffering from an incurable disease asks to be killed, the mercy killing of such a person is regarded as a much less serious crime than murder because, in such a case, the killer is not robbing the other of a good against his will. Suicide is not regarded as a real crime at all, for we take the view that a person can do with his own possessions what he likes.

However, from the fact that these are our normal opinions, we can infer nothing about their truth. After all, we could easily be mistaken. Whether life is or is not worthwhile, is a value judgment. Perhaps all this is merely a matter of opinion or taste. Perhaps no objective answer can be given. Fortunately, we need not enter deeply into these difficult and controversial questions. It is quite easy to show that the medieval evaluation of earthly life is based on a misguided procedure.

Let us remind ourselves briefly of how we arrive at our value judgments. When we determine the merits of students, meals, tennis players, bulls, or bathing belles, we do so on the basis of some criteria and some standard or norm. Criteria and standards notoriously vary from field to field and even from case to case. But that does not mean that we have *no* idea about what are the appropriate criteria or standards to use. It would not be fitting to apply the criteria for judging bulls to the judgment of students or bathing belles. They score on quite different points. And even where the same criteria are appropriate as in the judgment of students enrolled in different schools and universities the standards will vary from one institution to another. Pupils who would only just pass in one, would perhaps obtain honours in another. The higher the standard applied, the lower the marks, that is, the merit conceded to the candidate.

The same procedure is applicable also in the evaluation of a life. We examine it on the basis of certain criteria and standards. The medieval Christian view uses the criteria of the ordinary man: a life is judged by what the person concerned can get out of it: the balance of happiness over unhappiness, pleasure over pain, bliss over suffering. Our earthly life is judged not worth while because it contains much unhappiness, pain, and suffering, little happiness, pleasure, and bliss. The next life is judged worth while because it provides eternal bliss and no suffering.

Armed with these criteria, we can compare the life of this man and that, and judge which is more worth while, which has a greater balance of bliss over suffering. But criteria alone enable us merely to make comparative judgments of value, not absolute ones. We can say which is more and which is less worth while, but we cannot say which is worthwhile and which is not. In order to determine the latter, we must introduce a standard. But what standard ought we to choose?

Ordinarily, the standard we employ is the average of the kind. We call a man and a tree tall if they are well above the average of their kind. We do not say that Jones is a short man because he is shorter than a tree. We do not judge a boy a bad student because his answer to a question in the Leaving Examination is much worse than that given in reply to the same question by a young man sitting for his finals for the Bachelor's degree.

The same principles must apply to judging lives. When we ask whether a given life was or was not worth while, then we must take into consideration the range of worthwhileness which ordinary lives normally cover. Our end poles of the scale must be the best possible and the worst possible life that one finds. A good and worthwhile life is one that is well above average. A bad one is one well below.

The Christian evaluation of earthly lives is misguided because it adopts a quite unjustifiably high standard. Christianity singles out the major shortcomings of our earthly existence: there is not enough happiness; there is too much suffering; the good and bad points are quite unequally and unfairly distributed; the underprivileged and underendowed do not get adequate compensation; it lasts only a short time. It then quite accurately depicts the perfect or ideal life as that which does not have any of these shortcomings. Its next step is to promise the believer that he will be able to enjoy this perfect life later on. And then it adopts as its standard of judgment the perfect life, dismissing as inadequate anything that falls short of it. Having dismissed earthly life as miserable, it further damns it by characterizing most of the pleasures of which earthly existence allows as bestial, gross, vile, and sinful, or alternatively as not really pleasurable.

This procedure is as illegitimate as if I were to refuse to call anything tall unless it is infinitely tall, or anything beautiful unless it is perfectly flawless, or any one strong unless he is omnipotent. Even if it were true that there is available to us an after-life which is flawless and perfect, it would still not be legitimate to judge earthly lives by this standard. We do not fail every candidate who is not an Einstein. And if we do not believe in an after-life, we must of course use ordinary earthly standards.

I have so far only spoken of the worthwhileness, only of what a person can get out of a life. There are other kinds of appraisal. Clearly, we evaluate people's lives not merely from the point of view of what they yield to the persons that lead them, but also from that of other men on whom these lives have impinged. We judge a life more significant if the person has contributed to the happiness of others, whether directly by what he did for others, or by the plans, discoveries, inventions, and work he performed. Many lives that hold little in the way of pleasure or happiness for its owner are highly significant and valuable, deserve admiration and respect on account of the contributions made.

It is now quite clear that death is simply irrelevant. If life can be worthwhile at all, then it can be so even though it be short. And if it is not worthwhile at all, then an eternity of it is simply a nightmare. It may be sad that we have to leave this beautiful world, but it is so only if and because it is beautiful. And it is no less beautiful for coming to an end. I rather suspect that an eternity of it might make us less appreciative, and in the end it would be tedious.

It will perhaps be objected now that I have not really demonstrated that life has a meaning, but merely that it can be worthwhile or have value. It must be admitted that there is a perfectly natural interpretation of the question, "What is the meaning of life?" on which my view actually proves that life has no meaning. I mean the interpretation discussed in section 2 of this lecture, where I attempted to show that, if we accept the explanations of natural science, we cannot believe that living organisms have appeared on earth in accordance with the deliberate plan of some intelligent being. Hence, on this view, life cannot be said to have a purpose, in the sense in which man-made things have a purpose. Hence it cannot be said to have a meaning or significance in that sense.

However, this conclusion is innocuous. People are disconcerted by the thought that life as such has no meaning in that sense only because they very naturally think it entails that no individual life can have meaning either. They naturally assume that *this* life or *that* can have meaning only if *life as such* has meaning. But it should by now be clear that your life and mine may or may not have meaning (in one sense) even if life as such has none (in the other). Of course, it follows from this that your life may have meaning while mine has not. The Christian view guarantees a meaning (in one sense) to every life, the scientific view does not (in any sense). By relating the question of the meaningfulness of life to the particular circumstances of an individual's existence, the scientific view leaves it an open question whether an individual's life has meaning or not. It is, however, clear that the latter is the important sense of "having a meaning". Christians, too, must feel that their life is wasted and meaningless if they have not achieved salvation. To know that even such lost lives have a meaning in another sense is no consolation to them. What matters is not that life should have a guaranteed meaning, whatever happens here or here-after, but that, by luck (Grace) or the right temperament and attitude (Faith) or a judicious life (Works) a person should make the most of his life.

"But here lies the rub," it will be said. "Surely, it makes all the difference whether there is an after-life. This is where morality comes in." It would be a mistake to believe that. Morality is not the meting out of punishment and reward. To be moral is to refrain from doing to others what, if they followed reason, they would not do to themselves, and to do for others what, if they followed reason, they would want to have done. It is, roughly speaking, to recognize that others, too, have a right to a worthwhile life. Being moral does not make one's own life worthwhile, it helps others to make theirs so.

Conclusion

I have tried to establish three points: (i) that scientific explanations render their explicanda as intelligible as pre-scientific explanations; they differ from the latter only in that, having testable implications and being more precisely formulated, their truth or falsity can be determined with a high degree of probability; (ii) that science does not rob human life of purpose, in the only sense that matters, but, on the contrary, renders many more of our purposes capable of realization; (iii) that common sense, the Christian world view, and the scientific approach agree on the criteria but differ on the standard to be employed in the evaluation of human lives; judging human lives by the standards of perfection, as Christians do, is unjustified; if we abandon this excessively high standard and replace it by an everyday one, we have no longer any reason for dismissing earthly existence as not worthwhile.

On the basis of these three points I have attempted to explain why so many people come to the conclusion that human existence is meaningless and to show that this conclusion is false. In my opinion, this pessimism rests on a combination of two beliefs, both partly true and partly false: the belief that the meaningfulness of life depends on the satisfaction of at least three conditions, and the belief that this universe satisfies none of them. The conditions are, first, that the universe is intelligible, second, that life has a purpose, and third, that all men's hopes and desires can ultimately be satisfied. It seemed to medieval Christians and it seems to many Christians to-day that Christianity offers a picture of the world which can meet these conditions. To many Christians and non-Christians alike it seems that the scientific world picture is incompatible with that of Christianity, therefore with the view that these three conditions are met, therefore with the view that life has a meaning. Hence they feel that they are confronted by the dilemma of accepting either a world picture incompatible with the discoveries of science or the view that life is meaningless.

I have attempted to show that the dilemma is unreal because life can be meaningful even if not all of these conditions are met. My main conclusion, therefore, is that acceptance of the scientific world picture provides no reason for saying that life is meaningless, but on the contrary every reason for saying that there are many lives which are meaningful and significant. My subsidiary conclusion is that one of the reasons frequently offered for retaining the Christian world picture, namely, that its acceptance gives us a guarantee of a meaning for human existence, is unsound. We can see that our lives can have a meaning even if we abandon it and adopt the scientific world picture instead. I have, moreover, mentioned several reasons for rejecting the Christian world picture: (i) the biblical explanations of the details of our universe are often simply false; (ii) the so-called explanations of the whole universe are incomprehensible or absurd; (iii) Christianity's low evaluation of earthly existence (which is the main cause of the belief in the meaninglessness of life) rests on the use of an unjustifiably high standard of judgment.

V

An Absurd Reasoning*

Albert Camus

Absurdity and Suicide

There is but one truly serious philosophical problem, and that is suicide. Judging whether life is or is not worth living amounts to answering the fundamental question of philosophy. All the rest—whether or not the world has three dimensions, whether the mind has nine or twelve categories—comes afterwards. These are games; one must first answer. And if it is true, as Nietzsche claims, that a philosopher, to deserve our respect, must preach by example, you can appreciate the importance of that reply, for it will precede the definitive act. These are facts the heart can feel; yet they call for careful study before they become clear to the intellect.

If I ask myself how to judge that this question is more urgent than that, I reply that one judges by the actions it entails. I have never seen anyone die for the ontological argument. Galileo, who held a scientific truth of great importance, abjured it with the greatest ease as soon as it endangered his life. In a certain sense, he did right.[1] That truth was not worth the stake. Whether the earth or the sun revolves around the other is a matter of profound indiffer-

From *The Myth of Sisyphus and Other Essays* by Albert Camus, translated by Justin O'Brien. Copyright © 1955 by Alfred A. Knopf, Inc. Reprinted by permission of Alfred A. Knopf, Inc.

*When Camus writes of "the absurd man," he refers to a person who is aware of and attempts to comprehend absurdity, and such an attempt he calls "absurd reasoning" or "absurd logic". [Eds.]

[1]From the point of view of the relative value of truth. On the other hand, from the point of view of virile behavior, this scholar's fragility may well make us smile.

ence. To tell the truth, it is a futile question. On the other hand, I see many people die because they judge that life is not worth living. I see others paradoxically getting killed for the ideas or illusions that give them a reason for living (what is called a reason for living is also an excellent reason for dying). I therefore conclude that the meaning of life is the most urgent of questions. . . .

Suicide has never been dealt with except as a social phenomenon. On the contrary, we are concerned here, at the outset, with the relationship between individual thought and suicide. An act like this is prepared within the silence of the heart, as is a great work of art. The man himself is ignorant of it. One evening he pulls the trigger or jumps. Of an apartment-building manager who had killed himself I was told that he had lost his daughter five years before, that he had changed greatly since, and that that experience had "undermined" him. A more exact word cannot be imagined. Beginning to think is beginning to be undermined. Society has but little connection with such beginnings. The worm is in man's heart. That is where it must be sought. One must follow and understand this fatal game that leads from lucidity in the face of existence to flight from light. . . .

But if it is hard to fix the precise instant, the subtle step when the mind opted for death, it is easier to deduce from the act itself the consequences it implies. In a sense, and as in melodrama, killing yourself amounts to confessing. It is confessing that life is too much for you or that you do not understand it. Let's not go too far in such analogies, however, but rather return to everyday words. It is merely confessing that that "is not worth the trouble." Living, naturally, is never easy. You continue making the gestures commanded by existence for many reasons, the first of which is habit. Dying voluntarily implies that you have recognized, even instinctively, the ridiculous character of that habit, the absence of any profound reason for living, the insane character of that daily agitation, and the uselessness of suffering.

What, then, is that incalculable feeling that deprives the mind of the sleep necessary to life? A world that can be explained even with bad reasons is a familiar world. But, on the other hand, in a universe suddenly divested of illusions and lights, man feels an alien, a stranger. His exile is without remedy since he is deprived of the memory of a lost home or the hope of a promised land. This divorce between man and his life, the actor and his setting, is properly the feeling of absurdity. All healthy men having thought of their own suicide, it can be seen, without further explanation, that there is a direct connection between this feeling and the longing for death.

The subject of this essay is precisely this relationship between the absurd and suicide, the exact degree to which suicide is a solution to the absurd. The principle can be established that for a man who does not cheat, what he believes to be true must determine his action. Belief in the absurdity of existence must then dictate his conduct. It is legitimate to wonder, clearly and without false pathos, whether a conclusion of this importance requires forsaking as rapidly as possible an incomprehensible condition. I am speaking, of course, of men inclined to be in harmony with themselves. . . .

In a man's attachment to life there is something stronger than all the ills in the world. The body's judgment is as good as the mind's, and the body shrinks from annihilation. We get into the habit of living before acquiring the habit of thinking. In that race which daily hastens us toward death, the body maintains its irreparable lead. In short, the essence of that contradiction lies in what I shall call the act of eluding because it is both less and more than diversion in the Pascalian sense.* Eluding is the invariable game. The typical act of eluding, the fatal evasion that constitutes the third theme of this essay, is hope. Hope of another life one must "deserve" or trickery of those who live not for life itself but for some great idea that will transcend it, refine it, give it a meaning, and betray it. . . .

All great deeds and all great thoughts have a ridiculous beginning. Great works are often born on a street-corner or in a restaurant's revolving door. So it is with absurdity. The absurd world more than others derives its nobility from that abject birth. In certain situations, replying "nothing" when asked what one is thinking about may be pretense in a man. Those who are loved are well aware of this. But if that reply is sincere, if it symbolizes that odd state of soul in which the void becomes eloquent, in which the chain of daily gestures is broken, in which the heart vainly seeks the link that will connect it again, then it is as it were the first sign of absurdity.

It happens that the stage sets collapse. Rising, streetcar, four hours in the office or the factory, meal, streetcar, four hours of work, meal, sleep, and Monday Tuesday Wednesday Thursday Friday and Saturday according to the same rhythm—this path is easily followed most of the time. But one day the "why" arises and everything begins in that weariness tinged with amazement. "Begins"—this is important. Weariness comes at the end of the acts of a mechanical life, but at the same time it inaugurates the impulse of consciousness. It awakens consciousness and provokes what follows. What follows is the gradual return into the chain or it is the definitive awakening. At the end of the awakening comes, in time, the consequence: suicide or recovery. In itself weariness has something sickening about it. Here, I must conclude that it is

---

*A Pascalian "diversion" is any undertaking, serious or trivial, which keeps one from thinking about oneself—of realizing "our feeble and moral condition, so miserable that nothing can comfort us when we think of it closely." See Pascal's *Pensées*, sections 139-143. [Eds.]

good. For everything begins with consciousness and nothing is worth anything except through it. There is nothing original about these remarks. But they are obvious; that is enough for a while, during a sketchy reconnaissance in the origins of the absurd. Mere "anxiety," as Heidegger says, is at the source of everything.

Likewise and during every day of an unillustrious life, time carries us. But a moment always comes when we have to carry it. We live on the future: "tomorrow," "later on," "when you have made your way," "you will understand when you are old enough." Such irrelevancies are wonderful, for, after all, it's a matter of dying. Yet a day comes when a man notices or says that he is thirty. Thus he asserts his youth. But simultaneously he situates himself in relation to time. He takes his place in it. He admits that he stands at a certain point on a curve that he acknowledges having to travel to its end. He belongs to time, and by the horror that seizes him, he recognizes his worst enemy. Tomorrow, he was longing for tomorrow, whereas everything in him ought to reject it. That revolt of the flesh is the absurd.[2]

A step lower and strangeness creeps in: perceiving that the world is "dense," sensing to what a degree a stone is foreign and irreducible to us, with what intensity nature or a landscape can negate us. At the heart of all beauty lies something inhuman, and these hills, the softness of the sky, the outline of these trees at this very minute lose the illusory meaning with which we had clothed them, henceforth more remote than a lost paradise. The primitive hostility of the world rises up to face us across millennia. For a second we cease to understand it because for centuries we have understood in it solely the images and designs that we had attributed to it beforehand, because henceforth we lack the power to make use of that artifice. The world evades us because it becomes itself again. That stage scenery masked by habit becomes again what it is. It withdraws at a distance from us. Just as there are days when under the familiar face of a woman, we see as a stranger her we had loved months or years ago, perhaps we shall come even to desire what suddenly leaves us so alone. But the time has not yet come. Just one thing: that denseness and that strangeness of the world is the absurd.

Men, too, secrete the inhuman. At certain moments of lucidity, the mechanical aspect of their gestures, their meaningless pantomime makes silly everything that surrounds them. A man is talking on the telephone behind a glass partition; you cannot hear him, but you see his incomprehensible dumb show: you wonder why he is alive. This discomfort in the face of man's own inhumanity, this incalculable tumble before the image of what we are, this "nausea," as a writer of today calls it, is also the absurd. Likewise the stranger who at certain seconds comes to meet us in a mirror, the familiar and yet alarming brother we encounter in our own photographs is also the absurd.

[2]But not in the proper sense. This is not a definition, but rather an *enumeration* of the feelings that may admit of the absurd. Still, the enumeration finished, the absurd has nevertheless not been exhausted.

I come at last to death and to the attitude we have toward it. On this point everything has been said and it is only proper to avoid pathos. Yet one will never be sufficiently surprised that everyone lives as if no one "knew." This is because in reality there is no experience of death. Properly speaking, nothing has been experienced but what has been lived and made conscious. Here, it is barely possible to speak of the experience of others' deaths. It is a substitute, an illusion, and it never quite convinces us. That melancholy convention cannot be persuasive. The horror comes in reality from the mathematical aspect of the event. If time frightens us, this is because it works out the problem and the solution comes afterward. All the pretty speeches about the soul will have their contrary convincingly proved, at least for a time. From this inert body on which a slap makes no mark the soul has disappeared. This elementary and definitive aspect of the adventure constitutes the absurd feeling. Under the fatal lighting of that destiny, its uselessness becomes evident. No code of ethics and no effort are justifiable *a priori* in the face of the cruel mathematics that command our condition. . . .

Whatever may be the play on words and the acrobatics of logic, to understand is, above all, to unify. The mind's deepest desire, even in its most elaborate operations, parallels man's unconscious feeling in the face of his universe: it is an insistence upon familiarity, an appetite for clarity. Understanding the world for a man is reducing it to the human, stamping it with his seal. The cat's universe is not the universe of the anthill. The truism "All thought is anthropomorphic" has no other meaning. Likewise, the mind that aims to understand reality can consider itself satisfied only by reducing it to terms of thought. If man realized that the universe like him can love and suffer, he would be reconciled. If thought discovered in the shimmering mirrors of phenomena eternal relations capable of summing them up and summing themselves up in a single principle, then would be seen an intellectual joy of which the myth of the blessed would be but a ridiculous imitation. That nostalgia for unity, that appetite for the absolute illustrates the essential impulse of the human drama. But the fact of that nostalgia's existence does not imply that it is to be immediately satisfied. For if, bridging the gulf that separates desire from conquest, we assert with Parmenides the reality of the One (whatever it may be), we fall into the ridiculous contradiction of a mind that asserts total unity and proves by its very assertion its own difference and the diversity it claimed to resolve. This other vicious circle is enough to stifle our hopes. . . .

Hence the intelligence, too, tells me in its way that this world is absurd. Its contrary, blind reason, may well claim that all is clear; I was waiting for proof and longing for it to be right. But despite so many pretentious centuries and over the heads of so many eloquent and persuasive men, I know that is false. On this plane, at least, there is no happiness if I cannot know. That universal reason, practical or ethical, that determinism, those categories that explain everything are enough to make a decent man laugh. They have nothing to do with the mind. They negate its profound truth, which is to be enchained. In this unintelligible and limited universe, man's fate henceforth assumes its meaning. A horde of irrationals has sprung up and surrounds him until his ultimate end. In his recovered and now studied lucidity, the feeling of the absurd becomes clear and definite. I said that the world is absurd, that is all that can be said. But what is absurd is the confrontation of this irrational and the wild longing for clarity whose call echoes in the human heart. The absurd depends as much on man as on the world. For the moment it is all that links them together. It binds them one to the other as only hatred can weld two creatures together. This is all I can discern clearly in this measureless universe where my adventure takes place. Let us pause here. If I hold to be true that absurdity that determines my relationship with life, if I become thoroughly imbued with that sentiment that seizes me in face of the world's scenes, with that lucidity imposed on me by the pursuit of a science, I must sacrifice everything to these certainties and I must see them squarely to be able to maintain them. Above all, I must adapt my behavior to them and pursue them in all their consequences. I am speaking here of decency. But I want to know beforehand if thought can live in those deserts. . . .

All these experiences agree and confirm one another. The mind, when it reaches its limits, must make a judgment and choose its conclusions. This is where suicide and the reply stand. But I wish to reverse the order of the inquiry and start out from the intelligent adventure and come back to daily acts. The experiences called to mind here were born in the desert that we must not leave behind. At least it is essential to know how far they went. At this point of his effort man stands face to face with the irrational. He feels within him his longing for happiness and for reason. The absurd is born of this confrontation between the human need and the unreasonable silence of the world. This must not be forgotten. This must be clung to because the whole consequence of a life can depend on it. The irrational, the human nostalgia, and the absurd that is born of their encounter—these are the three characters in the drama that must necessarily end with all the logic of which an existence is capable. . . .

If I accuse an innocent man of a monstrous crime, if I tell a virtuous man that he has coveted his own sister, he will reply that this is absurd. His indignation has its comical aspect. But it also has its fundamental reason. The

virtuous man illustrates by that reply the definitive antinomy existing between the deed I am attributing to him and his lifelong principles. "It's
absurd" means "It's impossible" but also "It's contradictory." If I see a man
armed only with a sword attack a group of machine guns, I shall consider his
act to be absurd. But it is so solely by virtue of the disproportion between his
intention and the reality he will encounter, of the contradiction I notice
between his true strength and the aim he has in view. Likewise we shall deem
a verdict absurd when we contrast it with the verdict the facts apparently
dictated. And, similarly, a demonstration by the absurd is achieved by comparing the consequences of such a reasoning with the logical reality one wants
to set up. In all these cases, from the simplest to the most complex, the
magnitude of the absurdity will be in direct ratio to the distance between the
two terms of my comparison. There are absurd marriages, challenges, ran-
cors, silences, wars, and even peace treaties. For each of them the absurdity
springs from a comparison. I am thus justified in saying that the feeling of
absurdity does not spring from the mere scrutiny of a fact or an impression,
but that it bursts from the comparison between a bare fact and a certain
reality, between an action and the world that transcends it. The absurd is
essentially a divorce. It lies in neither of the elements compared; it is born of
their confrontation.

In this particular case and on the plane of intelligence, I can therefore say
that the Absurd is not in man (if such a metaphor could have a meaning) nor in
the world, but in their presence together. For the moment it is the only bond
uniting them. If I wish to limit myself to facts, I know what man wants, I know
what the world offers him, and now I can say that I also know what links them.
I have no need to dig deeper. A single certainty is enough for the seeker. He
simply has to derive all the consequences from it. . . .

And carrying this absurd logic to its conclusion, I must admit that that
struggle implies a total absence of hope (which has nothing to do with despair),
a continual rejection (which must not be confused with renunciation), and a
conscious dissatisfaction (which must not be compared to immature unrest).
Everything that destroys, conjures away, or exorcises these requirements
(and, to begin with, consent which overthrows divorce) ruins the absurd and
devaluates the attitude that may then be proposed. The absurd has meaning
only in so far as it is not agreed to. . . .

There exists an obvious fact that seems utterly moral: namely, that a man is
always a prey to his truths. Once he has admitted them, he cannot free himself
from them. One has to pay something. A man who has become conscious of
the absurd is forever bound to it. A man devoid of hope and conscious of being

so has ceased to belong to the future. That is natural. But it is just as natural that he should strive to escape the universe of which he is the creator. All the foregoing has significance only on account of this paradox. . . .

It is a matter of living in that state of the absurd. I know on what it is founded, this mind and this world straining against each other without being able to embrace each other. I ask for the rule of life of that state, and what I am offered neglects its basis, negates one of the terms of the painful opposition, demands of me a resignation. I ask what is involved in the condition I recognize as mine; I know it implies obscurity and ignorance; and I am assured that this ignorance explains everything and that this darkness is my light. But there is no reply here to my intent, and this stirring lyricism cannot hide the paradox from me. One must therefore turn away. Kierkegaard may shout in warning: "If man had no eternal consciousness, if, at the bottom of everything, there were merely a wild, seething force producing everything, both large and trifling, in the storm of dark passions, if the bottomless void that nothing can fill underlay all things, what would life be but despair?" This cry is not likely to stop the absurd man. Seeking what is true is not seeking what is desirable. If in order to elude the anxious question: "What would life be?" one must, like the donkey, feed on the roses of illusion, then the absurd mind, rather than resigning itself to falsehood, prefers to adopt fearlessly Kierkegaard's reply: "despair." Everything considered, a determined soul will always manage. . . .

Absurd Freedom

Now the main thing is done, I hold certain facts from which I cannot separate. What I know, what is certain, what I cannot deny, what I cannot reject—this is what counts. I can negate everything of that part of me that lives on vague nostalgias, except this desire for unity, this longing to solve, this need for clarity and cohesion. I can refute everything in this world surrounding me that offends or enraptures me, except this chaos, this sovereign chance and this divine equivalence which springs from anarchy: I don't know whether this world has a meaning that transcends it. But I know that I do not know that meaning and that it is impossible for me just now to know it. What can a meaning outside my condition mean to me? I can understand only in human terms. What I touch, what resists me—that is what I understand. And these two certainties—my appetite for the absolute and for unity and the impossibility of reducing this world to a rational and reasonable principle—I also know that I cannot reconcile them. What other truth can I admit without lying, without bringing in a hope I lack and which means nothing within the limits of my condition?

If I were a tree among trees, a cat among animals, this life would have a meaning, or rather this problem would not arise, for I should belong to this world. I should *be* this world to which I am now opposed by my whole consciousness and my whole insistence upon familiarity. This ridiculous reason is what sets me in opposition to all creation. I cannot cross it out with a stroke of the pen. What I believe to be true I must therefore preserve. What seems to me so obvious, even against me, I must support. And what constitutes the basis of that conflict, of that break between the world and my mind, but the awareness of it? If therefore I want to preserve it, I can through a constant awareness, ever revived, ever alert. This is what, for the moment, I must remember. At this moment the absurd, so obvious and yet so hard to win, returns to a man's life and finds its home there. At this moment, too, the mind can leave the arid, dried-up path of lucid effort. That path now emerges in daily life. It encounters the world of the anonymous impersonal pronoun "one," but henceforth man enters in with his revolt and his lucidity. He has forgotten how to hope. This hell of the present is his Kingdom at last. All problems recover their sharp edge. Abstract evidence retreats before the poetry of forms and colors. Spiritual conflicts become embodied and return to the abject and magnificent shelter of man's heart. None of them is settled. But all are transfigured. Is one going to die, escape by the leap, rebuild a mansion of ideas and forms to one's own scale? Is one, on the contrary, going to take up the heart-rending and marvelous wager of the absurd? Let's make a final effort in this regard and draw all our conclusions. The body, affection, creation, action, human nobility will then resume their places in this mad world. At last man will again find there the wine of the absurd and the bread of indifference on which he feeds his greatness.

Let us insist again on the method: it is a matter of persisting. At a certain point on his path the absurd man is tempted. History is not lacking in either religions or prophets, even without gods. He is asked to leap. All he can reply is that he doesn't fully understand, that it is not obvious. Indeed, he does not want to do anything but what he fully understands. He is assured that this is the sin of pride, but he does not understand the notion of sin; that perhaps hell is in store, but he has not enough imagination to visualize that strange future; that he is losing immortal life, but that seems to him an idle consideration. An attempt is made to get him to admit his guilt. He feels innocent. To tell the truth, that is all he feels—his irreparable innocence. This is what allows him everything. Hence, what he demands of himself is to live *solely* with what he knows, to accommodate himself to what is, and to bring in nothing that is not certain. He is told that nothing is. But this at least is a certainty. And it is with this that he is concerned: he wants to find out if it is possible to live *without appeal.* . . .

Now I can broach the notion of suicide. It has already been felt what solution might be given. At this point the problem is reversed. It was previously a question of finding out whether or not life had to have a meaning to be lived. It now becomes clear, on the contrary, that it will be lived all the better if it has no meaning. Living an experience, a particular fate, is accepting it fully. Now, no one will live this fate, knowing it to be absurd, unless he does everything to keep before him that absurd brought to light by consciousness. Negating one of the terms of the opposition on which he lives amounts to escaping it. To abolish conscious revolt is to elude the problem. The theme of permanent revolution is thus carried into individual experience. Living is keeping the absurd alive. Keeping it alive is, above all, contemplating it. Unlike Eurydice, the absurd dies only when we turn away from it. One of the only coherent philosophical positions is thus revolt. It is a constant confrontation between man and his own obscurity. It is an insistence upon an impossible transparency. It challenges the world anew every second. Just as danger provided man the unique opportunity of seizing awareness, so metaphysical revolt extends awareness to the whole of experience. It is that constant presence of man in his own eyes. It is not aspiration, for it is devoid of hope. That revolt is the certainty of a crushing fate, without the resignation that ought to accompany it.

This is where it is seen to what a degree absurd experience is remote from suicide. It may be thought that suicide follows revolt—but wrongly. For it does not represent the logical outcome of revolt. It is just the contrary by the consent it presupposes. Suicide, like the leap, is acceptance at its extreme. Everything is over and man returns to his essential history. His future, his unique and dreadful future—he sees and rushes toward it. In its way, suicide settles the absurd. It engulfs the absurd in the same death. But I know that in order to keep alive, the absurd cannot be settled. It escapes suicide to the extent that it is simultaneously awareness and rejection of death. It is, at the extreme limit of the condemned man's last thought, that shoelace that despite everything he sees a few yards away, on the very brink of his dizzying fall. The contrary of suicide, in fact, is the man condemned to death.

That revolt gives life its value. Spread out over the whole length of a life, it restores its majesty to that life. To a man devoid of blinders, there is no finer sight than that of the intelligence at grips with a reality that transcends it. The sight of human pride is unequaled. No disparagement is of any use. That discipline that the mind imposes on itself, that will conjured up out of nothing, that face-to-face struggle have something exceptional about them. To impoverish that reality whose inhumanity constitutes man's majesty is tantamount to impoverishing him himself. I understand then why the doctrines that explain everything to me also debilitate me at the same time. They relieve me of the weight of my own life, and yet I must carry it alone. At this juncture, I cannot conceive that a skeptical metaphysics can be joined to an ethics of renunciation.

Consciousness and revolt, these rejections are the contrary of renunciation. Everything that is indomitable and passionate in a human heart quickens them, on the contrary, with its own life. It is essential to die unreconciled and not of one's own free will. Suicide is a repudiation. The absurd man can only drain everything to the bitter end, and deplete himself. The absurd is his extreme tension, which he maintains constantly by solitary effort, for he knows that in that consciousness and in that day-to-day revolt he gives proof of his only truth, which is defiance. This is a first consequence. . . .

VI

Does Life Have A Meaning?

Richard Taylor

The question whether life has any meaning is difficult to interpret, and the more one concentrates his critical faculty on it the more it seems to elude him, or to evaporate as any intelligible question. One wants to turn it aside, as a source of embarrassment, as something that, if it cannot be abolished, should at least be decently covered. And yet I think any reflective person recognizes that the question it raises is important, and that it ought to have a significant answer.

If the idea of meaningfulness is difficult to grasp in this context, so that we are unsure what sort of thing would amount to answering the question, the idea of meaninglessness is perhaps less so. If, then, we can bring before our minds a clear image of meaningless existence, then perhaps we can take a step toward coping with our original question by seeing to what extent our lives, as we actually find them, resemble that image, and draw such lessons as we are able to from the comparison.

Meaningless Existence

A perfect image of meaninglessness, of the kind we are seeking, is found in the ancient myth of Sisyphus. Sisyphus, it will be remembered, betrayed divine secrets to mortals, and for this he was condemned by the gods to roll a stone to the top of a hill, the stone then immediately to roll back down, again to be pushed to the top by Sisyphus, to roll down once more, and so on again and again, *forever*. Now in this we have the picture of meaningless, pointless toil, of a meaningless existence that is absolutely *never* redeemed. It is not even redeemed by a death that, if it were to accomplish nothing more, would at least bring this idiotic cycle to a close. If we were invited to imagine Sisyphus struggling for awhile and accomplishing nothing, perhaps eventually falling from exhaustion, so that we might suppose him then eventually turning to something having some sort of promise, then the meaninglessness of the chapter of his life would not be so stark. It would be a dark and dreadful dream, from which he eventually awakens to sunlight and reality. But he does not awaken, for there is nothing for him to awaken to. His repetitive toil is his life and reality, and it goes on forever, and it is without any meaning whatever. Nothing ever comes of what he is doing, except simply, more of the same. Not by one step, nor by a thousand, nor by ten thousand does he even expiate by the smallest token the sin against the gods that led him into this fate. Nothing comes of it, nothing at all.

This ancient myth has always enchanted men, for countless meanings can be read into it. Some of the ancients apparently thought it symbolized the perpetual rising and setting of the sun, and others the repetitious crashing of the waves upon the shore. Probably the commonest interpretation is that it symbolizes man's eternal struggle and unquenchable spirit, his determination always to try once more in the face of overwhelming discouragement. This interpretation is further supported by that version of the myth according to which Sisyphus was commanded to roll the stone *over* the hill, so that it would finally roll down the other side, but was never quite able to make it.

I am not concerned with rendering or defending any interpretation of this myth, however. I have cited it only for the one element it does unmistakably contain, namely, that of a repetitious, cyclic activity that never comes to anything. We could contrive other images of this that would serve just as well, and no myth-makers are needed to supply the materials of it. Thus, we can imagine two persons transporting a stone—or even a precious gem, it does not matter—back and forth, relay style. One carries it to a near or distant point where it is received by the other; it is returned to its starting point, there to be recovered by the first, and the process is repeated over and over. Except in this relay nothing counts as winning, and nothing brings the contest to any close, each step only leads to a repetition of itself. Or we can imagine two groups of prisoners, one of them engaged in digging a prodigious hole in the ground that is no sooner finished than it is filled in again by the other group, the latter then digging a new hole that is at once filled in by the first group, and so on and on endlessly.

Now what stands out in all such pictures as oppressive and dejecting is not that the beings who enact these roles suffer any torture or pain, for it need not be assumed that they do. Nor is it that their labors are great, for they are no greater than the labors commonly undertaken by most men most of the time. According to the original myth, the stone is so large that Sisyphus never quite gets it to the top and must groan under every step, so that his enormous labor is all for nought. But this is not what appalls. It is not that his great struggle comes to nothing, but that his existence itself is without meaning. Even if we suppose, for example, that the stone is but a pebble that can be carried effortlessly, or that the holes dug by the prisoners are but small ones, not the slightest meaning is introduced into their lives. The stone that Sisyphus moves to the top of the hill, whether we think of it as large or small, still rolls back every time, and the process is repeated forever. Nothing comes of it, and the work is simply pointless. That is the element of the myth that I wish to capture.

Again, it is not the fact that the labors of Sisyphus continue forever that deprives them of meaning. It is, rather, the implication of this: that they come to nothing. The image would not be changed by our supposing him to push a different stone up every time, each to roll down again. But if we supposed that these stones, instead of rolling back to their places as if they had never been moved, were assembled at the top of the hill and there incorporated, say, in a beautiful and enduring temple, then the aspect of meaninglessness would disappear. His labors would then have a point, something would come of them all, and although one could perhaps still say it was not worth it, one could not say that the life of Sisyphus was devoid of meaning altogether. Meaningfulness would at least have made an appearance, and we could see what it was.

That point will need remembering. But in the meantime, let us note another way in which the image of meaninglessness can be altered by making only a very slight change. Let us suppose that the gods, while condemning Sisyphus to the fate just described, at the same time, as an afterthought, waxed perversely merciful by implanting in him a strange and irrational impulse; namely, a compulsive impulse to roll stones. We may if we like, to make this more graphic, suppose they accomplish this by implanting in him some substance that has this effect on his character and drives. I call this perverse, because from our point of view there is clearly no reason why anyone should have a persistent and insatiable desire to do something so pointless as that. Nevertheless, suppose that is Sisyphus' condition. He has but one obsession, which is to roll stones, and it is an obsession that is only for the moment appeased by his rolling them—he no sooner gets a stone rolled to the top of the hill than he is restless to roll up another.

Now it can be seen why this little afterthought of the gods, which I called perverse, was also in fact merciful. For they have by this device managed to give Sisyphus precisely what he wants—by making him want precisely what they inflict on him. However it may appear to us, Sisyphus' fate now does not appear to him as a condemnation, but the very reverse. His one desire in life is to roll stones, and he is absolutely guaranteed its endless fulfillment. Where otherwise he might profoundly have wished surcease, and even welcomed the quiet of death to release him from endless boredom and meaninglessness, his life is now filled with mission and meaning, and he seems to himself to have been given an entry to heaven. Nor need he even fear death, for the gods have promised him an endless opportunity to indulge his single purpose, without concern or frustration. He will be able to roll stones *forever*.

What we need to mark most carefully at this point is that the picture with which we began has not really been changed in the least by adding this supposition. Exactly the same things happen as before. The only change is in Sisyphus' view of them. The picture before was the image of meaningless activity and existence. It was created precisely to be an image of that. It has not lost that meaninglessness, it has now gained not the least shred of meaningfulness. The stones still roll back as before, each phase of Sisyphus' life still exactly resembles all the others, the task is never completed, nothing comes of it, no temple ever begins to rise, and all this cycle of the same pointless thing over and over goes on forever in this picture as in the other. The *only* thing that has happened is this: Sisyphus has been reconciled to it, and indeed more, he has been led to embrace it. Not, however, by reason or persuasion, but by nothing more rational than the potency of a new substance in his veins.

The Meaninglessness of Life

I believe the foregoing provides a fairly clear content to the idea of meaninglessness and, through it, some hint of what meaningfulness, in this sense, might be. Meaninglessness is essentially endless pointlessness, and meaningfulness is therefore the opposite. Activity, and even long, drawn-out and repetitive activity, has a meaning if it has some significant culmination, some more or less lasting end that can be considered to have been the direction and purpose of the activity. But the descriptions so far also provide something else; namely, the suggestion of how an existence that is objectively meaningless, in this sense, can nevertheless acquire a meaning for him whose existence it is.

Now let us ask: Which of these pictures does life in fact resemble? And let us not begin with our own lives, for here both our prejudices and wishes are great, but with the life in general that we share with the rest of creation. We shall find, I think, that it all has a certain pattern, and that this pattern is by now easily recognized.

We can begin anywhere, only saving human existence for our last consideration. We can, for example, begin with any animal. It does not matter where we begin, because the result is going to be exactly the same.

Thus, for example, there are caves in New Zealand, deep and dark, whose floors are quiet pools and whose walls and ceilings are covered with soft light. As one gazes in wonder in the stillness of these caves it seems that the Creator has reproduced there in microcosm the heavens themselves, until one scarcely remembers the enclosing presence of the walls. As one looks more closely, however, the scene is explained. Each dot of light identifies an ugly worm, whose luminous tail is meant to attract insects from the surrounding darkness. As from time to time one of these insects draws near it becomes entangled in a sticky thread lowered by the worm, and is eaten. This goes on month after month, the blind worm lying there in the barren stillness waiting to entrap an occasional bit of nourishment that will only sustain it to another bit of nourishment until. . . . Until what? What great thing awaits all this long and repetitious effort and makes it worthwhile? Really nothing. The larva just transforms itself finally to a tiny winged adult that lacks even mouth parts to feed and lives only a day or two. These adults, as soon as they have mated and laid eggs, are themselves caught in the threads and are devoured by the cannibalist worms, often without having ventured into the day, the only point to their existence having now been fulfilled. This has been going on for millions of years, and to no end other than that the same meaningless cycle may continue for another millions of years.

All living things present essentially the same spectacle. The larva of a certain cicada burrows in the darkness of the earth for seventeen years, through season after season, to emerge finally into the daylight for a brief flight, lay its eggs, and die—this all to repeat itself during the next seventeen years, and so on to eternity. We have already noted, in another connection, the struggles of fish, made only that others may do the same after them and that this cycle, having no other point than itself, may never cease. Some birds span an entire side of the globe each year and then return, only to insure that others may follow the same incredibly long path again and again. One is led to wonder what the point of it all is, with what great triumph this ceaseless effort, repeating itself through millions of years, might finally culminate, and why it should go on and on for so long, accomplishing nothing, getting nowhere. But then one realizes that there is no point to it at all, that it really culminates in nothing, that each of these cycles, so filled with toil, is to be followed only by more of the same. The point of any living thing's life is, evidently, nothing but life itself.

This life of the world thus presents itself to our eyes as a vast machine, feeding on itself, running on and on forever to nothing. And we are part of that life. To be sure, we are not just the same, but the differences are not so great as we like to think; many are merely invented, and none really cancels the kind of meaninglessness that we found in Sisyphus and that we find all around, wherever anything lives. We are conscious of our activity. Our goals, whether in any significant sense we choose them or not, are things of which we are at least partly aware and can therefore in some sense appraise. More significantly, perhaps men have a history, as other animals do not, such that each generation does not precisely resemble all those before. Still, if we can in imagination disengage our wills from our lives and disregard the deep interest each man has in his own existence, we shall find that they do not so little resemble the existence of Sisyphus. We toil after goals, most of them—indeed every single one of them—of transitory significance and, having gained one of them, we immediately set forth for the next, as if that one had never been, with this next one being essentially more of the same. Look at a busy street any day, and observe the throng going hither and thither. To what? Some office or shop, where the same things will be done today as were done yesterday, and are done now so they may be repeated tomorrow. And if we think that, unlike Sisyphus, these labors do have a point, that they culminate in something lasting and, independently of our own deep interests in them, very worthwhile, then we simply have not considered the thing closely enough. Most such effort is directed only to the establishment and perpetuation of home and family; that is, to the begetting of others who will follow in our steps to do more of the same. Each man's life thus resembles one of Sisyphus' climbs to the summit of his hill, and each day of it one of his steps; the difference is that whereas Sisyphus himself returns to push the stone up again, we leave this to our children. We at one point imagined that the labors of Sisyphus finally culminated in the creation of a temple, but for this to make any difference it had to be a temple that would at least endure, adding beauty to the world for the remainder of time. Our achievements, even though they are often beautiful, are mostly bubbles; and those that do last, like the sand-swept pyramids, soon become mere curiosities while around them the rest of mankind continues its perpetual toting of rocks, only to see them roll down. Nations are built upon the bones of their founders and pioneers, but only to decay and crumble before long, their rubble then becoming the foundation for others directed to exactly the same fate. The picture of Sisyphus is the picture of existence of the individual man, great or unknown, of nations, of the race of men, and of the very life of the world.

On a country road one sometimes comes upon the ruined hulks of a house and once extensive buildings, all in collapse and spread over with weeds. A curious eye can in imagination reconstruct from what is left a once warm and thriving life, filled with purpose. There was the hearth, where a family once talked, sang, and made plans; there were the rooms, where people loved, and babes were born to a rejoicing mother; there are the musty remains of a sofa, infested with bugs, once bought at a dear price to enhance an ever-growing comfort, beauty, and warmth. Every small piece of junk fills the mind with what once, not long ago, was utterly real, with children's voices, plans made, and enterprises embarked upon. That is how these stones of Sisyphus were rolled up, and that is how they became incorporated into a beautiful temple, and that temple is what now lies before you. Meanwhile other buildings, institutions, nations, and civilizations spring up all around, only to share the same fate before long. And if the question "What for?" is now asked, the answer is clear: so that just this may go on forever.

The two pictures—of Sisyphus and of our own lives, if we look at them from a distance—are in outline the same and convey to the mind the same image. It is not surprising, then, that men invent ways of denying it, their religions proclaiming a heaven that does not crumble, their hymnals and prayer books declaring a significance to life of which our eyes provide no hint whatever.[1] Even our philosophies portray some permanent and lasting good at which all may aim, from the changeless forms invented by Plato to the beatific vision of St. Thomas and the ideals of permanence contrived by the moderns. When these fail to convince, then earthly ideals such as universal justice and brotherhood are conjured up to take their places and give meaning to man's seemingly endless pilgrimage, some final state that will be ushered in when the last obstacle is removed and the last stone pushed to the hilltop. No one believes, of course, that any such state will be final, or even wants it to be in case it means that human existence would then cease to be a struggle; but in the meaning such ideas serve a very real need.

The Meaning of Life

We noted that Sisyphus' existence would have meaning if there were some point to his labors, if his efforts ever culminated in something that was not just an occasion for fresh labors of the same kind. But that is precisely the meaning it lacks. And human existence resembles his in that respect. Men do achieve things—they scale their towers and raise their stones to their hilltops—but every such accomplishment fades, providing only an occasion for renewed labors of the same kind.

But here we need to note something else that has been mentioned, but its significance not explored, and that is the state of mind and feeling with which such labors are undertaken. We noted that if Sisyphus had a keen and unappeasable desire to be doing just what he found himself doing, then, although his life would in no way be changed, it would nevertheless have a

---

[1]A popular Christian hymn, sung often at funerals and typical of many hymns, expresses this thought:
Swift to its close ebbs out life's little day;
Earth's joys grow dim, its glories pass away;
Change and decay in all around I see:
O thou who changest not, abide with me.

meaning for him. It would be an irrational one, no doubt, because the desire itself would be only the product of the substance in his veins, and not any that reason could discover, but a meaning nevertheless.

And would it not, in fact, be a meaning incomparably better than the other? For let us examine again the first kind of meaning it could have. Let us suppose that, without having any interest in rolling stones, as such, and finding this, in fact, a galling toil, Sisyphus did nevertheless have a deep interest in raising a temple, one that would be beautiful and lasting. And let us suppose he succeeded in this, that after ages of dreadful toil, all directed at this final result, he did at last complete his temple, such that now he could say his work was done and he could rest and forever enjoy the result. Now what? What picture now presents itself to our minds? It is precisely the picture of infinite boredom! Of Sisyphus doing nothing ever again, but contemplating what he has already wrought and can no longer add anything to, and contemplating it for an eternity! Now in this picture we have a meaning for Sisyphus' existence, a point for his prodigious labor, because we have put it there; yet, at the same time, that which is really worthwhile seems to have slipped away entirely. Where before we were presented with the nightmare of eternal and pointless activity, we are now confronted with the hell of its eternal absence.

Our second picture, then, wherein we imagined Sisyphus to have had inflicted on him the irrational desire to be doing just what he found himself doing, should not have been dismissed so abruptly. The meaning that picture lacked was no meaning that he or anyone could crave, and the strange meaning it had was perhaps just what we were seeking.

At this point, then, we can reintroduce what has been until now, it is hoped, resolutely pushed aside in an effort to view our lives and human existence with objectivity; namely, our own wills, our deep interest in what we find ourselves doing. If we do this we find that our lives do indeed still resemble that of Sisyphus, but that the meaningfulness they thus lack is precisely the meaningfulness of infinite boredom. At the same time, the strange meaningfulness they possess is that of the inner compulsion to be doing just what we were put here to do, and to go on doing it forever. This is the nearest we may hope to get to heaven, but the redeeming side of that fact is that we do thereby avoid a genuine hell.

If the builders of a great and flourishing ancient civilization could somehow return now to see archaeologists unearthing the trivial remnants of what they had once accomplished with such effort—see the fragments of pots and vases, a few broken statues, and such tokens of another age and greatness—they could indeed ask themselves what the point of it all was, if this is all it finally came to. Yet, it did not seem so to them then, for it was just the building, and not what was finally built, that gave their life meaning. Similarly, if the builders of the ruined home and farm that I described a short while ago could be brought back to see what is left, they would have the same feelings. What we construct in our imaginations as we look over these decayed and rusting pieces would reconstruct itself in their very memories, and certainly with unspeakable sadness. The piece of a sled at our feet would revive in them a warm Christmas. And what rich memories would there be in the broken crib? And the weed-covered remains of a fence would reproduce the scene of a great herd of livestock, so laboriously built up over so many years. What was it all worth, if this is the final result? Yet, again, it did not seem so to them through those many years of struggle and toil, and they did not imagine they were building a Gibraltar. The things to which they bent their backs day after day, realizing one by one their ephemeral plans, were precisely the things in which their wills were deeply involved, precisely the things in which their interests lay, and there was no need then to ask questions. There is no more need of them now—the day was sufficient to itself, and so was the life.

This is surely the way to look at all of life—at one's own life, and each day and moment it contains; of the life of a nation; of the species; of the life of the world; and of everything that breathes. Even the glow worms I described, whose cycles of existence over the millions of years seem so pointless when looked at by us, will seem entirely different to us if we can somehow try to view their existence from within. Their endless activity, which gets nowhere, is just what it is their will to pursue. This is its whole justification and meaning. Nor would it be any salvation to the birds who span the globe every year, back and forth, to have a home made for them in a cage with plenty of food and protection, so that they would not have to migrate any more. It would be their condemnation, for it is the doing that counts for them, and not what they hope to win by it. Flying these prodigious distances, never ending, is what it is in their veins to do, exactly as it was in Sisyphus' veins to roll stones, without end, after the gods had waxed merciful and implanted this in him.

A human being no sooner draws his first breath than he responds to the will that is in him to live. He no more asks whether it will be worthwhile, or whether anything of significance will come of it, than the worms and the birds. The point of his living is simply to be living, in the manner that it is his nature to be living. He goes through his life building his castles, each of these beginning to fade into time as the next is begun; yet, it would be no salvation to rest from all this. It would be a condemnation, and one that would in no way be redeemed were he able to gaze upon the things he has done, even if these were beautiful and absolutely permanent, as they never are. What counts is that one should be able to begin a new task, a new castle, a new bubble. It counts only because it is there to be done and he has the will to do it. The same will be the life of his children and of theirs; and if the philosopher is apt to see in this a pattern similar to the unending cycles of the existence of Sisyphus, and to despair, then it is indeed because the meaning and point he is seeking is not there—but mercifully so. The meaning of life is from within us, it is not bestowed from without, and it far exceeds in both its beauty and permanence any heaven of which men have ever dreamed or yearned for.

VII

Meaning and Value of Life

Paul Edwards

To the questions "Is human life ever worthwhile?" and "Does (or can) human life have any meaning?" many religious thinkers have offered affirmative answers with the proviso that these answers would not be justified unless two of the basic propositions of most Western religions were true—that human life is part of a divinely ordained cosmic scheme and that after death at least some human beings will be rewarded with eternal bliss. Thus, commenting on Bertrand Russell's statement that not only must each individual human life come to an end but that life in general will eventually die out, C. H. D. Clark contrasts this "doctrine of despair" with the beauty of the Christian scheme. "If we are asked to believe that all our striving is without final consequence," then "life is meaningless and it scarcely matters how we live if all will end in the dust of death." According to Christianity, on the other hand, "each action has vital significance." Clark assures us that "God's grand design is life eternal for those who walk in the steps of Christ. Here is the one grand incentive to good living. . . . As life is seen to have purpose and meaning, men find release from despair and the fear of death" (*Christianity and Bertrand Russell*, p. 30). In a similar vein, the Jewish existentialist Emil Fackenheim claims that "whatever meaning life acquires" is derived from the encounter between God and man. The meaning thus conferred upon human life "cannot be understood in terms of some finite human purpose, supposedly more ultimate than the meeting itself. For what could be more ultimate than the Presence of God?" It is true that God is not always "near," but "times of

Divine farness" are by no means devoid of meaning. "Times of Divine nearness do not light up themselves alone. Their meaning extends over all of life." There is a "dialectic between Divine nearness and Divine farness," and it points to "an eschatological future in which it is overcome" ("Judaism and the Meaning of Life").

Among unbelievers not a few maintain that life can be worthwhile and have meaning in some humanly important sense even if the religious world view is rejected. Others, however, agree with the religious theorists that our two questions must be given negative answers if there is no God and if death means personal annihilation. Having rejected the claims of religion, they therefore conclude that life is not worthwhile and that it is devoid of meaning. These writers, to whom we shall refer here as "pessimists," do not present their judgments as being merely expressions of certain moods or feelings but as conclusions that are in some sense objectively warranted. They offer reasons for their conclusions and imply that anybody reaching a contradictory conclusion is mistaken or irrational. Most pessimists do not make any clear separation between the statements that life is not worthwhile and that life is without meaning. They usually speak of the "futility" or the "vanity" of life, and presumably they mean by this both that life is not worth living and that it has no meaning. For the time being we, too, shall treat these statements as if they were equivalent. However, later we shall see that in certain contexts it becomes important to distinguish between them.

Our main concern in this article will be to appraise pessimism as just defined. We shall not discuss either the question whether life is part of a divinely ordained plan or the question whether we survive our bodily death. Our question will be whether the pessimistic conclusions are justified if belief in God and immortality are rejected. . . .

Strengths of the Pessimist Position

Is it possible for somebody who shares the pessimists' rejection of religion to reach different conclusions without being plainly irrational? Whatever reply may be possible, any intelligent and realistic person would surely have to concede that there is much truth in the pessimists' claims. That few people achieve real and lasting happiness, that the joys of life (where there are any) pass away much too soon, that totally unpredictable events frequently upset the best intentions and wreck the noblest plans—this and much more along the same lines is surely undeniable. Although one should not dogmatize that there will be no significant improvements in the future, the fate of past revolutions, undertaken to rid man of some of his apparently avoidable suffering, does not inspire great hope. The thought of death, too, even in those who are not so overwhelmed by it as Tolstoy, can be quite unendurable. Moreover, to many who have reflected on the implications of physical theory it seems plain that because of the constant increase of entropy in the universe all life anywhere will eventually die out. Forebodings of this kind moved Bertrand Russell to write his famous essay "A Free Man's Worship," in which he concluded that "all the labors of the ages, all the devotion, all the inspiration, all the noonday brightness of human genius, are destined to extinction in the vast death of the solar system, and the whole temple of man's achievement must inevitably be buried beneath the debris of a universe in ruins." Similarly, Wilhelm Ostwald observed that "in the longest run the sum of all human endeavor has no recognizable significance." Although it is disputed whether physical theory really has such gloomy implications, it would perhaps be wisest to assume that the position endorsed by Russell and Ostwald is well-founded.

Comparative Value Judgments about Life and Death

Granting the strong points in the pessimists' claims, it is still possible to detect certain confusions and dubious inferences in their arguments. To begin with, there is a very obvious inconsistency in the way writers like Darrow* and Tolstoy arrive at the conclusion that death is better than life. They begin by telling us that death is something terrible because it terminates the possibility of any of the experiences we value. From this they infer that nothing is really worth doing and that death is better than life. Ignoring for the moment the claim that in view of our inevitable death nothing is "worth doing," there very plainly seems to be an inconsistency in first judging death to be such a horrible evil and in asserting later on that death is better than life. Why was death originally judged to be an evil? Surely because it is the termination of life. And if something, y, is bad because it is the termination of something, x, this can be so only if x is good or has positive value. If x were not good, the termination of x would not be bad. One cannot consistently have it both ways.

To this it may be answered that life did have positive value prior to one's realization of death but that once a person has become aware of the inevitability of his destruction life becomes unbearable and that this is the real issue. This point of view is well expressed in the following exchange between Cassius and Brutus in Shakespeare's *Julius Caesar* (III.i. 102-105):

> CASSIUS: Why he that cuts off twenty years of life
> Cuts off so many years of fearing death.
> BRUTUS: Grant that, and then is death a benefit:
> So are we Caesar's friends that have abridged
> His time of fearing death.

There is a very simple reply to this argument. Granting that some people after

---

*Clarence Darrow (1857-1938), controversial American trial lawyer, author of two pessimistic pamphlets, "Is Life Worth Living?" and "Is the Human Race Getting Anywhere?" [Eds.]

once realizing their doom cannot banish the thought of it from their minds, so much so that it interferes with all their other activities, this is neither inevitable nor at all common. It is, on the contrary, in the opinion of all except some existentialists, morbid and pathological. The realization that one will die does not in the case of most people prevent them from engaging in activities which they regard as valuable or from enjoying the things they used to enjoy. To be told that one is not living "authentically" if one does not brood about death day and night is simply to be insulted gratuitously. A person who knows that his talents are not as great as he would wish or that he is not as handsome as he would have liked to be is not usually judged to live "inauthentically," but on the contrary to be sensible if he does not constantly brood about his limitations and shortcomings and uses whatever talents he does possess to maximum advantage.

There is another and more basic objection to the claim that death is better than life. This objection applies equally to the claim that while death is better than life it would be better still not to have been born in the first place and to the judgment that life is better than death. It should be remembered that we are here concerned with such pronouncements when they are intended not merely as the expression of certain moods but as statements which are in some sense true or objectively warranted. It may be argued that a value comparison—any judgment to the effect that A is better or worse than B or as good as B—makes sense only if both A and B are, in the relevant respect, in principle open to inspection. If somebody says, for example, that Elizabeth Taylor is a better actress than Betty Grable, this seems quite intelligible. Or, again, if it is said that life for the Jews is better in the United States than it was in Germany under the Nazis, this also seems readily intelligible. In such cases the terms of the comparison are observable or at any rate describable. These conditions are fulfilled in some cases when value comparisons are made between life and death, but they are not fulfilled in the kind of case with which Tolstoy and the pessimists are concerned. If the conception of an afterlife is intelligible, then it would make sense for a believer or for somebody who has not made up his mind to say such things as "Death cannot be worse than this life" or "I wonder if it will be any better for me after I am dead." Achilles, in the *Iliad*, was not making a senseless comparison when he exclaimed that he would rather act

> . . . as a serf of another,
> A man of little possessions, with scanty means of subsistence,
> Than rule as a ghostly monarch the ghosts of all the departed.

Again, the survivors can meaningfully say about a deceased individual "It is better (for the world) that he is dead" or the opposite. For the person himself, however, if there is no afterlife, death is not a possible object of observation or experience, and statements by him that his own life is better than, as good as, or worse than his own death, unless they are intended to be no more than expressions of certain wishes or moods, must be dismissed as senseless. At first sight the contention that in the circumstances under discussion value comparisons between life and death are senseless may seem implausible because of the widespread tendency to think of death as a shadowy kind of life—as sleep, rest, or some kind of home-coming. Such "descriptions" may be admirable as poetry or consolation, but taken literally they are simply false.

Irrelevance of the Distant Future

These considerations do not, however, carry us very far. They do not show either that life is worth living or that it "has meaning." Before tackling these problems directly, something should perhaps be said about the curious and totally arbitrary preference of the future to the present, to which writers like Tolstoy and Darrow are committed without realizing it. Darrow implies that life would not be "futile" if it were not an endless cycle of the same kind of activities and if instead it were like a journey toward a destination. Tolstoy clearly implies that life would be worthwhile, that some of our actions at least would have a "reasonable meaning," if the present life were followed by eternal bliss. Presumably, what would make life no longer futile as far as Darrow is concerned is some feature of the destination, not merely the fact that it is a destination; and what would make life worthwhile in Tolstoy's opinion is not merely the eternity of the next life but the "bliss" which it would confer—eternal misery and torture would hardly do. About the bliss in the next life, if there is such a next life, Tolstoy shows no inclination to ask "What for?" or "So what?" But if bliss in the next life is not in need of any further justification, why should any bliss that there might be in the present life need justification?

The Logic of Value Judgments

Many of the pessimists appear to be confused about the logic of value judgments. It makes sense for a person to ask about something "Is it really worthwhile?" or "Is it really worth the trouble?" if he does not regard it as intrinsically valuable or if he is weighing it against another good with which it may be in conflict. It does not make sense to ask such a question about something he regards as valuable in its own right and where there is no conflict with the attainment of any other good. (This observation, it should be noted, is quite independent of what view one takes of the logical status of intrinsic value judgments.) A person driving to the beach on a crowded Sunday, may, upon finally getting there, reflect on whether the trip was really worthwhile. Or, after undertaking a series of medical treatments, somebody may ask whether it was worth the time and the money involved. Such questions make sense because the discomforts of a car ride and the time and money spent on medical treatments are not usually judged to be valuable for their own sake. Again, a woman who has given up a career as a physician in order to raise a family may ask herself whether it was worthwhile, and in this case the question would make sense not because she regards the raising of a family as no more than a means, but because she is weighing it against another good. However, if somebody is very happy, for any number of reasons—because he is in love, because he won the Nobel prize, because his child recovered from a serious illness—and if this happiness does not prevent him from doing or experiencing anything else he regards as valuable, it would not occur to him to ask "Is it worthwhile?" Indeed, this question would be incomprehensible to him, just as Tolstoy himself would presumably not have known what to make of the question had it been raised about the bliss in the hereafter.

It is worth recalling here that we live not in the distant future but in the present and also, in a sense, in the relatively near future. To bring the subject down to earth, let us consider some everyday occurrences: A man with a toothache goes to a dentist, and the dentist helps him so that the toothache disappears. A man is falsely accused of a crime and is faced with the possibility of a severe sentence as well as with the loss of his reputation; with the help of a devoted attorney his innocence is established, and he is acquitted. It is true that a hundred years later all of the participants in these events will be dead and none of them will *then* be able to enjoy the fruits of any of the efforts involved. But this most emphatically does not imply that the dentist's efforts were not worthwhile or that the attorney's work was not worth doing. To bring in considerations of what will or will not happen in the remote future is, in such and many other though certainly not in all human situations, totally irrelevant. Not only is the finality of death irrelevant here; equally irrelevant are the facts, if they are facts, that life is an endless cycle of the same kind of activities and that the history of the universe is not a drama with a happy ending.

This is, incidentally, also the answer to religious apologists like C. H. D. Clark who maintain that all striving is pointless if it is "without final consequence" and that "it scarcely matters how we live if all will end in the dust of death." Striving is not pointless if it achieves what it is intended to achieve even if it is without *final* consequence, and it matters a great deal how we live if we have certain standards and goals, although we cannot avoid "the dust of death."

The Vanished Past

In asserting the worthlessness of life Schopenhauer remarked that "what has been exists as little as what has never been" and that "something of great importance now past is inferior to something of little importance now present." Several comments are in order here. To begin with, if Schopenhauer is right, it must work both ways: if only the present counts, then past sorrows no less than past pleasures do not "count." Furthermore, the question whether "something of great importance now past is inferior to something of little importance now present" is not, as Schopenhauer supposed, a straightforward question of fact but rather one of valuation, and different answers, none of which can be said to be mistaken, will be given by different people according to their circumstances and interests. Viktor Frankl, the founder of "logotherapy," has compared the pessimist to a man who observes, with fear and sadness, how his wall calendar grows thinner and thinner as he removes a sheet from it every day. The kind of person whom Frankl admires, on the other hand, "files each successive leaf neatly away with its predecessors" and reflects "with pride and joy" on all the richness represented by the leaves removed from the calendar. Such a person will not in old age envy the young. " 'No, thank you,' he will think. 'Instead of possibilities, I have realities in my past' " *(Man's Search for Meaning,* pp. 192-193). This passage is quoted not because it contains any great wisdom but because it illustrates that we are concerned here not with judgments of fact but with value judgments and that Schopenhauer's is not the only one that is possible. Nevertheless, his remarks are, perhaps, a healthy antidote to the cheap consolation and the attempts to cover up deep and inevitable misery that are the stock in trade of a great deal of popular psychology. Although Schopenhauer's judgments about the inferior value of the past cannot be treated as objectively true propositions, they express only too well what a great many human beings are bound to feel on certain occasions. To a man dying of cancer it is small consolation to reflect that there was a time when he was happy and flourishing; and while there are undoubtedly some old people who do not envy the young, it may be suspected that more often the kind of talk advocated by the prophets of positive thinking is a mask for envy and a defense against exceedingly painful feelings of regret and helplessness in the face of aging and death and the now unalterable past. . . .

Is Human Life Ever Worthwhile?

Let us now turn to the question of whether life is ever worth living. This also appears to be denied by the pessimists when they speak of the vanity or the futility of human life. We shall see that in a sense it cannot be established that the pessimists are "mistaken," but it is also quite easy to show that in at least two senses which seem to be of importance to many people, human lives frequently are worth living. To this end, let us consider under what circumstances a person is likely to raise the question "Is my life (still) worthwhile?" and what is liable to provoke somebody into making a statement like "My life has ceased to be worth living." We saw in an earlier section that when we say of certain acts, such as the efforts of a dentist or a lawyer, that they were worthwhile we are claiming that they achieved certain goals. Something similar seems to be involved when we say that a person's life is (still) worthwhile or worth living. We seem to be making two assertions: first, that the person has some goals (other than merely to be dead or to have his pains eased) which do not seem to him to be trivial and, second, that there is some genuine possibility that he will attain these goals. These observations are confirmed by various systematic studies of people who contemplated suicide, of others who unsuccessfully attempted suicide, and of situations in which people did commit suicide. When the subjects of these studies declared that their lives were no longer worth living they generally meant either that there was nothing left in their lives about which they seriously cared or that there was no real likelihood of attaining any of the goals that mattered to them. It should be noted that in this sense an individual may well be mistaken in his assertion that his life is or is not worthwhile any longer: he may, for example, mistake a temporary indisposition for a more permanent loss of interest, or, more likely, he may falsely estimate his chances of achieving the ends he wishes to attain.

Different Senses of "Worthwhile"

According to the account given so far, one is saying much the same thing in declaring a life to be worthwhile and in asserting that it has meaning in the "terrestrial" sense of the word.* There is, however, an interesting difference. When we say that a person's life has meaning (in the terrestrial sense) we are not committed to the claim that the goal or goals to which he is devoted have any positive value. (This is a slight oversimplification, assuming greater uniformity in the use of "meaning of life" than actually exists, but it will not seriously affect any of the controversial issues discussed here.) The question "As long as his life was dedicated to the spread of communism it has meaning to *him*, but was it really meaningful?" seems to be senseless. We are inclined to say, "If his life had meaning to him, then it had meaning—that's all there is to it." We are not inclined (or we are much less inclined) to say something of this kind when we speak of the worth of a person's life. We might say—for example, of someone like Eichmann—"While he was carrying out the extermination program, his life *seemed* worthwhile to him, but since his goal was so horrible, his life *was not* worthwhile." One might perhaps distinguish between a "subjective" and an "objective" sense of "worthwhile." In the sub-

*Edwards here refers to the sense of 'meaning' according to which certain purposes are to be found *in* a particular person's life. The distinction between a 'terrestrial' and a 'cosmic' sense of 'meaning' is derived from Baier. [Eds.]

jective sense, saying that a person's life is worthwhile simply means that he is attached to some goals which he does not consider trivial and that these goals are attainable for him. In declaring that somebody's life is worthwhile in the objective sense, one is saying that he is attached to certain goals which are both attainable and of positive value.

It may be held that unless one accepts some kind of rationalist or intuitionist view of fundamental value judgments one would have to conclude that in the objective sense of "worthwhile" no human life (and indeed no human action) could ever be shown to be worthwhile. There is no need to enter here into a discussion of any controversial questions about the logical status of fundamental value judgments. But it may be pointed out that somebody who favors a subjectivist or emotivist account can quite consistently allow for the distinction between ends that only seem to have positive value and those that really do. To mention just one way in which this could be done: one may distinguish between ends that would be approved by rational and sympathetic human beings and those that do not carry such an endorsement. One may then argue that when we condemn such a life as Eichmann's as not being worthwhile we mean not that the ends to which he devoted himself possess some non-natural characteristic of badness but that no rational or sympathetic person would approve of them.

The Pessimists' Special Standards

The unexciting conclusion of this discussion is that some human lives are at certain times not worthwhile in either of the two senses we have distinguished, that some are worthwhile in the subjective but not in the objective sense, some in the objective but not in the subjective sense, and some are worthwhile in both senses. The unexcitingness of this conclusion is not a reason for rejecting it, but some readers may question whether it meets the challenge of the pessimists. The pessimist, it may be countered, surely does not deny the plain fact that human beings are on occasions attached to goals which do not seem to them trivial, and it is also not essential to his position to deny (and most pessimists do not in fact deny) that these goals are sometimes attainable. The pessimist may even allow that in a superficial ("immediate") sense the goals which people try to achieve are of positive value, but he would add that because our lives are not followed by eternal bliss they are not "really" or "ultimately" worthwhile. If this is so, then the situation may be characterized by saying that the ordinary man and the pessimist do not mean the same by "worthwhile," or that they do mean the same in that both use it as a positive value expression but that their standards are different: the standards of the pessimist are very much more demanding than those of most ordinary people.

Anybody who agrees that death is final will have to concede that the pessimist is not mistaken in his contention that judged by *his* standards, life is never worthwhile. However, the pessimist is mistaken if he concludes, as frequently happens, that life is not worthwhile by ordinary standards because it is not worthwhile by his standards. Furthermore, setting aside the objection mentioned earlier (that there is something arbitrary about maintaining that eternal bliss makes life worthwhile but not allowing this role to bliss in the present life), one may justifiably ask why one should abandon ordinary standards in favor of those of the pessimist. Ordinarily, when somebody changes standards (for example, when a school raises or lowers its standards of admission) such a change can be supported by reasons. But how can the pessimist justify his special standards? It should be pointed out here that our ordinary standards do something for us which the pessimist's standards do not: they guide our choices, and as long as we live we can hardly help making choices. It is true that in one type of situation the pessimist's standards also afford guidance—namely, in deciding whether to go on living. It is notorious, however, that whether or not they are, by their own standards, rational in this, most pessimists do not commit suicide. They are then faced with much the same choices as other people. In these situations their own demanding standards are of no use, and in fact they avail themselves of the ordinary standards. Schopenhauer, for example, believed that if he had hidden his antireligious views he would have had no difficulty in obtaining an academic appointment and other worldly honors. He may have been mistaken in this belief, but in any event his actions indicate that he regarded intellectual honesty as worthwhile in a sense in which worldly honors were not. Again, when Darrow had the choice between continuing as counsel for the Chicago and North Western Railway and taking on the defense of Eugene V. Debs and his harassed and persecuted American Railway Union, he did not hesitate to choose the latter, apparently regarding it as worthwhile to go to the assistance of the suppressed and not worthwhile to aid the suppressor. In other words, although no human action is worthwhile, some human actions and presumably some human lives are less unworthwhile than others.

VIII

'Nothing Matters'

Is 'the Annihilation of Values' something that could happen?

R. M. Hare

I

I want to start by telling you a story about something which once happened in my house in Oxford—I cannot remember now all the exact details, but will do my best to be accurate. It was about nine years ago, and we had staying with us a Swiss boy from Lausanne; he was about 18 years old and had just left school. He came of a Protestant family and was both sincerely religious and full of the best ideals. My wife and I do not read French very well, and so we had few French books in the house; but those we had we put by his bedside; they included one or two anthologies of French poetry, the works of Villon, the confessions of Rousseau and, lastly, *L'Etranger* by Camus. After our friend had been with us for about a week, and we thought we were getting to know him as a cheerful, vigourous, enthusiastic young man of a sort that anybody is glad to know, he surprised us one morning by asking for cigarettes—he had not smoked at all up till then—and retiring to his room, where he smoked them one after the other, coming down hurriedly to meals, during which he would say nothing at all. After dinner in the evening, at which he ate little, he said he would go for a walk. So he went out and spent the next

Excerpted from R. M. Hare, " 'Nothing Matters,' "*Applications of Moral Philosophy* (1972), pp. 32–39; reprinted by permission of R. M. Hare. A French version of this essay was published in the proceedings of the Cercle Cultural de Royaumont, under the title *La Philosophie Analytique* (Cahiers de Royaumont, no. IV, Editions de Minuit, 1959).

three hours—as we learnt from him later—tramping round and round Port Meadow (which is an enormous, rather damp field beside the river Thames on the outskirts of Oxford). Since we were by this time rather worried about what could be on his mind, when he came back at about eleven o'clock we sat him down in an armchair and asked him what the trouble was. It appeared that he had been reading Camus's novel, and had become convinced that *nothing matters.* I do not remember the novel very well; but at the end of it, I think, the hero, who is about to be executed for a murder in which he saw no particular point even when he committed it, shouts, with intense conviction, to the priest who is trying to get him to confess and receive absolution, "Nothing matters." It was this proposition of the truth of which our friend had become convinced: *Rien, rien n'avait d'importance.*

Now this was to me in many ways an extraordinary experience. I have known a great many students at Oxford, and not only have I never known one of them affected in this way, but when I have told this story to English people they have thought that I was exaggerating, or that our Swiss friend must have been an abnormal, peculiar sort of person. Yet he was not; he was about as well-balanced a young man as you could find. There was, however, no doubt at all about the violence with which he had been affected by what he had read. And as he sat there, it occurred to me that as a moral philosopher I ought to have something to say to him that would be relevant to his situation.

Now in Oxford, moral philosophy is thought of primarily as the study of the concepts and the langauge that we use when we are discussing moral questions: we are concerned with such problems as 'What does it mean to say that something *matters,* or *does not matter?*' We are often accused of occupying ourselves with trivial questions about words; but this sort of question is not really trivial; if it were, philosophy itself would be a trivial subject. For philosophy as we know it began when Socrates refused to answer questions about, for example, what *was* right or wrong before he had discussed the question '*What is it to be* right or wrong?'; and it does not really make any difference if this question is put in the form 'What is rightness?' or 'What is the meaning of the word "right"?' or 'What is its use in our language?' So, like Socrates, I thought that the correct way to start my discussion with my Swiss friend was to ask what was the meaning or function of the word 'matters' in our language; what is it to be important?

He very soon agreed that when we say something matters or is important what we are doing, in saying this, is to express concern about that something. If a person is concerned about something and wishes to give expression in language to this concern, two ways of doing this are to say 'This is important' or 'It matters very much that so and so should happen and not so and so'. Here, however, I must utter a warning lest I be misunderstood. The word 'express' has been used recently as a technical term by a certain school of moral philosophers known as the Emotivists. The idea has therefore gained currency that if a philosopher says that a certain form of expression is used to *express* something, there must be something a bit shady or suspicious about that form of expression. I am not an emotivist, and I am using the word 'express' as it is normally used outside philosophical circles, in a perfectly neutral sense. When I say that the words 'matters' and 'important' are used to express concern, I am no more committed to an emotivist view of the meaning of those words than I would be if I said 'The word "not" is used in English to express negation' or 'Mathematicians use the symbol "+" to express the operation of addition'.

Having secured my friend's agreement on this point, I then pointed out to him something that followed immediately from it. This is that when somebody says that something matters or does not matter, we want to know *whose* concern is being expressed or otherwise referred to. If the function of the expression 'matters' is to express concern, and if concern is always *somebody's* concern, we can always ask, when it is said that something matters or does not matter, 'Whose concern?' The answer to these questions is in most cases obvious from the context. In the simplest cases it is the speaker who is expressing his own concern. If we did not know what it meant in these simple cases to say that something matters, we should not be able to understand what is meant by more complicated, indirect uses of the expression. We know what it is to be concerned about something and to express this concern by saying that it matters. So we understand when anybody else says the same thing; he is then expressing his own concern. But sometimes we say things like 'It matters (or doesn't matter) to *him* whether so and so happens'. Here we are not expressing our own concern; we are referring indirectly to the concern of the person about whom we are speaking. In such cases, in contrast to the more simple cases, it is usual to give a clear indication of the person whose concern is being referred to. Thus we say, 'It doesn't matter *to him*'. If we said 'It doesn't matter', and left out the words 'to him', it could be assumed in ordinary speech, in the absence of any indication to the contrary, that the speaker was expressing his *own* unconcern.

II

With these explanations made, my friend and I then returned to the remark at the end of Camus's novel, and asked whether we really understood it. 'Nothing matters' is printed on the page. So somebody's unconcern for absolutely everything is presumably being expressed or referred to. But whose? As soon as we ask this question we see that there is something funny, not indeed about the remark as made by the character in the novel, in the context in which he is described as making it (though there is something funny even about that, as we shall see), but about the effect of this remark upon my friend. If we ask whose unconcern is being expressed, there are three people to be considered, one imaginary and two real: the character in the novel, the writer of the novel, and its reader, my Swiss friend. The idea that Camus was expressing his *own* unconcern about everything can be quickly dismissed. For to produce a work of art as good as this novel is something which cannot be done by someone who is not most deeply concerned, not only with the form of the work, but with its content. It is quite obvious that it mattered very much to Camus to say as clearly and tellingly as possible what he had to say; and this argues a concern not only for the work, but for its readers.

As for the character in the novel, who thus expresses his unconcern, a writer of a novel can put what sentiments he pleases in the mouths of his characters—subject to the limits of verisimilitude. By the time we have read this particular novel, it seems to us not inappropriate that the character who is the hero of it should express unconcern about absolutely everything. In fact, it has been pretty clear right from the beginning of the novel that he has not for a long time been deeply concerned about anything; that is the sort of person he is. And indeed there are such people. I do not mean to say that there has ever been anybody who has literally been concerned about *nothing*. For what we are concerned about comes out in what we choose to *do*; to be concerned about something is to be disposed to make certain choices, certain efforts, in the attempt to affect in some way that about which we are concerned. I do not think that anybody has ever been *completely* unconcerned about *everything,* because everybody is always doing something, choosing one thing rather than another; and these choices reveal what it is he thinks matters, even if he is not able to express this in words. And the character in Camus's novel, though throughout the book he is depicted as a person who is rather given to unconcern, is depicted at the end of it, when he says these words, as one who is spurred by something—it is not clear what: a sense of conviction, or revelation, or merely irritation—to seize the priest by the collar of his cassock with such violence, while saying this to him, that they had to be separated by the warders. There is something of a contradiction in being so violently concerned to express unconcern; if nothing *really* mattered to him, one feels, he would have been too bored to make this rather dramatic scene.

Still, one must allow writers to portray their characters as their art seems to require, with all their inconsistencies. But why, because an imaginary Algerian prisoner expressed unconcern for the world which he was shortly to leave, should my friend, a young Swiss student with the world before him, come to share the same sentiments? I therefore asked him whether it was really true that nothing mattered to him. And of course it was not true. He was not in the position of the prisoner but in the position of most of us; he was concerned not about nothing, but about many things. His problem was not to find something to be concerned about—something that mattered—but to reduce to some sort of order those things that were matters of concern to him; to decide which mattered most; which he thought worth pursuing even at the expense of some of the others—in short, to decide what he really wanted.

III

The values of most of us come from two main sources; our own wants and our imitation of other people. If it be true that to imitate other people is, especially in the young, one of the strongest desires, these two sources of our values can be seen to have a common head. What is so difficult about growing up is the integration into one stream of these two kinds of values. In the end, if we are to be able sincerely to say that something matters for *us*, we must ourselves be concerned about it; other people's concern is not enough, however much in general we may want to be like them. Thus, to take an aesthetic example, my parents may like the music of Bach, and I may want to be like my parents; but this does not mean that I can say sincerely that I like the music of Bach. What often happens in such cases is that I *pretend* to like Bach's music; this is of course in fact *mauvaise foi*—hypocrisy; but none the less it is quite often by this means that I come in the end to like the music. Pretending to like something, if one does it in the right spirit, is one of the best ways of getting really to like it. It is in this way that nearly all of us get to like alcohol. Most developed art is so complex and remote from what people like at the first experience, that it would be altogether impossible for new generations to get to enjoy the developed art of their time, or even that of earlier generations, without at least some initial dishonesty.

Nevertheless, we also often rebel against the values of our elders. A young man may say, 'My parents think it matters enormously to go to church every Sunday; but *I* can't feel at all concerned about it'. Or he may say, 'Most of the older generation think it a disgrace not to fight for one's country in time of war; but isn't it more of a disgrace not to make a stand against the whole murderous business by becoming a pacifist?' It is by reactions such as these that people's values get altered from generation to generation.

Now to return to my Swiss friend. I had by this time convinced him that many things did matter for him, and that the expression 'Nothing matters' in his mouth could only be (if he understood it) a piece of play-acting. Of course he didn't actually understand it. It is very easy to assume that all words work in the same way; to show the differences is one of the chief ways in which philosophers can be of service to mankind. My friend had not understood that the function of the word 'matters' is to express concern; he had thought mattering was something (some activity or process) that things did, rather like chattering; as if the sentence 'My wife matters to me' were similar in logical function to the sentence 'My wife chatters to me'. If one thinks that, one may begin to wonder what this activity is, called mattering; and one may begin to observe the world closely (aided perhaps by the clear cold descriptions of a novel like that of Camus) to see if one can catch anything doing something that could be called 'mattering'; and when we can observe nothing going on which seems to correspond to this name, it is easy for the novelist to persuade us that after all *nothing matters*. To which the answer is, ' "Matters" isn't that sort of word; it isn't intended to *describe* something that things do, but to express our concern about what they do; so of course we can't *observe* things mattering; but that doesn't mean that they don't matter (as we can be readily assured if, as I told my friend to do, we follow Hume's advice and "turn our reflexion into our own breast"[1])'.

There are real struggles and perplexities about what matters most; but alleged worries about whether anything matters at all are in most cases best dispelled by Hume's other well-known remedy for similar doubts about the possibility of causal reasoning—a good game of backgammon.[2] For people who (understanding the words) say that nothing matters are, it can safely be declared, giving but one example of that hypocrisy or *mauvaise foi* which Existentialists are fond of castigating.

I am not saying that no *philosophical* problem arises for the person who is perplexed by the peculiar logical character of the word 'matters': there is one, and it is a real problem. There are no pseudo-problems in philosophy; if anything causes philosophical perplexity, it is the philosopher's task to find the cause of this perplexity and so remove it. My Swiss friend was not a hypocrite. His trouble was that, through philosophical naïveté, he took for a real moral problem what was not a moral problem at all, but a philosophical one—a problem to be solved, not by an agonising struggle with his soul, but by an attempt to understand what he was saying.

I am not denying, either, that there may be people who can sincerely say that very little matters to them, or even almost nothing. We should say that they are psychologically abnormal. But for the majority of us to become like this is a contingency so remote as to excite neither fear nor attraction; we just are not made like that. We are creatures who feel concern for things—creatures who think one course of action better than another and act accordingly. And I easily convinced my Swiss friend that he was no exception.

So then, the first thing I want to say in this talk is that you cannot annihilate values—not values as a whole. As a matter of empirical fact, a man is a valuing

[1]*Treatise*, III 1 i.
[2]*Treatise*, I 4 vii.

creature, and is likely to remain so. What may happen is that one set of values may get discarded and another set substituted; for indeed our scales of values are always changing, sometimes gradually, sometimes catastrophically. The suggestion that *nothing* matters naturally arises at times of perplexity like the present, when the claims upon our concern are so many and conflicting that we might indeed wish to be delivered from all of them at once. But this we are unable to do. The suggestion may have one of two opposite effects, one good and one bad. On the one hand, it may make us scrutinise more closely values to which we have given habitual allegiance, and decide whether we really prize them as much as we have been pretending to ourselves that we do. On the other, it may make us stop thinking seriously about our values at all, in the belief that nothing is to be preferred to anything else. The effect of this is not, as might be thought, to overthrow our values altogether (that, as I have said, is impossible); it merely introduces a shallow stagnation into our thought about values. We content ourselves with the appreciation of those things, like eating, which most people can appreciate without effort, and never learn to prize those things whose true value is apparent only to those who have fought hard to reach it. . . .

IX

The Far Side of Despair

Hazel E. Barnes

Among the accusing adjectives which hostile critics have attached to humanistic existentialism, one of the most frequently heard is "nihilistic." Existentialists, it appears, believe in *nothing;* hence nothing stands to block their destructive impulses, and we may expect *anything* from them. Whether spoken naively or formulated with philosophical sophistication, this attitude contains an important assumption: that there is a logical connection between what one believes about ultimate reality, one's sense of purpose, one's values, and one's concrete action. . . .

It is generally assumed that a lack of higher meaning or over-all purpose in the Universe is a terribly bad thing. Even Sartre has remarked that it would be much better if God the Father existed. Our forlornness is due to our discovery that He is not there. It is worthwhile to ask ourselves just what this hypothesis of higher meaning and purpose really does and has meant to man and why he has felt the necessity to project it. Most of the time I believe it has been bound up with the hope for immortality. Certainly in traditional Christianity, as in any religion which promises a personal afterlife, the significant part of the idea of historical development is not that God and His Universe are infinitely good and eternal but that the individual shares in this destiny. Most important of all for our present selves is the thought that the specific role we play in this far future is determined by the way we conduct ourselves here and now. This life on earth is our trial and test, and the grade we receive indicates the eternal class we go into. The undeniable positive element here is the conviction that

Excerpted from Hazel E. Barnes, *An Existentialist Ethic* (1967), pp. 98, 102–5, 106–9, and 113–15; reprinted by permission of Alfred A. Knopf, Inc. and Hazel E. Barnes.

what we do matters forever. If taken literally—or as near to literally as today's fundamentalist is willing to take it—the pragmatic value of this doctrine is overwhelming. Meaning, purpose, and progress toward some definite destination are clearly defined and omnipresent. The catch is that the more concrete and specific the positive promise, the darker the negative side. The Medieval Heaven gains part of its shining light from the contrast with the smoky darkness of the Hell which lies below it. "Here pity or here piety must die," says Dante; and I, for one, would at this point bid piety a hasty adieu. A God who would for eternity subject even one person to horrors surpassing those of Buchenwald, a Creator who would create souls capable of deserving such punishment seems to me to echo man's ignoble desire for vengeance more than his aspirations for an understanding Justice. Of course very few people today believe in everlasting punishment, and it is easy to see why. Only the most hardened sinner could bear to live with this sort of anticipation for any of his acquaintances—let alone the fear of being condemned himself.

In a more acceptable form, Christianity for today's average believer stresses the mercy of God. Although it may not be put in quite this way, the idea seems to be that since God views each life from within, He sees each man's good intentions. *"Tout comprendre, c'est tout pardonner."* Hell isn't left quite empty, but like the Greeks' realm of Hades, it is reserved for the really great sinners—like Hitler, perhaps—who are condemned by almost everybody and sufficiently remote so as not to concern us. Heaven and Hell are less concrete and precisely located than they used to be. If one gets liberal enough in his Christian commitment, he may think of Heaven as simply the eternal consciousness of God's presence and Hell as the painful awareness of His absence. At this point, even if individual immortality is not lost, we are in danger of floating off into a vague pantheism which is no longer specifically Christian. In itself, this makes no difference for our present discussion. The issue is not specifically between existentialism and Christianity. Yet we may note that the more the old idea of Heaven and Hell is subjected to ethical purification and intellectual criticism, the feebler becomes any specific hypothesis as to the meaning and ultimate goal of the individual life. If Christianity reaches the point of no longer postulating any afterlife for the specific person, then we may well ask what remains of what centuries have found most valuable—the infinite value of every human soul, its eternal existence, and its freedom of choice to determine the quality of that existence.

Not all hypotheses of the existence of a higher meaning necessarily postulate eternal life for the individual consciousness, whether separate or absorbed in some ultimate Unity. Aristotelianism does not—despite the First Cause, the Unmoved Mover which thinks itself and by its very presence draws all other forms upward toward pure Thought. The Hebrew prophets, too, speak of no future life for man. It is in the present that man must walk humbly and righteously in the sight of the Just God, who will champion those whose cause is right. These interpretations of reality are not oriented toward any eternal Future, but they do serve as some sort of absolute guarantee and point of reference. If the Universe is rationally organized, whether ordered by a Deist Creator, or simply sustained by an Unmoved Mover, it at least serves as a mirror for man wherein he can find himself and his proper place. If the order of the Universe both corresponds to human reason and exists independently of it, one may conclude, at the very least, that Reason is our essence and guide, that to develop it to its greatest extent is our highest good. It is an easy step from there to the notion that Reason may discover absolutes in the ethical sphere as well and that the ultimate attainment of rationality will be a culmination of all that is best in ourselves and a steadfast bond between us and the outside world. Similarly, the belief that the structure of things is permeated with the spirit of Justice offers a sustenance and guarantee to man which come from outside himself. Not only will God reward the Just. He furnishes the assurance that we *ought* to be just and that we may know what Justice is.

Existentialism rejects all of these blandishments. In the early writing of French existentialists, man's recognition that he stood alone in an irrational world without God was expressed in an attitude in which revolt and despair were equally mingled. Things ought not to be this way, was the cry. We will never accept our fate with resignation, but we will live it—in our own way—against the Universe. At the end of *The Flies*, Orestes declares: "On the far side of despair, life begins." But the life which was to start involved no change in the view of things which precipitated Orestes' self-chosen exile. Camus said that his thought had gone beyond what he formulated early in *The Myth of Sisyphus*, but he added that he had never renounced the vision of the absurd which led him to ask, "Can I live without appeal? Can Thought live in this desert?" It is important not to forget this tragic vision of man against the Universe. Humanistic existentialism finds no divine presence, no ingrained higher meaning, no reassuring Absolute. At the same time, no humanistic existentialist will allow that the only alternative is despair and irresponsibility. Camus has pointed out the fallacy involved in leaping from the premise "The Universe has no higher meaning" to the conclusion, "Therefore my life is not worth living." The individual life may have an intrinsic value, both to the one who lives it and to those in the sphere of his influence, whether the Universe knows what it is doing or not.

Merleau-Ponty has remarked, "Life makes no sense, but it is ours to make sense of." In a popular lecture, Sartre expressed somewhat the same idea, explaining in simple terms both what he means by creating or "inventing" values and by value itself.

> To say that we invent values means nothing except this: life has no meaning a priori. Before you live it, life is nothing, but it is for you to give it a meaning. Value is nothing other than this meaning which you choose.[1]

[1]Sartre: *L'Existentialisme est un humanisme*, pp. 89–90.

. . . In contrasting traditional and existentialist attitudes toward the question of the meaning of life, I should like to use a homely example as an illustration. Let us imagine reality to have the shape of a gigantic Chinese checkerboard—without even the logically arranged spacing of the regularly shaped holes as in the usual game board, and with various-sized marbles, only some of which will fit into the spaces provided. The traditional attitude of religion and philosophy has been that we faced two alternatives. Theological and rational positions have assumed that there exists some correct pattern, impressed into the board itself, which can be discovered and which will then show us how we may satisfactorily and correctly arrange the piles of marbles near us. They have assumed—and so have the Nihilists—that if there is no such pattern, then there is no reason to play at all. If there is no motive for making a particular pattern, they have concluded that one might as well destroy the patterns set up by others or commit suicide. Existentialism holds that there is a third possibility. There is no pre-existing pattern. No amount of delving into the structure of the board will reveal one inscribed there in matter. Nor is it sensible to hope for some nonmaterial force which might magnetically draw the marbles into their correct position if we put ourselves in touch with such a power by prayer or drugs or any other device which man might think of. But while this lack deprives man of guide and certain goal, it leaves him free to create his own pattern. It is true that there is no external model according to which one may pronounce the new pattern good or bad, better or worse. There are only the individual judgments by him who makes it and by those who behold it, and these need not agree. If the maker finds value in his own creation, if the process of making is satisfying, if the end result compares sufficiently favorably with the intention, then the pattern *has* value and the individual life has been worthwhile. I must quickly add that no such pattern exists alone. Although its unique form and color remain distinctly perceptible, it is intermeshed with the edges of the patterns of others—like the design of a paisley print. The satisfaction in a life may well result in large part from the sense that these intermeshings have positive significance for the individual pattern. There is another kind of satisfaction—that which comes from the knowledge that other persons have declared one's pattern good. Still a third derives from the realization that what one has done has helped make it easier for others to live patterns intrinsically satisfying to them.

That a positive value is present in experiencing a delight in what one has created and in the approval of others cannot be denied. For many people this is not enough. The sense that there is something missing is sufficient to undermine any quiet content with what one has. We hear most frequently three basic complaints, and these refer respectively to (1) the starting point, (2) the here and now, and (3) the farther on. First, there is the feeling that we need some sort of eternal archetype or measuring stick. Existentialism admits that there is nothing of the sort and that life is harder without it. Yet we may well ask whether the privilege of having such an authority would not come at too high a price, and cost more than it is worth. Pragmatically, the over-all destiny and purpose of the Universe play a small part in the daily projects of Western man—with the possible exception of those remaining fundamentalists who still take the promise of Heaven and Hell quite literally. Mostly it is there as a kind of consolation at moments of failure, cheering our discouragement with the idea that things may be better sometime in a way that we cannot begin to comprehend. I do not deny the psychic refreshment of such comfort. But if the belief in any such authority and plan is sufficiently specific to be more than a proud hope, it must be restrictive as well. If man can be sure that he is right by any nonhuman standard, then his humanity is strictly confined by the nonhuman. He is not free to bring anything new into the world. His possibilities are those of the slave or the well-bred child. Higher meaning is itself a limitation for a being-who-is-a-process. Such a future is not open but prescribed. Man as a tiny being in an impersonal world may be without importance from the theoretical but nonexistent point of view of an omniscient objective observer. Man in the theological framework of the medieval man-centered Universe has only the dignity of the child, who must regulate his life by the rules laid down by adults. The human adventure becomes a conducted tour. It is in this sense that I seriously question the sincerity or the wisdom of Sartre's statement that it would be better if God the Father existed. The time has come for man to leave his parents and to live in his own right by his own judgments.

The second disturbing aspect of a life of self-created patterns emerges when we compare ourselves with our fellow man. Obviously some people are satisfied with patterns which others regard as deplorable. Can we allow this chaos of judgments and still cling to the belief in the positive value of whatever patterns we ourselves have made? Is the result not such an anarchy of the arbitrary that to speak of pattern at all is nonsense? Here existentialism begins by saying that up to a point, arbitrariness, inconsistency, and the simultaneous existence of divergent value systems are not to be lamented but welcomed. The creative freedom to choose and structure one's own pattern would be worthless if we were to agree that we would all work in the same way toward the same end. Just as we expect persons to differ in their specific projects, so we should allow for those individual over-all orientations which bestow upon the project its significance and which are, in turn, colored by it. Sartre has declared that the creation of a value system by which one is willing to live and to judge one's life is man's most important creative enterprise. This means more than the working out of standards of right and wrong and the regulation of one's own demands in the light of our relations with others. It involves the whole context of what we might call "the style" of a life—not just the moral but the aesthetic, the temperamental—everything which goes to make up the personality which continues, with varying degrees of modification, until death and which even then will leave behind it an objectified "Self for Others." Every such life is unique, no matter how hard the one who lives it may have tried to mold himself after the pattern of his contemporaries. Existentialism prizes this uniqueness and resists all attempts to reduce it to the lowest possible minimum. Existentialism recognizes and exults in the fact that since everyone *is* a point of view, there is no more possibility of all persons becoming the same than there is of reducing to one perspective the views of two people looking at a landscape from different spots. . . .

The absence of any discernible higher meaning in the Universe takes on a new and special significance when we confront the future, not merely my own but that of the world as a whole. What difference does it make, some will ask, whether I fashion one kind of pattern rather than another or none at all? All patterns will be blotted out as though they had never been. If this world is all, how can one attach any significance whatsoever to the individual life in the face of the immensity of space, the staggering infinity of Time? "We are sick with space!" cries Robert Frost. The French keep reminding us of the futility of all endeavor "from the point of view of Sirius." Again, I feel that we suffer still from Christianity's insistence that all of us together and the Universe with us are going somewhere definite and that the destination bestows its meaning on the present mile of the journey. Deprived of this forward voyaging, we find no delight in the nonpurposeful development of an impersonal cosmos which has no prearranged destination. Whether this drifting Universe will eventually become cold and lifeless, or whether there will occur once again—or many times—the coming together of organized matter and the appearance of other forms of consciousness, it seems unlikely that man will be remembered any more than we have reason to think that all of this present world of matter was put here for his express benefit.

Is there any reason *why* we should try to adopt the point of view of Sirius? We should realize that observation of a dead planet through a telescope is neither more nor less true as a vision of the Universe than is the examination of living organisms through a microscope. To see the big without the small is to exclude much of reality just as surely as to stay within the limits of the microscopic. If there is a falsification of boundaries at the one end, there is a blurring of details and elimination of foreground at the other. William James has commented that inasmuch as death comes at the end to cut off all human projects, every life is finally a failure. The point of view of Sirius reveals the same message on the cosmic scale. Yet if it were possible for one to stand on Sirius at the instant before the final disappearance of all life, that moment of conclusion would be no more real or significant than any one of the moments preceding it. If there is an absolute negative quality in the absence of what will not be, then there is a corresponding positive value in what will have been.

This last awareness might just as well take pride in what had been there as despair in the knowledge that it will no longer be. One does not choose to eat something bitter today simply because tomorrow it will make no difference which food one has chosen. The addition of positive moments does not add up to zero even if the time arrives when nothing more is added to the series. One might say that there is never any adding up of the sum, but this is not quite true. The new digits carry the weight of those which have gone before.

It is illogical to conclude that human values and meanings are unreal and of no importance simply because they do not originate in the structure of the nonhuman Universe. It is enough that the world serves to support these subjective structures for the consciousness which lives them. At the same time it is only natural that an individual man, whose being is a self-projection, should rebel at the prospect of seeing his projects suddenly brought to a stop. If the patterns and meanings which a consciousness creates were restricted to those experiences which we can live directly, then despair would in truth seem to be our only proper response. But man's being is that of a creature who is always about-to-be. In a peculiar sense also, he is, in his being, always outside or beyond himself, out there in the objects of his intentions or—more accurately—in his projects in the world. An impersonal Universe cannot sustain these subjective structures. But we do not exist in an impersonal Universe. We live in a human world where multitudes of other consciousnesses are ceaselessly imposing their meanings upon Being-in-itself and confronting the projects which I have introduced. It is in the future of these intermeshed human activities that I most fully transcend myself. In so far as "I" have carved out my being in his human world, "I" go on existing in its future.

X

Questions about the Meaning of Life

R. W. Hepburn

Claims about 'the meaning of life' have tended to be made and discussed in conjunction with bold metaphysical and theological affirmations. For life to have meaning, there must (it is assumed) be a comprehensive divine plan to give it meaning, or there must be an intelligible cosmic process with a 'telos' that a man needs to know if his life is to be meaningfully orientated. Or, it is thought to be a condition of the meaningfulness of life, that values should be ultimately 'conserved' in some way, that no evil should be unredeemable and irrational. And it may be claimed that if death were to end our experience, meaninglessness would triumph.

Because of this rich metaphysical background, the agnostic or naturalist faces a problem when he asks himself, 'Does life have meaning, for me?': or more formally, 'Can the vocabulary of life as "meaningful" or "meaningless" still play a role in my naturalistic interpretation of things?' The answer is not simple; for the informal logic of the vocabulary itself is not simple. This is a situation in which the naturalistic philosopher is tempted in one of two directions: either to renounce the vocabulary—as too deeply entangled with unacceptable beliefs, or to radically redefine the terms 'meaning', 'meaning-ful' and their cognates, thereby giving them work to do, but misleadingly different from their traditional work. The task for such a philosopher may be to mediate delicately between these poles, and in the course of trying to do that a good many complexities in the language of 'meaning' may come to light—

From Ronald W. Hepburn, "Questions about the Meaning of Life," *Religious Studies* (April 1966), Vol. 1, pp. 125–140; reprinted by permission of Ronald W. Hepburn and the Cambridge University Press.

complexities of interest perhaps not only to the naturalistic philosopher himself.

In the last few years some analytical philosophers have in fact written on the expression 'the meaning of life'; for instance, Kurt Baier, Inaugural Lecture, 'The Meaning of Life' (Canberra, 1957), Anthony Flew, 'Tolstoi and the Meaning of Life', *Ethics* (Jan. 1963), Kai Nielsen, 'Linguistic Philosophy and "The Meaning of Life" ', *Cross-Currents* (Summer, 1964). Their analyses overlap at many points, though not completely. I shall first of all offer a very brief, compressed and somewhat schematised account of these analyses, conflating them where they overlap, and then discuss some of the issues they raise.[1]

According to the interpretations being now worked out, questions about the meaning of life are, very often, conceptually obscure and confused. They are amalgams of logically diverse questions, some coherent and answerable, some neither. A life is not a statement, and cannot therefore have linguistic meaning. But admittedly we do use the word 'meaning' outside linguistic contexts. We speak of the meaning of a gesture, of a transaction, of a disposition of troops; and in such cases we are speaking of the point or purpose or end of an act or set of acts. This usage suggests an equation between meaningfulness and purposiveness. For a life to be meaningful, it must be purposeful: or—to make life meaningful is to pursue valuable ends.

To adopt this schema, however, already involves a shift from traditional ways of speaking about life as meaningful. Meaning is not now something to be found, as awaiting discovery, but is imparted to it by the subject himself. A person looks in vain for meaning and is needlessly frustrated when he cannot find it—if he conceives it as somehow existing prior to his decisions about what policies to pursue.

To say that 'making life meaningful' is a matter of 'pursuing valuable, worthwhile ends' is to say that it is an activity that indispensably involves value judgment. The description of cosmic patterns, tendencies or trends does not obviate the need to make autonomous judgments about the worthwhileness or otherwise of following, or promoting or opposing any of these. This is true no less of statements about God or a hereafter. Since claims about God and hereafter are ultimately claims about what is the case, not what ought to be, no conclusions will follow deductively from them about values. Even in the religious context, the question (as now analysed) still arises, 'What ends are *worthy* of pursuit?' Religious propositions cannot guarantee meaningfulness. Conversely, it is argued, loss of religious or metaphysical belief does not entail the denial of meaningfulness.

If we concentrate on the question 'What is the purpose of life?' rather than

[1] I had completed this article before seeing relevant studies by John Wisdom—*Paradox and Discovery* (1966), Ch. IV, and by Ilham Dilman—*Philosophy*, Oct. 1965.

on 'What is its meaning?', we are still dealing with the questions 'What ends shall I choose?' 'What purposes shall I hold to?' The analytical philosopher characteristically and quite intentionally changes the question from singular to plural, from 'purpose' to 'purposes'. He will claim that the original question contains a presupposition that must be rejected, the presupposition that life, if purposeful, can have only a single purpose, that only a single policy is worthwhile. Why may not a purposeful existence be a network of many purposes, with trajectories of varying reach, scope and seriousness? 'We are not and cannot always be doing or caring about one big thing.'[2]

The phrase, 'the purpose of human life', can be offensive on a second count, because it may suggest an analogy with the purpose of an instrument, utensil, tool or organ in a living body. The theist, who does take this analogy seriously, sees human life (with its help) as subordinated to the intentions, activities of another being, who 'assigns' (Baier) tasks and roles to men, and thereby imbues his life with purpose. Two senses of 'purpose' must be contrasted: the first, the sense in which one has a purpose if one 'purposes' or plans to do something, perhaps with the help of an artefact, an instrument, or other means: the second is the sense in which an artefact itself has a purpose, that is, a function. Only the first of these senses is compatible with moral autonomy, with being an autonomous purposer. To subordinate oneself wholly to the purposes of another is to forfeit moral status. This amounts to a moral argument against the manner in which theism seeks to secure purpose for human life. We must resist the temptation to translate 'What is the purpose of life?' into 'What are people *for*?'

We have seen two ways in which recent analyses of questions about the meaning of life seek to disconnect those questions from metaphysical and religious claims, or at least try to deprive such claims of any unique, privileged importance in the handling of the questions. Religious and metaphysical statements are still statements of fact, and therefore logically cannot in themselves be answers to questions about meaning. Second: if human life is given purpose by virtue of man's fulfilling the task assigned him by God, it will be 'purpose' in the autonomy-denying, dignity-destroying sense. Two further arguments tend to the same general conclusion.

Consider the familiar claim that life is meaningless if death ends all, that a necessary condition of life being meaningful is immortality or resurrection. Against this it is argued that there is no entailment between temporal finiteness and disvalue, futility. We can and do love flowers that fade; and the knowledge that they will fade may even enhance their preciousness. To be everlasting, that is, is no necessary or sufficient condition of value and worthwhileness, nor therefore of meaningfulness. An eternity of futility is not logically impossible.

[2]H. D. Aiken, *Reason and Conduct* (New York, 1962), p. 374. See chapter XVI as a whole.

Again, the quest for the meaning of life is very often thought of, but thought of confusedly, as a quest for *esoteric wisdom,* metaphysical or theological. On this, Flew's discussion of Tolstoi is interesting and relevant. First, we find in Tolstoi's *A Confession* (O.U.P. ed., 1940) an account of a period of 'arrest of life', the loss of a sense that life has any meaning or purpose, an inner deadness and disorientation. Tolstoi asked, 'What is it for?' 'What does it lead to?' His reflection took various pessimistic turns, including notably a refusal to account anything worthwhile, if death ends all. It struck him eventually, however, that the vanity and brevity of life were well enough known to very simple and unreflective people: yet in their cases there was seldom any 'arrest of life'. Tolstoi concluded that these people must know the meaning of life, the meaning that eluded the learned Tolstoi himself: it must be, not a piece of rational knowledge, but some non-rational or supra-rational knowledge to which they somehow had access. Flew now contests the assumption that these people necessarily had any esoteric, mystical knowledge that Tolstoi lacked. 'What we surely need here is Ryle's distinction between knowing *how* and knowing *that;* the peasants may indeed know how to live their lives free of all sophisticated psychological disabilities, but this by no means presupposes the possession of any theoretical knowledge' hidden from such a man as Tolstoi. In fact, the characters in Tolstoi's novels know better. In *War and Peace* Pierre's 'mental change' is a coming to have (a learning how to have) peace of mind, not a matter of acquiring new information, new dogma. The same is true of Levin and Hadji Murad. In so far as this kind of discovery of meaning is religious, it is so in a way that may be 'analysable in terms of ethics and psychology only'. Crucially, to know the meaning of life is to know how to live, as at one stage Tolstoi did not.

If we continue thus and develop these last themes, it becomes clear that the first-mentioned schematic account of the meaning of life is quite misleadingly oversimple. To give life meaning cannot be just a matter of pursuing worthy projects, for that account fails to cope with phenomena like Tolstoi's arrest of life—or John Stuart Mill's during his mental crisis of 1826. More generally, it is quite possible to make various value-judgments in cold blood, while yet suffering from a sense of meaninglessness. One may fill one's days with honest, useful and charitable deeds, not doubting them to be of value, but without feeling that these give one's life meaning or purpose. It may be profoundly boring. To seek meaning is not just a matter of seeking justification for one's policies, but of trying to discover how to organise one's vital resources and energies around these policies. To find meaning is not a matter of judging these to be worthy, but of seeing their pursuit as in some sense a fulfilment, as involving self-realisation as opposed to self-violation, and as no less opposed to the performance of a dreary task. Baier's account of 'meaning' includes reference to the pursuit of worthwhile projects, both in the sense of 'projects that afford satisfaction to the pursuer', and in the sense of 'morally worthwhile projects'—concerning, for instance, the well-being of others. Questions of the meaning of life, I suggest, are typically questions of how these two sorts of pursuit can be *fused*. I do not think that the use of such words as 'fulfilment' and 'self-realisation' need force one into a refined form of egoism, nor that the price of avoiding such is to empty the words of all sense. It need not be claimed that the values, duties, etc. involved *derive their force* from their ability to gratify the agent. If a particular agent fails to see the pursuit of moral and social goals as conferring meaning on his life, he need not be lamenting that he has failed to envisage how their pursuit could yield gratification for him. Nor is he necessarily revealing *Akrasia*. He may actually rise to his duty, but he rises to it as one rises from a warm bed to a chill morning's tasks. If he is asking how his duties (and other pursuits) can be represented as of 'interest' to him, it need not be in the sense of 'interest' that egoism requires, but in the sense *of concern'* to him. What one often finds, on reading the reflective autobiographies and semiautobiographies that are un-doubtedly our best source-books here, is that in asking questions about the meaning of his life, the author is asking how he can relate the pursuit of various valuable ends to the realising of a certain kind or form of life, the thought of which evokes in him the response: 'The pursuit of these goals really concerns me, matters to me!' He may achieve this by way of an imaginative vivifying of the objectives (moral, social, religious . . .) of his policies and pursuits, by summoning up and dwelling upon a vision of the ideal that facilitates self-identification with it. The writer may be helped in this by some extant public myth (compare R. B. Braithwaite on religious belief), or he may elaborate a private myth in which he casts himself in the role of a person dedicated to the pursuit of the valuable ends, whatever they are.[3]

I have kept the plural—'goals', 'ends'—following the tendency (noted above) to repudiate 'monolithic' accounts of the good life. But it needs to be remarked that there are perfectly intelligible occurrences of the singulars in many contexts; occurrences that do not stem from bad metaphysics or bad moral philosophy. A life may be said to acquire 'new meaning' through the rallying and ordering of resources that have hitherto been dispersed and conflicting in disunity. This is a sort of 'integrating' that is independent of any claims about all goods being ultimately one. Vronsky, in love with Anna Karenina, 'felt that all his powers, hitherto dissipated and scattered, were now concentrated and directed with terrible energy toward one blissful aim . . . He knew that . . . all the happiness of life and the only meaning of life for him now was in seeing and hearing her' (I, ch. xxxi). In the same novel, Levin,

---

[3]Obviously relevant autobiographical quarries include *The Prelude, Dichtung und Wahrheit*, Chesterton's *Autobiography* and Berdyaev's *Dream and Reality*. I have discussed some other aspects of these topics in 'Vision and Choice in Morality', *Proc. Arist. Soc.* Suppl. vol. 1956, reprinted in *Christian Ethics and Contemporary Philosophy*, ed. I. T. Ramsey (S.C.M. 1966). The present article is generally complementary to that paper.

having seen Kitty passing in a coach, reflects: 'in the whole world there was only one being able to unite in itself the universe and the meaning of life for him. It was Kitty' (III, ch. xii).

All these complexities are reflected in the complexity of the criteria we are likely to use in commenting upon or appraising discourse about the meaning a person's life has for him. Where we are moved to disapproval, our criticism may certainly be in part a *moral* criticism: one may disapprove, for instance, of a person's commitment to the Don Juan pattern of life, its goals and priorities. But such criticism may involve other factors besides the moral. Suppose someone does take the Don Juan pattern as fitting his life as lived at present and as setting 'tasks' for his future. But suppose also that in this particular case, the life as it is being lived is totally ineffectual in the relevant respects. We shall want to say, '*This* meaning cannot be given to *this* life'; and the cost of trying to impose it is a falsification of the course the life is taking in fact. The effect of such blunders in self-commitment to a pattern of life may be grotesque or pathetic, or, as in the case of the other Don—Don Quixote—it may be richly comic. Or again, although we may not wish to speak of falsification, of events and pattern at loggerheads, we might detect that there is a self-conscious, self-dramatising and only half-sincere playing-out of a role. Whereas, on the other hand, we should count integrity, the refusal of stereotyped, paste-board *personae*, as pre-eminent among grounds for approval in this domain. The agent himself may come to see, in a dawning self-knowledge, that some attempt to give meaning or purpose has been proceeding on the wrong lines. Once more, in *Anna Karenina* (Part II, ch. xxxv), Kitty's attempt to find meaning through adopting Varenka's religious way of life ends unhappily. She decides it has not risen above the level of an imitation, and has involved pretence and self-deception. Some pages later, Anna reflects on her efforts to love Karenin: 'Have I not tried, . . . with all my might, to find a purpose in my life? Have I not tried to love him . . . ? But the time came when I could no longer deceive myself . . .' (Part III, ch. xvi). Where we can estimate them, the ease or difficulty, 'slickness' or strenuousness involved in the quest for meaning may figure in criticism. We sometimes say that someone has found meaning in too facile or superficial a way, or that an autobiography discloses a 'lack of probing', 'a relaxed mood' or a cocksureness that replaces the tension of real self-exploration.[4]

The pursuit of meaning, in the senses we have been examining, is a sophisticated activity, involving a discipline of attention and imagination. Is this true of *all* relevant senses? The case of Tolstoi and the peasants, as discussed by Flew, suggests otherwise. To look back at that may help to plot further ramifications.

What makes it plausible to say that the peasants knew the meaning of life,

[4]Roy Pascal, *Design and Truth in Autobiography* (1960), pp. 191, 181.

and in what sense, if any, did they *not* know it? On Flew's Rylean account (*ibid.* p. 116) 'the secret of the peasants . . . [is] knowledge of *how* to go on living, [and this is] only another way of saying that they . . . enjoy rude mental health'. This 'no nonsense' analysis relies on a very weak sense of 'knowing how'. It is not being claimed that the peasants had mastered techniques for banishing depression—for they did not suffer from it; nor even rules, skills by which to steer their lives round the hazards of depression and mental arrests. They could hardly know of such states of mind as Tolstoi's or J. S. Mill's or Coleridge's in 'dejection'. They are unaware of the perils they have missed. If for the peasants 'knowing the meaning of life' equals 'knowing how to live', it amounts to no more than this: that as a matter of fact the peasants were not vulnerable to the malaise that Tolstoi suffered. One might want to say, 'This is surely not a "knowing" *at all*', but just a fortunate combination of circumstances *happening* to produce 'rude mental health'. It is true, however, that ordinary language allows this weak sense of 'knowing how', a sense that is consistent with Flew's account of the peasants. It is applicable, for instance, to the baby who 'knows how to cry', even to the bird who 'knows how to build a nest'.

On the other hand, if one's aim is (like Flew's) 'to throw light upon the meaning of the question: "What is the meaning of life?"' (*ibid.* p. 110), one must keep in mind that a quite important element of meaning is not covered by this weak sense of 'knowing how . . .', 'knowing how to live', etc. Tolstoi may well have been mistaken in thinking that the peasants had an esoteric knowledge that he lacked, a knowledge that gave a key to the problem of life's meaning. But, in thinking so, he was testifying to that side of the logic of 'the meaning of life' that has to drop out in the case of the peasants: namely, that questions about the meaning of life involve a problem, see life as a problem, and involve a search for an answer. This is so frequently presupposed in discourse about the meaning of life, that such discourse is felt as curiously attenuated, if it is thought away. If we do take the problematic context as built in to the logic, then the sense of 'knowing how to live' that is correlative with solving the problem and coming to know that meaning, will be a stronger sense than can be used of the peasants. It will involve awareness of the hurdles, the threats of futility, and the devising of tactics to overcome them.

Could a man's life have or fail to have meaning, without his knowing that it did or did not have meaning? This question could be answered either way, according to the interpretation given to 'the meaning of life'. We can answer Yes: his own awareness of his life's meaning is not a necessary condition for its being meaningful. This is so, if 'having meaning' is equated with 'contributing to valuable projects', 'achieving useful results'. But it may be felt, again, that such an answer goes against the grain of language: that it is too odd to say, for instance, 'White did not himself find the meaning of his life: but Black (White's biographer, writing after White's death) did find it'. Finding the meaning of White's life may be deemed to be something only White is logically able to do. The giving of meaning to life is seen as essentially a task for the liver of it. Conversely, in the case of people who have not worked at it, seen it as a task, who have been unreflectively happy or unhappy, it would be most natural to say that they have neither found nor failed to find the meaning of life.

It must, of course, be admitted that the peasants had something Tolstoi wanted to have but did not have. In the sense we have been elucidating, if Tolstoi succeeded in getting it, he could be said to have found the meaning of life, but we should not say the same of the peasants, since they had never been conscious of a problem. If this is logically curious, it is not unintelligible. Were life never problematic, were people never subject to arrests of life, it is unlikely that we should ever have acquired the expressions we are discussing. But having once acquired them in the problematic context, they can be extended to other and non-problematic contexts. The former seem to remain primary, however, and it distorts the logic of 'the meaning of life' if we take as paradigmatic instances of success in discovering meaning, people who have never been troubled by the problematic aspects of life, its limits, contingency and the like.

(Two smaller, related points may be mentioned in passing. Flew's statement that the characters in Tolstoi's novels know better than Tolstoi is contestable. In the case of Levin there is a good deal about the revelation of 'a knowledge unattainable by reasoning'. The knowledge of 'what we should live for . . . cannot be explained by reason' (Part VIII, chs. xix, xii, etc.). Again, Tolstoi does permit himself to use the expression, 'the meaning of life' in a remarkably different sense from that on which our discussion, and Flew's, has centered. When Anna, just before her suicide, discerned the hopelessness of her position, 'she saw it clearly in the piercing light which now revealed to her the meaning of life and of human relations' (Part VII, ch. xxx)—a diabolical, not a benign, pattern being revealed. To have seen this 'meaning' was not to be enabled to live, but was to judge, on the contrary, that a continuance of life was unendurable. This is an eccentric but noteworthy usage.)

On the highly particularised problems of giving meaning to an individual life, philosophy may not have much to say: but it is certainly concerned with what seem to be general threats to meaningfulness arising out of the human situation as such. For the non-theist, the chief threat may well appear to come from the realisation of mortality. The relation between meaning and mortality is, as we have noted, a focus of attention in current discussions. On the one side are writers (Tolstoi is again among them—as Flew brings out) who in some contexts virtually identify the question of meaningfulness with the question of immortality: deny immortality and you necessarily deny meaningfulness. This account plainly distorts the logic of the question about the meaning of life, not least by reducing its complexity to a single issue of fact. On the other side, a naturalistic account oversimplifies and dogmatises if it claims that 'death is irrelevant' (Baier) to questions of value, worthwhileness—and hence to meaningfulness. The argument that values are not devalued by mortality, although unassailable on grounds of logic, may be used to express a naturalism that is more optimistic and brash than it is entitled to be. For a person may heed the argument that mortality and value are compatible, and yet may be burdened with a sense of futility that the argument cannot dispel. His malaise may range from occasional vague misgivings over the worth-whileness of his activities, to a thoroughgoing arrest of life.

We can most usefully consider this sort of malaise at a still more general level. A complaint of meaninglessness can be a complaint about a felt dispro-portion between preparation and performance; between effort expended and the effect of effort, actual or possible. Yeats expressed the complaint in well-known words: 'When I think of all the books I have read, wise words heard, anxieties given to parents, . . . of hopes I have had, all life weighed in the balance of my own life seems to me *a preparation for something that never happens.*' (Compare again, Tolstoi's question, 'What does it *lead* to?')

A useful vocabulary in which to discuss this can be borrowed from aes-thetics. In Monroe Beardsley's book, *Aesthetics* (New York, 1958, pp. 196 f.), he distinguishes, in a musical composition, passages that have 'Introduction quality' and passages that have 'Exhibition quality': the one is felt as leading up to the other, the first as preparation and the second as fulfilment. He quotes, *apropos*, an amusing criticism by Tovey of Liszt's tone poem, *Ce qu'on Entend sur La Montagne.* The work consists of 'an introduction to an introduction to a connecting link to another introduction . . . , etc.' Beardsley adds: 'When [the tone poem] stops it is still promising something that never arrives.'

In music this sort of disappointment can be due to more causes than one. It may be the listener's expectations, not the music, that are at fault. He may be simply misinformed about the programme he is to hear; expecting a sym-phony, but getting only a concert overture. A musical idiom may disappoint him: he awaits a fully-fashioned melody in the style of Brahms, but—since the music happens to be in the style of Webern—it provides none. In different cases, different kinds of correction are required: to study the programme, to familiarise himself with musical development after Brahms. What sounded prefatory can come to sound performatory. But, as in the Liszt-Tovey case, the fault may lie with the music, and nothing the listener can do can give it an exhibition quality.

How far can the analogy be applied? To draw first its limits: a piece of music is 'given' to a listener in a way that his life, being partly shaped by his choices, is not given. The nearest to a given in the latter case is an awareness of the general conditions and scope of human existence, of what it is open for men to do and to be, of what they can reasonably count on doing and being. Suppose a person who has lost belief in immortality has a sense of futility due to the feeling that life is all prefatory, has no exhibition quality. An analytical philosopher points out to him that things can be valuable although not eternal, and so on. This is rather like pointing out that a symphony was never on the programme, but that other valuable things were. The implication is that just as a satisfactory short piece of music can be heard as having exhibition quality, so can life within the limits of earthly existence be perceived as having it.

This suggestion may dispel the sense of futility, or it may not. It may dispel it, because to some considerable extent it does lie within our power to take a particular experience either in a prefatory or exhibitory way, although how this is done we cannot inquire here in any detail. In general, and very obviously, many activities can be understood both as leading to anticipated worthwhile ends, and as worthwhile in themselves also. A person may sometimes successfully counsel himself to dwell less upon the possible future effects of his various activities, and relish the present activities themselves. (To do so, there must, admittedly, be something relishable about the activities.)

Suppose, then, the suggestion does not dispel the sense of futility. To follow the analogy a step further: life may be found recalcitrant in the way that Liszt's tone-poem was recalcitrant to Tovey. Clearly there are experiences, of prolonged and unrelievable ill-health, for instance, that can be regarded as valuable, in the sense of disciplinary, only so long as death is not believed to be the end. Lacking such belief, a person cannot simply be counselled to endow a life pervaded by pain with exhibition quality. It is of such suffering that people tend to use words like 'pointless' and 'senseless'. If this experience is followed by no 'exhibition-section', it is unredeemably futile.

What follows? The existence of unsuccessful musical compositions exposed to the Tovey criticism does not devalue those that are not exposed. Must one say any more, in the case of lives, than that some lives are without meaning, in the present sense; but that others are meaningful? Or, in terms of the earlier discussion, that some people are confronted with a stiffer problem than others in giving meaning to their lives, and that the task may sometimes be impossible for them. This would be enough to qualify an over-optimistic naturalism that implies that (where meaning is concerned) everything remains as it was in the days of belief in immortality and Providence.[5] As an index of the difficulty of nicely proportioning prefatory and exhibitory quality in life, one may instance an aesthetic theory like John Dewey's, according to which the distinctiveness of art is its capacity to provide just such completeness and balance in experience—in contrast to the ordinary experience of life, which seldom can maximise these qualities and can never *guarantee* them.[6]

---

[5] In the studies from which this discussion started, Baier and Nielson, e.g., acknowledge that, on their analysis, particular lives may, in particular extreme situations, be 'meaningless'.

[6] For instance: 'Art celebrates with peculiar intensity the moments in which the past reenforces the present and in which the future is a quickening of what now is' (Dewey, *Art as Experience* (1934), p. 18).

If it is a condition for life-in-general to be meaningful that these qualities *should* be guaranteed, then life-in-general is without meaning to the naturalist or agnostic—though individual lives may happen to attain it, by practical wisdom and good fortune.

Judgments about the value or futility of human projects are problematic in yet another way. Our appraisal of the value of our activities tends to vary according to the 'backcloth' against which they are viewed. To the naturalist, human endeavour viewed *sub specie aeternitatis*, may seem to shrivel, frighteningly. (Compare Sartre's troubled musings on the heat-death of the sun, in his autobiographical essay, *Les Mots*, p. 208.) He may nonetheless judge as entirely worthwhile some social reform, viewed against the backcloth of a dozen years, or months, of social abuse. Yet it is not only a vestigial romanticism that prompts one to give privileged importance to the widest and broadest backcloth. For the more fully synoptic one's view, the more confident one becomes that one is reckoning with all possible threats of vilification. The movement is towards the discarding of blinkers and frames that artificially confine attention to a narrow context and which might equally artificially boost a sense of importance and worthwhileness. Only: on naturalist assumptions, the *sub specie aeternitatis* view must at least seem to vilify, by revealing human history in an ocean of emptiness before and after. Some of the logical darkness around the meaning-of-life questions comes from the uneasy awareness that there *are* alternative views, perspectives, more or less synoptic or selective in different ways, giving very different answers to questions of value, importance, futility. From this bewildering diversity the questioner seeks some release.

He may come to the problem with the belief or half-belief that there must be an authoritative view; and that if life is to be shown to be meaningful, this authoritative view will also be a value-confirming, value-enhancing view. On authoritativeness, however, I think he is asking for what cannot be given. Either a 'view' is a sheer psychological fact about how someone sees human activity, in which case it has nothing that can properly be called 'authority'— though it may have strikingness and imaginative force. Or, if we judge that a particular view does have authority, this is to make a judgment of value and not simply to describe one's imaginings. Now, the estimate of the importance of human life implied in the 'authoritative' view may or may not conflict with the estimate one makes on other bases. If it does not conflict, there is no further problem: if it does conflict, then we must ask, Which has to yield, the judgment that the perspective is authoritative, or the independent (perhaps workaday) estimate of worthwhileness? The criteria for authoritativeness, crucially, are no less challengeable than the independent value-judgment: only by the agent weighing up, arbitrating between, or oscillating between, the two clashing sets of evaluations, can he deal with his dilemma. If he resolves the dilemma, it is resolved by his own autonomous value-judgments:

and therefore the promise of having it resolved for him by some self-evident authoritativeness is not fulfilled.

Despite this argument, the naturalist ought to admit to substantial difference between his position and that of the Christian theist. There must in fact remain, with the naturalist, an uncomfortable tension or conflict between the 'close-up', anthropocentric view or perspective that can sustain his sense of meaningfulness and worthwhileness, and on the other hand his sense of intellectual obligation to the objective, scientific and anti-anthropocentric view—which tends to vilify, if not logically, then psychologically. The Christian is not exposed to this tension in the same way or to the same extent. The doctrines of divine creation and of incarnation combine to rule out the judgment that, in leaving the arena of the human, one is leaving simultaneously the theatre of mind and purpose and value. For the theist, that is, there is the implicit promise of a *harmony* of perspectives. To challenge that is to challenge the ultimate coherence of theism.

Once again, the meaning-of-life vocabulary may be so used (with exacting criteria of application), that only where such a harmony is promised can human life be properly called meaningful. Or at least the reluctance of a theist to concede that life can be meaningful to the unbeliever may reflect this, perhaps unanalysed but sensed, difference between their views of the world.

In the greater part of this discussion we have been assuming that the paradigm case of a satisfactory answer to problems about the meaning of life is contained in Christian theism, and that the question for the non-Christian is whether anything at all can be rescued from a collapse of meaning. This assumption, however, may be questioned in various ways. Two of these must be briefly mentioned.

That Christianity is able to provide a satisfactory answer is implicitly denied by those critics who claim that no hereafter, even of endless beatitude, could compensate for some of the evils actually endured by men here and now.[7] To revert to the musical analogy: in a 'meaningful' work, the exhibition passages fulfil and complete the anticipatory passages, which are unsatisfying by themselves. We can conceive of an anticipatory passage, however, which is so atrocious musically that nothing that followed it, even of high quality, could be said to fulfil or complete it. It may be argued that some 'passages' in some people's lives are so evil that nothing could conceivably justify them. As with a *privatio* theory of evil, so with analysis in terms of 'introductory quality': it makes out evil to be what we cannot by any means always see it to be, as able to be supplemented so as to become ingredient in an aesthetically and morally valuable whole. Here, therefore, the meaning-of-life problem runs into the problem of evil. To the extent that one is baffled by the problem of evil, to the same extent one must be baffled by the meaning of life. We cannot open up that problem here.

---

[7]Dostoevsky's is the classic statement: see *The Brothers Karamazov*, Book V, chap. 4.

Secondly, in his aggressively anti-theistic argument, Kurt Baier claims that theism seeks to give meaning and purpose to human life in a morally objectionable way. Understanding one's life as given purpose by God involves a thoroughgoing self-abasement or self-annulment quite incompatible with the stance of a moral agent. This self-abasement is a correlative of the recognition of God's holiness (on current accounts), the realisation in numinous dread that God is 'wholly other'.

The objection is impressive and serious, and certainly effective against some forms and formulations of theism. If the 'otherness' of God and the *tremendum* side of the mystery are one-sidedly stressed, then human moral judgment and divine purpose are bound to be seen as incommensurable. An attitude of worshipfulness will involve an abrogating of moral autonomy.

It seems equally clear, however, that this is not the only posture a theist can adopt. Worship is by no means a simple, single-stranded concept. To worship is not only to yield to an overwhelming of the intellect or engage in unthinking, undiscerning adulation. Something very different from this is expressed, for instance, in the *B Minor Mass* or Stravinsky's *Symphony of Psalms*. An act of worship need not be a submitting of oneself, without insight, to the wholly inscrutable. Moral perfection and beauty, fused in an intensifying strangeness, are being celebrated, as these are believed to inhere in God. Evaluative reflection is being exercised: it is very far from abdicating. The worshipper is not passively, heteronomously, accepting claims about divine greatness: he is actively and autonomously recognising and relishing them. His worship is not a preface to a life of submission to commands *ab extra*. The very ingredients of his worship itself—in attitude and feeling—become part of his own inner life, the stillness of soul, the wonderment and solemnity.

The element of strangeness, of *mysterium*, has however a further role to play. Without cancelling the values, moral and aesthetic, that are celebrated in the act of worship, it powerfully intimates that they are nonetheless open to further transformation. It forbids thinking that the human vision of the good is precisely congruent with the nature of divine goodness. There is both recognition of affinity and awareness of disparity. But the latter need not be taken as a command to surrender autonomy: rather to extend progressively the zone of 'recognition'.

If it is true that a worshipful stance does not involve abrogating moral autonomy, neither need an acceptance of a divine purpose or meaning to the worshipper's life. This would indeed involve a regulating of one's life, a limiting of one's projects to what, rightly or wrongly, one judged to be compatible with God's will and intention. But such a limiting or circumscribing is a common feature of familiar moral situations, where one acts say, as a member of a trust, or has a special status in a group, a status that prescribes special obligations. In many, if not all such cases—and the case of divine purpose is no exception—the regulating of action is necessary, if some good or goods is to be realised. A rational person will make it his business to understand how the relevant moral institution does bring about that good. In the theistic case one needs reasons for believing that God's wisdom, goodness and power are such that the following of his will is a surer way to achieving goods in general than by carving out patterns of life that ignore or transgress his will.

Nevertheless, this sort of language quickly brings one to difficulties more stubborn than the original problem of autonomy. The fact that some worship-ful activity expresses morally and aesthetically valuable states of mind does nothing to guarantee the existence of the God who is the primary object of the worship. It cannot show that God, if he exists, has the qualities celebrated in the act of worship, that these qualities are mutually compatible in a single being or that God can have these qualities and the world be the sort of world it is. And we confront the problem of how one can meaningfully speak of God, an infinite being, as having such features of finite person-hood as willing, intending, purposing. In a word, there remain difficulties enough in the theistic conception of the meaning and purpose of life, but they are the general difficulties of theism itself. The objection that the theist must abdi-cate his moral status is by no means decisive against all forms of theism, although valid against some. [8]

At the start of this article I mentioned one terse and gruff dismissal of the whole topic, the meaning of life: 'Life is not a statement, is not a linguistic entity, so cannot strictly be said to have or lack meaning.' We evaded this objection by way of a part-equating of 'meaning', in this context, with 'point' or 'purpose'. Yet it is worth asking whether, in discussing the meaning of life, some analogy with linguistic meaning may not often be operative—either in the background or the foreground of attention, helpfully or misleadingly. In what ways could it operate?

The words in a meaningful sentence 'cohere'. Words in a random list do not: like the events of a 'meaningless' life, they merely succeed each other discretely and atomistically, and are no more. The 'past' of a piece of discourse to which one is listening is felt as active and as bearing upon the presently uttered words. It is not a 'lost' past. Neither is it an obsessively dominant past, that imposes a static and completed pattern in place of the developing and novel pattern that the piece of discourse builds up. Certainly life is not a piece of discourse, and the motifs that supply coherence and continuity to it are very different from a rule-governed syntax. But if not pressed to breaking-point, the analogy may have a regulative function in the managing of our relation to our own past. Extreme cases of *failure* in this task can be seen in schizo-phrenics to whom every day is 'a separate island with no past or future', and who lack all sense of continuity, coherence; and, at the other pole, those who feel 'nailed' to their past, unable to distance it at all. [9]

[8]Further arguments on this topic can be found in C. C. J. Webb's criticism of N. Hartmann, *Religion and Theism* (1934), pp. 69–86, 87, 144 to end.

[9]On these forms of schizophrenia, see R. May, *Existence* (1958), pp. 66 (quoting Minkowski), 68.

The vocabulary of 'meaning', however, can obviously do no detailed regulating or managing by itself. If it appears to do much more than hold the bare form of the task before the attention, it may be spellbinding its user into illusion. It may suggest that the pattern of our life as a whole has a unity, and an availability to recollection *in* its unity, beyond what is in fact possible. We may say of apparent unity and coherence in life what Proust said of 'the total value of our spiritual nature': 'At whatever moment we estimate it, . . . it is more or less fictitious; . . . notwithstanding the long inventory of its treasures, . . . now one, now another of these unrealisable . . . It is an illusion that our inward wealth is perpetually in our possession.'[10]

The linguistic analogy may lure one on still further. The words of a sentence are uttered as the clock ticks, and the events of a life occur as the clock ticks: but the meaning of the sentence is not an episode in time—and the meaning of life . . . ? To yield to the suggestion, and to say 'timeless' of the patterns of continuities, overlapping motifs of a life would be no more illegitimate than to say the same thing of logical relations and patterns. Nevertheless, one cannot use the language of 'timelessness', in respect of life, without evoking a whole syndrome of distinctive aspirations, for 'deliverance from time', for experience as a *'totum simul'*, for 'eternal life': and, seductive though these are, would they not surely be out of place in such reflections?

Yet some writers might not hurry to exorcise them. Santayana, for instance, argued that eternal life cannot be satisfactorily conceived as an endless succession of events, nor, coherently, as a *totum simul;* and concluded that eternity is experienced only in the contemplating of timeless objects and structures.[11] To contemplate the web of one's life's aims, its themes and articulating images, might count, on such a view, as affording as much fulfilment of the longing for eternity as the nature of things affords, everything beyond that being ultimately delusory.

It is natural and not at all absurd for a naturalistic philosopher to seek some (inevitably limited and provisional) substitute for a metaphysical or religious doctrine of eternal life. If he judges that doctrine to be logically incoherent anyway, there is all the less reason to protest if he chooses to savour those facets of experience that give a *partial* backing to the doctrines. The important thing is that he should himself be under no illusions. When he uses the vocabulary of timelessness, the 'metaphysical pathos' of his discourse must be appropriate to his real beliefs and must not borrow illegitimate splendour from the theism and mysticism he rejects.

It is possible (and we have remarked on this briefly already) to take note of all the senses we have been discussing, senses in which life may be held to have meaning within a non-theistic philosophy, to share, at least in outline, the value-theory of the philosophers with whom we started, and yet to insist

[10]*Sodome et Gomorrhe*, vol. I. p. 213 (Eng. tr., *Cities of the Plain*, vol. I, p. 218).
[11]*The Philosophy of Santayana*, ed. I. Edman (1953), pp. 206–11.

that life and individual lives are without meaning—'really'. What is a person doing who insists on this answer?

He may be claiming that life could be thought of as having meaning only so long as that meaning was believed to be a matter for discovery, not for creation and value-decision. He may be claiming that, to be meaningful, life would have to be *comprehensively* meaningful and its meaning invulnerable to assault. Worthwhile objectives must be ultimately realisable, despite appearances. If the Kantian postulates cannot be made, meaningfulness goes: it is for him an all-or-nothing matter. Otherwise expressed, the question about meaning can be put as a question about contingency and fortuitousness. If our attempts to impose or discover coherence and purpose in a life can operate only within the narrow *Spielraum* left by an unplanned and patternless 'facticity', in the end by accidents of birth and death, then the language of meaning is far more misleading (sardonically so) than it is useful.[12] If Nietzsche speaks of how desirable it is to 'die at the right time', of the 'free death' that 'consummates', he succeeds only in throwing into stronger relief the impossibility of guaranteeing anything of the sort, and we recall his own lingering ('meaningless') end as a case in point.

The vocabulary of meaning can thus be rejected *en bloc*, as for instance atheist existentialists have tended to reject it. In criticism, perhaps only this can be said: that it is a pity to expend in one rhetorical gesture a piece of discourse that can be used to express important distinctions between and within individual human lives. The gesture, though impressive, is extravagant and linguistically wasteful. But, so far as the rejection is a piece of (negative) verbal stipulation, one is free to opt for it: the language of the meaning of life is not indispensable. Alternatively, as we saw, one may prune and rationalise and redefine the vocabulary, restricting it to judgments about purposefulness or knowledge how to live. Perhaps there is most to be said for the third option, an elucidatory and conservative tracing of senses of 'the meaning of life' in literature and philosophy, and an attempt to see how differently the tasks of a life can look when they are viewed in the light of the many analogies of meaning.

Our sample of these analogies in this article, if not random, is certainly not complete.[13]

---

[12]Sartre: 'All existing things are born for no reason, continue through weakness and die by accident. . . . It is meaningless that we are born; it is meaningless that we die.'

[13]A version of this study was included in my Stanton Lectures, at the University of Cambridge, Lent Term 1966.

XI

Linguistic Philosophy and 'The Meaning of Life'

Kai Nielsen

I

Anglo-Saxon philosophy has in various degrees "gone linguistic". From the faithful attention to the niceties of plain English practiced by John Austin, to the use of descriptive linguistics initiated by Paul Ziff in his *Semantic Analysis*, to the deliberately more impressionistic concern with language typical of Isaiah Berlin and Stuart Hampshire, there is a pervasive emphasis by English-speaking philosophers on what can and cannot be said, on what is intelligible, and on what is nonsensical. When linguistic philosophy was first developing, many things were said to be nonsense which were not nonsense. However, this is something of the past, for linguistic philosophy has for a long time been less truculent and more diffident about what it makes sense to say, but only to become—some would say—unbelievably bland, dull and without a rationale that is of any general interest.[1]

Critics from many quarters have raised their voices to assault linguistic philosophy as useless pedantry remote from the perennial concerns of philosophy or the problems of belief and life that all men encounter when, in

This essay is a revised version of "Linguistic Philosophy and 'The Meaning of Life'," *Cross-Currents* (Summer 1964), Vol. XIV, pp. 313–34; printed, with some alterations by the Editors, with permission of Kai Nielsen.

[1]John Passmore remarks in his brief but thoroughly reliable and judicious *Philosophy in the Last Decade* (Sydney University Press: 1969) "Philosophy is once again cultivating areas it had declared wasteland, or had transferred without compunction to other owners." p. 5.

Hesse's terms, they feel to the full "the whole riddle of human destiny". Traditionally the philosophical enterprise sought, among other things, to give us some enlightenment about our human condition, but as philosophy "goes linguistic", it has traitorously and irresponsibly become simply talk about the uses of talk. The philosopher has left his "high calling" to traffic in linguistic trivialities.

Criticism of linguistic philosophy has not always been this crude, but there has typically been at least the implied criticism that linguistic philosophy could not really do justice to the profound problems of men with which Plato, Spinoza or Nietzsche struggled.

It is my conviction that such a charge is unfounded. In linguistic philosophy there is a partially new technique but no "abdication of philosophy". Surely most linguistic philosophy is dull, as is most philosophy, as is most anything else. Excellence and insight in any field are rare. But at its best linguistic philosophy is not dull and it is not without point; furthermore, though it often is, it need not be remote from the concerns of men. It is this last claim—the claim that linguistic philosophy can have nothing of importance to say about the perplexities of belief and life that from time to time bedevil us—that I wish to challenge.

With reference to the concepts of human purpose, religion and the problematical notion 'the meaning of Life', I want to show how in certain crucial respects linguistic philosophy can be relevant to the perplexities about life and conduct that reflective people actually face. 'What is the meaning of Life?' has been a standby of both the pulpiteer and the mystagogue. It has not come in for extended analysis by linguistic philosophers, though Ayer, Wisdom, Baier, Edwards, Flew, Hepburn and Dilman have had some important things to say about this obscure notion which when we are in certain moods perplexes us all and indeed, as it did Tolstoy and Dostoevsky, may even be something that forces itself upon us in thoroughly human terms.[2] I want to show how the use of the analytical techniques of linguistic philosophy can help us in coming to grips with the problems of human purpose and the meaning of Life.

Part of the trouble centers around puzzles about the use of the word 'meaning' in 'What is the meaning of Life?' Since the turn of the century there has been a lot of talk in philosophical circles about 'meanings' or 'a meaning criterion' and a good measure of attention has been paid to considerations about the meanings of words and sentences. But the mark (token) 'meaning' in 'What is the meaning of Life?' has a very different use than it has in 'What is the meaning of "obscurantist"?', 'What is the meaning of "table"?', 'What is the meaning of "good"?', 'What is the meaning of "science"?' and 'What is the

---

[2]A.J. Ayer, "The Claims of Philosophy" in M. Natanson (ed.) *Philosophy of the Social Sciences* (Random House, 1963). [The relevant articles by Baier, Edwards, and Hepburn are found in the present volume. (Eds.)]

meaning of "meaning"?'. In these other cases we are asking about the meaning or use of the word or words, and we are requesting either a definition of the word or an elucidation or description of the word's use. But in asking: 'What is th meaning of Life?' we are not asking—or at least this is not our central perplexity—about 'What is the meaning of the word "Life"? What then are we asking?

Indirection is the better course here. Consider some of the uses of the general formula: 'What is the meaning of that?' How, in what contexts, and for what purposes does it get used? Sometimes we may simply not know the meaning of a word, as when we come across a word we do not understand and look it up in a dictionary or ask the person using it in conversation what it means. It is not that he is using the word in an odd sense and we want to know what *he means* by it, but that we want to know what is meant by that word as it is employed in the public domain.

There is the quite different situation in which it is not about words that we are puzzled but about someone's non-linguistic behavior. A friend gives us a dark look in the middle of a conversation in which several people are taking part and afterwards we ask him 'What was the meaning of those dark looks?' We were aware when we noticed his dark look that he was disapproving of something we were doing but we did not and still do not know what. Our 'What was the meaning of that?' serves to try to bring out what is the matter. Note that in a way here we are not even puzzled about the meaning of words. The recipient of the dark look may very well know he is being disapproved of; but he wants to know what for. Here 'What is the meaning of that?' is a request for the point or the purpose of the action. In this way, as we shall see, it is closer to the question 'What is the meaning of Life?' than questions about the meaning of a word or a sentence.

We also ask 'What is the meaning of that?' when we want to know how a particular person on a particular occasion intends something. We want to know what *he means* by that. Thus if I say of some author that he writes 'chocolate rabbit stories' you may well ask me what I mean by that. Here you are puzzled both about the meaning of the phrase 'chocolate rabbit stories', for as with 'the pine cone weeps' or 'the rock cogitates' it is a deviant collection of words of indeterminate meaning, and about the point or purpose of making such a remark. After all, the point of making such an utterance may not be evident. Suppose I had said it to a stupid and pompous writer blown up with a false sense of his own importance. I could explain my meaning by saying that I was obliquely giving him to understand that his stories, like chocolate rabbits, were all out of the same mold: change the names and setting and you have the same old thing all over again. And the point of my utterance would also become evidence, i.e. to deflate the pompous windbag. The phrase 'chocolate rabbit stories' has no fixed use in human discourse, but language is sufficiently elastic for me to be able to give it a use without generating any linguistic or conceptual shock. To explain my meaning I must make clear the use I am giving it and make evident why I choose to use such an odd phrase.

'What is the meaning of Life?' is in some very significant respects like this last question though it is of course also very different. It is different in being non-deviant and in being a profoundly important question in the way the other question clearly is not. But note the likeness. In the first place when we or other people ask this question we are often not at all sure what we are asking. In this practical context we may in a way even be puzzled about the word 'life', though, as I have said, the question does not primarily function as a request for the explanation of the use of a word. There is a sense in which life does and there is a sense in which life does not begin and end in mystery. And when we ask about life here we are not asking Schrodinger's question or J.B.S. Haldane's. We are not in search of some property or set of properties that is common to and distinctive of all those things we call 'living things.' We are typically concerned with something very different and much vaguer. We are asking: Is life just one damn thing after another until finally one day we die and start to rot? Or can I sum it up and find or at least give it some point after all? Or is this just a silly illusion born of fear and trembling?' These are desperately vague, amorphous questions, but—as Wisdom would surely and rightly say—not meaningless for all that. And for some of us, and perhaps for all of us, *sometimes*, they are haunting, edging questions, questions we agonize over, then evade, then again try to come to grips with.

First, I want to say that, like 'What is the meaning of calling them chocolate rabbit stories?', 'What is the meaning of Life?' does *not* have a clear use; but that it does not have a clear use does not, I repeat, entail or in any way establish that it does not have a use or even that it does not have a supremely important use.[3] Secondly, 'What is the meaning of life?', most typically—though not always—functions as a request for the goals *worth* seeking in life though sometimes it may serve to ask if there are *any* goals worth seeking in life.[4] We are asking what (if anything) is the point to our lives? What (if anything) could give our lives purpose or point? In anguish we struggle to find the purpose, point or rationale of our grubby lives. But if this is the nature of the question, what would an answer look like? For this to be a fruitful question, all of us must ask ourselves individually: what would we take as an answer? When we ask this we are apt to come up with a blank; and if we are readers of philosophical literature we may remember that, along with others, a philosopher as persuasive and influential as A.J. Ayer has said that all such

---

[3]John Wisdom has driven home this point with force. In particular see his "The Modes of Thought and the Logic of 'God' " in his *Paradox and Discovery* (California, 1965).

[4]Ronald Hepburn has correctly stressed that this for some people may not be what is uppermost in their minds when they ask that question. See Hepburn's essay in this volume. See also Ilham Dilman's remarks about Hepburn's analysis in "Life and Meaning," *Philosophy*, 40 (October 1965).

questions are unanswerable. But if they are really unanswerable—or so it would seem—then they are hardly genuine questions.

I will concede that *in a sense* such questions are unanswerable, but in a much more important sense they *are* answerable. We can be intelligent about and reason about such questions. Any analysis which does not bring this out and elucidate it is confused and inadequate. In destroying pontifical pseudo-answers the baby has frequently gone down with the bath. In showing what kind of answers could not be answers to this question, the temptation is to stress that there are no answers at all and that indeed no answers are needed. I want to try to show why this is wrong and what an answer would look like.

II

How then is it possible for our life to have a meaning or a purpose? For a while, oddly enough, Ayer in his "The Claims of Philosophy" is a perfectly sound guide.[5] We do know what it is for a man to have a purpose. "It is a matter," Ayer remarks, "of his intending, on the basis of a given situation, to bring about some further situation which for some reason or other he conceives to be desirable."

But, Ayer asks, how is it possible for life *in general* to have a meaning or a purpose?

Well, there is one very simple answer. Life in general has a purpose if all living beings are tending toward a certain specifiable end. To understand the meaning of life or the purpose of existence it is only necessary to discover this end.

As Ayer makes perfectly clear, there are overwhelming difficulties with such an answer. In the first place there is no good reason to believe living beings are tending toward some specifiable end. But even if it were true that they are all tending toward this end such a discovery would not at all answer the question 'What is the meaning or purpose of life?' This is so because when we human beings ask this exceedingly vague question we are not just asking for *an explanation of* the facts of existence; we are asking for a *justification* of these facts. In asking this question we are seeking a way of life, trying as suffering, perplexed, and searching creatures to find what the existentialists like to call an "authentic existence." And as Ayer goes on to explain,

a theory which informs them merely that the course of events is so arranged as to lead inevitably to a certain end does nothing to meet their need. For the end in

[5]See Ayer, *op cit.* The rest of the references to Ayer in the text are from this essay. His brief remarks in his "What I Believe" in *What I Believe* (London: 1966) pp. 15–16 and in his introduction to *The Humanist Outlook*, A. J. Ayer (ed.), (London: 1968) pp. 6–7 are also relevant as further brief statements of his central claims about the meaning of life.

question will not be one that they themselves have chosen. As far as they are concerned it will be entirely arbitrary; and it will be a no less arbitrary fact that their existence is such as necessarily to lead to its fulfillment. In short, from the point of view of justifying one's existence, there is no essential difference between a teleological explanation of events and a mechanical explanation. In either case, it is a matter of brute fact that events succeed one another in the ways they do and are explicable in the ways they are.

In the last analysis, an attempt to answer a question of why events are as they are must always resolve itself into saying only *how* they are. Every explanation of why people do such and such and why the world is so and so finally depends on a very general description. And even if it is the case, as Charles Taylor powerfully argues, that teleological explanations of human behavior are irreducible, Ayer's point here is not all weakened, for in explaining, teleologically or otherwise, we are still showing how things are; we are not justifying anything.[6]

When we ask: 'What is the meaning of life?' we want an answer that is more than *just* an explanation or description of *how* people behave or *how* events are arranged or *how* the world is constituted. We are asking for a *justification* for our existence. We are asking for a justification for why life is as it is, and not even the most complete explanation and/or description of *how* things are ordered can answer this quite different question. The person who demands that some general description of man and his place in nature should entail a statement that man ought to live and die in a certain way is asking for something that can no more be the case than it can be the case that ice can gossip. To ask about the meaning of our lives involves asking how we should live, or whether any decision to live in one way is more *worthy* of acceptance than any other. Both of these questions are clearly questions of value; yet no statement of *fact* about how we in fact do live can by itself be sufficient to answer such questions. No statement of what ought to be the case can be deduced from a statement of what is the case. If we are demanding such an answer, then Ayer is perfectly right in claiming the question is unanswerable.

Let me illustrate. Suppose, perhaps as a result of some personal crisis, I want to take stock of myself. As Kierkegaard would say, I want to appropriate, take to heart, the knowledge I have or can get about myself and my condition in order to arrive at some decision as to what sort of life would be most meaningful for me, would be the sort of life I would truly want to live if I could act rationally and were fully apprised of my true condition. I might say to myself, though certainly not to others, unless I was a bit of an exhibitionist, 'Look Nielsen, you're a little bit on the vain side and you're arrogant to boot. And why do you gossip so and spend so much of your time reading science

[6]Charles Taylor, *The Explanation of Behavior* (Routledge and Kegan Paul, 1964).

fiction? And why do you always say what you expect other people want you to say? You don't approve of that in others, do you? And why don't you listen more? And weren't you too quick with Jones and too indulgent with Smith'? In such a context I would put these questions and a host of questions like them to myself. And I might come up with some general explanations, good or bad, like 'I act this way because I have some fairly pervasive insecurities'. And to my further question, 'Well, why do you have these insecurities?' I might dig up something out of my past such as 'My parents died when I was two and I never had any real home'. To explain why this made me insecure I might finally evoke a whole psychological theory and eventually perhaps even a biological and physiological theory, and these explanations about the nature of the human animal would themselves finally rest, in part at least, on various descriptions of how man does behave. In addition, I might, if I could afford it and were sufficiently bedevilled by these questions, find my way to a psychiatrist's couch and there, after the transference had taken place, I would eventually get more quite personalized explanations of my behavior and attitudes. But none of these things, in themselves, could tell me the meaning of life or even the meaning of my life, though they indeed might help me in this search. I might discover that I was insecure because I could never get over the wound of the loss of my father. I might discover that unconsciously I blamed myself. As a child I wished him dead and then he died so somehow I did it, really. And I would, of course, discover how unreasonable this is. I would come to understand that people generally react this way in those situations. In Tolstoy's phrase, we are all part of the "same old river." And, after rehearsing it, turning it over, taking it to heart, I might well gain control over it and eventually gain control over some of my insecurities. I could see and even live through again what *caused* me to be vain, arrogant and lazy. But suppose, that even after all these discoveries I really didn't want to change. After stock-taking, I found that I was willing to settle for the *status quo*. Now I gratefully acknowledge that this is very unlikely, but here we are concerned with the *logical* possibilities. 'Yes, there are other ways of doing things,' I say to myself, 'but after all is said and done I have lived this way a long time and I would rather go on this way than change. This sort of life, is after all, the most meaningful one. This is how I really want to act and this is how I, and others like me, ought to act.' What possible facts could anyone appeal to which would prove, in the sense of logically entail, that I was wrong and that the purpose of life or the meaning of life was very different than I thought it was? It is Ayer's contention, and I think he is right, that there are none.

'But you have left out God,' someone might say. 'You have neglected the possibility that there is a God and that God made man to His image and likeness and that God has a plan for man. Even Sartre, Heidegger and Camus agree that to ask 'What is the Meaning of Life?' or 'What is the purpose of human existence?' is, in effect, to raise the question of God. If there is a God your conclusion would not follow, and, as Father Copleston has said, if there is *no* God human existence can have no end or purpose other than that given by man himself.[7]

I would want to say, that the whole question of God or no God, Jesus or no Jesus, is entirely beside the point. Even if there were a God human existence can, in the relevant sense of 'end', 'purpose' or 'meaning', have no other end, purpose or meaning than what we as human beings give it by our own deliberate choices and decisions.

Let us see how this is so. Let us suppose that everything happens as it does because God intends that it should. Let us even assume, as we in reality cannot, that we can know the purpose or intentions of God. Now, as Ayer points out, either God's "purpose is sovereign or it is not. If it is sovereign, that is, if everything that happens is necessarily in accordance with it, then it is true also of our behavior. Consequently, there is no point in our deciding to conform to it, for the simple reason that we cannot do otherwise." No matter what, we do God's purpose. There is no sense in saying it is *our* purpose, that it is something we have made our own by our own deliberate choice. I have not *discovered* a meaning for my life and other people have not *discovered* a meaning for their lives. If it were possible for us *not* to fulfill it, the purpose would not be God's *sovereign* purpose and if it is His sovereign purpose, it cannot, in the requisite sense, be *our* purpose, for it will not be something of which it would make sense to say that we chose it. It is just something that necessarily happens to us because of God's intentions. If we are compelled to do it, it is not *our* purpose. It is only our purpose if we want to do it and if we could have done otherwise.

On the other hand, if God's purpose is not sovereign and we are not inexorably compelled to do what God wills, we have no reason to conform to God's purpose unless we independently judge it to be *good* or by our own independent decision make it our purpose. We cannot derive the statement 'x is good' from 'that Being whom people call "God" says "x is good" ' or from 'that Being whom people call "God" wills x' unless we *independently* judge that whatever this Being *says* is good *is good* or whatever that Being wills *ought* to be done. Again, as Ayer remarks, this "means that the significance of our behavior depends finally upon our own judgments of value; and the concurrence of a diety then becomes superfluous."[8]

The basic difficulty, as Ayer makes clear, is that in trying to answer the questions as we have above, we have really misunderstood the question.

---

[7]See his discussion of existentialism in his *Contemporary Philosophy*.

[8]While I completely agree with the central thrust of Ayer's argument here, he has, I believe, overstated his case. Even if our behaviour finally depends on our own standards of value, it does not follow that the concurrence of the deity, if there is one, is superfluous, for we could still find crucial moral guidance from our grasp of something of God's wisdom.

'What-is-the-meaning-of-that?' and 'What-is-the-purpose-of-that?' questions can be very different. We have already noted some of the differences among 'What-is-the-meaning-of-that?' questions, and we have seen that 'What is the meaning of Life?' in many contexts at least can well be treated as a 'What-is-the-purpose-of-that?' question. But 'What is the purpose of life?' is only very superficially like 'What is the purpose of a blotter?', 'What is the purpose of brain surgery?' or 'What is the purpose of the liver?' The first is a question about a human artifact and in terms of certain assumed ends we can say quite explicitly, independently of whether or not we want blotters, what the purpose of blotters is. Similarly brain surgery is a well-known human activity and has a well-known rationale. Even if we are Christian Scientists and disapprove of surgery altogether, we can understand and agree on what the purpose of brain surgery is, just as we all can say Fearless Fosdick is a good safecracker, even though we disapprove of safecrackers. And again, in terms of the total functioning of the human animal we can say what livers are for, even though the liver is not an artifact like a blotter. If there is a God and God made man, we *might* say the question 'What is the purpose of human life?' is very like 'What is the purpose of umbrellas'?. The human animal then becomes a Divine artifact. But, even if all this were so, we would not—as we have already seen—have an answer to the *justifactory* question we started with when we asked, 'What is the meaning of life?'. If we knew God's purpose for man, we would know what man was made for. But we would not have an answer to our question about the meaning of life, for we would not know if there was purpose *in* our lives or if we could find a point in acting one way rather than another. We would only know that there was something—which may or may not be of value—that we were constructed, "cut out", to be.

Similarly, if an Aristotelian philosophy is correct, "What is the purpose of life?' would become very like 'What is the purpose of the liver?' But here again a discovery of what end man is as a matter of fact tending toward would not answer the perplexity we started from, that is to say, it would not answer the question, 'What is the meaning of life, how should men live and die?' We would only learn that 'What is the purpose of life?' could admit of two very different uses. As far as I can see, there are no good reasons to believe either that there is a God or that the human animal has been ordered for some general end; but even if this were so it would not give us an answer to the question: 'What is the meaning of life?'

This is so because the question has been radically misconstrued. When we ask: 'What is the meaning of life?' or 'What is the purpose of human existence?' we are normally asking, as I have already said, questions of the following types: 'What should we seek?', 'What ends—if any—are worthy of attainment?' Questions of this sort require a very different answer than any answer to: 'What is the meaning of "obscurantism"?', 'What is the purpose of the ink-blotter?' and 'What is the purpose of the liver?'. Ayer is right when he says: "what is required by those who seek to know the purpose of their existence is not a factual description of the way that people actually do conduct themselves, but rather a decision as to how they *should* conduct themselves." Again he is correct in remarking: "There is—a sense in which it can be said that life does have a meaning. It has for each of us whatever meaning we severally *choose* to give it. The purpose of a man's existence is constituted by the ends to which he, consciously or unconsciously, devotes himself."

Ayer links this with another crucial logical point, a point which the existentialists have dramatized as some kind of worrisome "moral discovery." Ayer points out that "in the last resort . . . each individual has the responsibility of making the choice of how he ought to live and die" and that it is logically impossible that someone else, in some authoritative position, can make that choice for him. If someone gives me moral advice in the nature of the case I must decide whether or not to follow his advice, so again the choice is finally my own. This is true because moral questions are primarily questions about what to do. In asking how I ought to live, I am trying to make up my mind how to act. And to say I deliberately acted in a certain way implies that I decided to do it. There is no avoiding personal choice in considering such questions.

But Ayer, still writing in the tradition of logical empiricism, often writes as if it followed from the truth of what we have said so far, that there could be no reasoning about 'How ought man to live?' or 'What is the meaning of life?'. Thus Ayer says at one point in "The Claims of Philosophy": "He [the moral agent] cannot prove his judgments of value are correct, for the simple reason that no judgment of value is capable of proof." He goes on to argue that people have no way of demonstrating that one judgment of value is superior to another. A decision between people in moral disagreement is a "subject for persuasion and finally a matter of individual choice."

As we have just seen there is a sound point to Ayer's stress on choice vis-a-vis morality, but taken as a whole his remarks are at best misleading. There is reasoning about moral questions and there are arguments and proofs in morality. There are principles in accordance with which we appraise our actions, and there are more general principles, like the principle of utility or the principles of distributive justice in accordance with which we test our lower-level moral rules. And there is a sense of 'being reasonable' which, as Hume and Westermarck were well aware, has distinctive application to moral judgments. Thus, if I say, 'I ought to be relieved of my duties, I'm just too ill to go on' I not only must believe I am in fact ill, I must also be prepared to say, of any of my colleagues or anyone else similarly placed, that in like circumstances they too ought to be relieved of their duties if they fall ill. There is a certain *generality* about moral discourse and a man is not reasoning morally or 'being reasonable' if he will not allow those inferences. Similarly, if I say 'I want x' or 'I prefer x' I need not, though I may, be prepared to give reason why I want it or prefer it, but if I say 'x is the right thing to do' or 'x is good' or 'I ought to do x' or 'x is worthy of attainment', I must—perhaps with the exception of judgments of intrinsic goodness—be prepared to give *reasons* for saying 'x is the right thing to do', 'x is good', 'I ought to do x' and the like. (Note, this remark has the status of what Wittgenstein would call a grammatical remark.)

It is indeed true in morals and in reasoning about human conduct generally that justification must come to an end; but this is also true in logic, science and in common sense empirical reasoning about matters of fact; but it is also true that the end point in reasoning over good and evil is different than in science and the like, for in reasoning about how to act, our judgment finally terminates in a choice—a decision of principle. And here is the truth in Ayer's remark that moral judgments are *"finally* a matter of individual choice."* But, unless we are to mislead, we must put the emphasis on 'finally', for a dispassionate, neutral analysis of the uses of the language of human conduct will show, as I have indicated, that there is reasoning, and in a relevant sense, 'objective reasoning', about moral questions. It is not at all a matter of pure persuasion or goading someone into sharing your attitudes.

I cannot, of course, even begin to display the full range of the reasoning which has sought to establish this point. But I hope I have said enough to block the misleading implications of Ayer's otherwise very fine analysis. Early linguistic philosophy was primarily interested in 1) the descriptive and explanatory discourse of the sciences, and 2) in logico-mathematico discourse; the rest was rather carelessly labelled, "expressive or emotive discourse." But the thrust of the work of linguistic philosophers since the Second World War has corrected that mistaken emphasis as recent analytical writing in ethics makes evident. Here I commend to you R.M. Hare's *The Language of Morals,* and his *Freedom and Reason,* Stephen Toulmin's *An Examination of the Place of Reason in Ethics,* Kurt Baier's *The Moral Point of View,* Marcus Singer's *Generalization in Ethics,* P.H. Nowell-Smith's *Ethics,* Bernard Mayo's *Ethics and the Moral Life,* or George von Wright's *The Varieties of Goodness.* They would also reinforce the point I tried briefly to make against Ayer, as would an examination of the essays of Philippa Foot or John Rawls.[9]

III

There are, however, other considerations that may be in our minds when we ask 'What is the meaning of life?' or 'Does life have a meaning?'. In asking such questions, we may *not* be asking 'What should we seek?' or 'What goals

---

[9]I have discussed these issues in my "Problems of Ethics" and "History of Contemporary Ethics", both in Vol. 3 of *The Encyclopedia of Philosophy,* Paul Edwards, ed., (Macmillan, 1967).

are worth seeking really?' Instead we may be asking 'Is *anything* worth seeking?' Does it matter finally what we do?' Here, some may feel, we finally meet the real tormenting "riddle of human existence".

Such a question is not simply a moral question: it is a question concerning human conduct, a question about how to live one's life or about whether to continue to live one's life. Yet when we consider what an answer would look like here we draw a blank. If someone says 'Is anything worthwhile?' we gape. We want to reply: 'Why, sitting in the sunshine in the mornings, seeing the full moon rise, meeting a close friend one hasn't seen in a long time, sleeping comfortably after a tiring day, all these things and a million more are most assuredly worthwhile. Any life devoid of experiences of this sort would most certainly be impoverished.'

Yet this reply is so obvious we feel that something different must be intended by the questioner. The questioner knows that we, and most probably he, ordinarily regard such things as worthwhile, but he is asking if these things or *anything* is worthwhile *really?* These things *seem* worthwhile but are they in reality? And here we indeed do not know what to say. If someone queries whether it is really worthwhile leaving New York and going to the beach in August we have some idea of what to say; there are some criteria which will enable us to make at least a controversial answer to this question. But when it is asked, in a philosophical manner, *if anything, ever* is really worthwhile, it is not clear that we have a genuine question before us. The question borrows its form from more garden-variety questions but when we ask it in this general way do we actually know what we mean? If someone draws a line on the blackboard, a question over the line's straightness can arise only if some criterion for a line's being straight is accepted. Similarly only if some criterion of worthiness is accepted can we intelligibly ask if a specific thing or anything is worthy of attainment.

But if a sensitive and reflective person asks, 'Is anything worthwhile, really?' could he not be asking this because, 1) he has a certain vision of human excellence, and 2) his austere criteria for what is worthwhile have developed in terms of that vision? Armed with such criteria, he might find nothing that man can in fact attain under his present and foreseeable circumstances *worthy* of attainment. Considerations of this sort seem to be the sort of considerations that led Tolstoy and Schopenhauer to come to such pessimistic views about life. Such a person would be one of those few people, who as one of Hesse's characters remarks, "demand the utmost of life and yet cannot come to terms with its stupidity and crudeness." In terms of his ideal of human excellence nothing is worthy of attainment.

To this, it is natural to respond, 'If this is our major problem about the meaning of life, then this is indeed no intellectual or philosophical riddle about human destiny. We need not like Steppenwolf return to our lodging lonely and disconsolate because life's "glassy essence" remains forever hidden, for we can well envisage, in making such a judgment, what would be worthwhile. We can say what a meaningful life would look like even though we can't attain it. If such is the question, there is no "riddle of human existence", though there is a pathos to human life and there is the social-political pattern problem of how to bring the requisite human order into existence. Yet only if we have a conception of what human life should be can we feel such pathos.'

If it is said in response to this that what would really be worthwhile could not possibly be attained, an absurdity has been uttered. To say something is worthy of attainment implies that, everything else being equal, it ought to be attained. But to say that something ought to be attained implies that it *can* be attained. Thus we *cannot* intelligibly say that something is worthy of attainment but that it cannot possibly be attained. So in asking 'Is anything worthy of attainment?' we must acknowledge that there are evaluative criteria operative which guarantee that what is sincerely said to be worthy of attainment is at least in principle attainable. And as we have seen in speaking of morality, 'x is worthy of attainment' does not mean 'x is preferred', though again, in asserting that something is worthy of attainment, or worthwhile, we imply that we would choose it, everything else being equal, in preference to something else. But we cannot intelligibly speak of a choice if there is no possibility of doing one thing rather than another.

Life is often hard and, practically speaking, the ideals we set our hearts on, those to which we most deeply commit ourselves, may in actual fact be impossible to achieve. A sensitive person may have an ideal of conduct, an ideal of life, that he assents to without reservation. But the facts of human living being what they are, he knows full well that this ideal cannot be realized. His ideals are intellgible enough, logically their achievement is quite possible, but as a matter of *brute fact* his ideals are beyond his attainment. If this is so, is it worthwhile for him and others like him to go on living or to strive for anything at all? Can life, under such circumstances, be anything more than an ugly habit? For such a man, 'What is the meaning of life?' has the force of 'What *point* can a life such as mine have under these circumstances?'. And in asking whether such a life has a point he is asking the very question we put above, viz. can life be worth living under such conditions.

Again such a question is perfectly intelligible and is in no way unanswerable any more than any other question about how to act, though here too we must realize that the facts of human living *cannot* be sufficient for a man simply to read off an answer without it in any way affecting his life. Here, too, *any* answer will require a decision or some kind of effective involvement on the part of the person involved. A philosopher can be of help here in showing what kind of answers we cannot give, but it is far less obvious that he can provide us with a set of principles that together with empirical facts about his condition and prospects, will enable the perplexed man to know what he ought to do. The philosopher or any thoughtful person who sees just what is involved in the question can give some helpful advice. Still the person involved must work out an answer in anguish and soreness of heart.

However, I should remind him that no matter how bad his own life was, there would always remain something he could do to help alleviate the sum total of human suffering. This certainly has value and if he so oriented his life, he could not say that his life was without point. I would also argue that in normal circumstances he could not be sure that his ideals of life would permanently be frustrated, and if he held ideals that would be badly frustrated under almost any circumstances, I would get him to look again at his ideals. Could such ideals really be adequate? Surely man's reach must exceed his grasp, but how far should we go? Should not any ideal worth its salt come into some closer involvement with the realities of human living? And if one deliberately and with self-understanding plays the role of a Don Quixote can one justifiably complain that one's ideals are not realized? Finally, it does not seem to me reasonable to expect that *all* circumstances can have sufficient meaning to make them worthwhile. Under certain circumstances life is not worth living. As a philosopher, I would point out this possibility and block those philosophical-religious claims that would try to show that this could not possibly be.

Many men who feel the barbs of constant frustration, come to feel that their ideals have turned out to be impossible, and ask in anguish—as a consequence—'Does life really have any meaning?'. To a man in such anguish I would say all I have said above and much more, though I am painfully aware that such an approach may seem cold and unfeeling. I know that these matters deeply affect us; indeed they can even come to obsess us, and when we are so involved it is hard to be patient with talk about what can and cannot be said. But we need to understand these matters as well; and, after all, what more can be done along this line than to make quite plain what is involved in his question and try to exhibit a range of rational attitudes that could be taken toward it, perhaps stressing the point that though Dr. Rieux lost his wife and his best friend, his life, as he fought the plague, was certainly not without point either for him or for others. But I would also try to make clear that finally an answer to such a question must involve a decision or the having or adopting of a certain attitude on the part of the person involved. This certainly should be stressed and it should be stressed that the question 'Is such a life meaningful?' is a sensible question, which admits of a non-obscurantist, non-metaphysical treatment.

IV

There are many choices we must make in our lives and some choices are more worthwhile than others, though the criteria for what is worthwhile are in large measure at least context-dependent. 'It's worthwhile going to Leningrad to see the Hermitage' is perfectly intelligible to someone who knows and cares about art. Whether such a trip to Leningrad is worthwhile for such people can be determined by these people by a visit to the Museum. 'It's worthwhile fishing the upper Mainistee' is in exactly the same category, though the criteria for worthwhileness are not the same. Such statements are most assuredly perfectly intelligible; and no adequate grounds have been given to give us reason to think that we should philosophically tinker with the ordinary criteria of 'good art museum' or 'good trout fishing'. And why should we deny that these and other things are really worthwhile? To say 'Nothing is worthwhile since all pales and worse still, all is vain because man must die' is to mistakenly assume that because an eternity of even the best trout fishing would be not just a bore but a real chore, that trout fishing is therefore not worthwhile. Death and the fact (if it is a fact) that there is nothing new under the sun need not make all vanity. That something must come to an end can make it all the more precious: to know that love is an old tale does not take the bloom from your beloved's cheek.

Yet some crave a more general answer to 'Is anything worthwhile?' This some would say, is what they are after when they ask about the meaning of life.

As I indicated, the criteria for what is worthwhile are surely in large measure context-dependent, but let us see what more we can say about this need for a more general answer.

In asking 'Why is anything worthwhile?' if the 'why' is a request for *causes,* a more general answer can be given. The answer is that people have preferences, enjoy, admire and approve of certain things and they can and sometimes do reflect. Because of this they find some things worthwhile. This, of course, is not what 'being worthwhile' *means,* but if people did not have these capacities they would not find anything worthwhile. But *reasons* why certain things are worthwhile are dependent on the thing in question.

If people find x worthwhile they generally prefer x, approve of x, enjoy x, or admire x on reflection. If people did not prefer, approve of, enjoy or admire things then nothing would be found to be worthwhile. If they did not have these feelings the notion of 'being worthwhile' would have no role to play in human life; but it does have a role to play and, as in morality, justification of what is worthwhile must finally come to an end with the reflective choices we make.

Moral principles, indeed, have a special onerousness about them. If something is a moral obligation, it is something we ought to do through and through. It for most people at least and from a moral point of view for everyone overrides (but does not exhaust) all non-moral considerations about what is worthwhile. If we are moral agents and we are faced with the necessity of choosing either A or B, where A, though very worthwhile, is a non-moral end and where B is a moral one, we must choose B. The force of the 'must' here is logical. From a moral point of view there is no alternative but to choose B. Yet we do not escape the necessity of decision for we still must *agree* to *adopt* a moral point of view, to *try* to act as moral agents. Here, too, we must finally make a decision of principle.[10] There are good Hobbesian reasons for adopting the moral point of view but if one finally would really prefer "a state of nature" in which all were turned against all, rather than a life in which there was a freedom from this and at least a minimum of cooperation between human beings, then these reasons for adopting the moral point of view would not be compelling to such a person. There is, in the last analysis, no escape from making a choice.

In asking 'What is the meaning of Life?' we have seen how this question is in reality a question concerning human conduct. It asks either 'What should we seek?' or 'What ends (if any) are really worthwhile?'. I have tried to show in what general ways such questions are answerable. We can give reasons for our moral judgments and moral principles and the whole activity of morality can be seen to have a point, but not all questions concerning what is worthwhile are moral questions. Where moral questions do not enter we must make a decision about what, on reflection, we are going to seek. We must ascertain what—all things considered—really answers to our interests or, where there is no question of anything answering to our interests or failing to answer to our interests, we should decide what on reflection we prefer. What do we really want, wish to approve of, or admire? To ask 'Is anything worthwhile?' involves our asking 'Is there nothing that we, on reflection, upon knowledge of ourselves and others, want, approve of, or admire?' When we say 'So-and-so is worthwhile' we are making a normative judgment that cannot be derived from determining what we desire, admire or approve of. That is to say, these statements do not entail statements to the effect that so and so is worthwhile. But in determining what is worthwhile this is finally all we have to go on. In saying something is worthwhile, we 1) *express* our preference, admiration or approval; 2) in some sense imply that we are prepared to defend our choice with *reasons:* and 3) in effect, indicate our belief that others like us in the relevant respects and similarly placed, will find it worthwhile too. And the answer to our question is that, of course, there are things we humans desire, prefer, approve of, or admire. This being so, our question is not unanswerable. Again we need not fly to a metaphysical enchanter.

As I said, 'Is anything really worthwhile, really worth seeking?' makes us gape. And 'atomistic analyses', like the one I have just given, often leave us with a vague but persistent feeling of dissatisfaction, even when we cannot clearly articulate the grounds of our dissatisfaction. 'The real question,' we want to say, 'has slipped away from us amidst the host of distinctions and analogies. We've not touched the deep heart of the matter at all.'

---

[10]I have discussed the central issues involved here at length in my "Why Should I Be Moral?", *Methodos,* 15 (1963).

Surely, I have not exhausted the question for, literally speaking, it is not one question but a cluster of loosely related questions all concerning 'the human condition'—how man is to act and how he is to live his life even in the face of the bitterest trials and disappointments. Questions here are diverse, and a philosopher, or anyone else, becomes merely pretentious and silly when he tries to come up with some formula that will solve, resolve or dissolve the perplexities of human living. But I have indicated in skeletal fashion how we can approach general questions about 'What (if anything) is worth seeking?' And I have tried to show how such questions are neither meaningless nor questions calling for esoteric answers.

V

We are not out of the woods yet. Suppose someone were to say: 'Okay, you've convinced me. Some things are worthwhile and there is a more or less distinct mode of reasoning called moral reasoning and there are canons of validity distinctive of this *sui generis* type reasoning. People do reason in the ways that you have described, but it still remains the case that here one's attitudes and final choices are relevant in a way that it isn't necessarily the case in science or in arguments over plain matters of fact. But when I ask: "How ought men act?", "What is the meaning of life?" and "What is the meaning of *my* life?, how should I live and die?" I want an answer that is logically independent of any human choice or any pro-attitude toward any course of action or any state of affairs. Only if I can have that kind of warrant for my moral judgments and ways-of-life will I be satisfied.

If a man demands this and continues to demand this after dialectical examination we must finally leave him unsatisfied. As linguistic philosophers there is nothing further we can say to him. In dialectical examination we can again point out to him that he is asking for the logically impossible, but if he recognizes this and persists in asking for that which is impossible there are no further rational arguments that we can use to establish our point. But, prior to this last-ditch stand, there are still some things that we can say. We can, in detail and with care, point out to him, describe fully for him, the rationale of the moral distinctions we do make and the functions of moral discourse. A full description here will usually break this kind of obsessive perplexity. Furthermore, we can make the move Stephen Toulmin makes in the last part of his *The Place of Reason in Ethics*. We can describe for him another use of 'Why' that Toulmin has well described as a "limiting question."[11]

[11]Stephen Toulmin, *An Examination of the Place of Reason in Ethics* (Cambridge University Press, 1950).

Let me briefly explain what this is and how it could be relevant. When we ask a "limiting question" we are not really asking a question at all. We are in a kind of "land of shadows" where there are no clear-cut uses of discourse. If we just look at their grammatical form, "limiting questions" do not appear to be extra-rational in form, but in their depth grammar—their actual function— they clearly are. 'What holds the universe up?' looks very much like 'What holds the Christmas tree up?' but the former, in common sense contexts at least, is a limiting question while the latter usually admits of a perfectly obvious answer. As Toulmin himself puts it, limiting questions are "questions expressed in a form borrowed from a familiar mode of reasoning, but not doing the job which they normally do within that mode of reasoning."[12] A direct answer to a limiting question never satisfies the questioners. Attempted "answers" only regenerate the question, though often a small change in the questions themselves or their context will make them straightforward questions. Furthermore, there is no standard interpretation for limiting questions sanctioned in our language. And limiting questions do not present us with any genuine alternatives from which to choose.

Now "limiting questions" get used in two main contexts. Sometimes, they merely express what Ryle, rather misleadingly, called a "category mistake." Thus someone who was learning English might ask: 'How hot is blue?' or 'Where is anywhere?' And, even a native speaker of English might ask as a *moral* agent, 'Why ought I to do what is right?'. We "answer" such questions by pointing out that blue cannot be hot, anywhere is not a particular place, and that if something is indeed right, this entails that it ought to be done. Our remarks here are grammatical remarks, though our speaking in the material mode may hide this. And if the questioner's "limiting question" merely signifies that a category mistake has been made, when this is pointed out to the questioner, there is an end to the matter. But more typically and more interestingly, limiting questions do not *just* or at all indicate category mistakes but express, as well or independently, a *personal predicament*. Limiting questions may express anxiety, fear, hysterical apprehensiveness about the future, hope, despair, and any number of attitudes. Toulmin beautifully illustrates from the writings of Dostoevsky an actual, on-the-spot use, of limiting questions:

> He was driving somewhere in the steppes. . . . Not far off was a village, he could see the black huts, and half the huts were burnt down, there were only the charred beams sticking out. As they drove in, there were peasant women drawn up along the road . . .
> 'Why are they crying? Why are they crying?', Mitya [Dmitri] asked, as they dashed gaily by.
> 'It's the babe,' answered the driver, 'the babe is weeping.'

[12]*Ibid.*, p. 205.

And Mitya was struck by his saying, in his peasant way, 'the babe', and he liked the peasant's calling it a 'babe'. There seemed more pity in it.

'But why is it weeping?', Mitya persisted stupidly. 'Why are its little arms bare? Why don't they wrap it up?'

'The babe's cold, its little clothes are frozen and don't warm it.'

'But why is it? Why?' foolish Mitya still persisted.

'Why, they're poor people, burnt out. They've no bread. They're begging because they've been burnt out.'

'No, no,' Mitya, as it were still did not understand. 'Tell me why it is those poor mothers stand there? Why are people poor? Why is the babe poor? Why is the steppe barren? Why don't they hug each other and kiss? Why don't they sing songs of joy? Why are they so dark from black misery? Why don't they feed the babe?'

And he felt that, though his questions were unreasonable, and senseless, yet he wanted to ask just that, and he had to ask it just in that way. And he felt that a passion of pity, such as he had never known before, was rising in his heart, that he wanted to cry, that he wanted to do something for them all, so that the babe should weep no more, so that the dark-faced, dried-up mother should not weep, that no one should shed tears again from that moment . . .

'I've had a good dream, gentlemen,' he said in a strange voice, with a new light, as of joy, in his face.[13]

It is clear that we need not, may not, from the point of view of analysis, condemn these uses of language as illicit. We can point out that it is a muddle to confuse such questions with literal questions, and that such questions have no fixed *literal* meaning, and that as a result there are and can be no fixed literal ways of answering them, but they are indeed, genuine uses of language, and not the harum-scarum dreams of undisciplined metaphysics. When existentialist philosophers and theologians state them as profound questions about an alleged ontological realm there is room for complaint, but as we see them operating in the passage I quoted from *The Brothers Karamazov*, they seem to be not only linguistically proper but also an extremely important form of discourse. It is a shame and a fraud when philosophers 'sing songs' as a substitute for the hard work of philosophizing, but only a damn fool would exclude song-singing, literal or metaphorical, from the life of reason, or look down on it as a somehow inferior activity. Non-literal 'answers' to these non-literal, figurative questions, when they actually express personal predicaments or indeed more general human predicaments may, in a motivational sense, *goad* people to do one thing or another that they *know* they ought to do or they may comfort them or give them hope in time of turmoil and anxiety. I am not saying this is their only use or that they have no other respectable rationale. I do not at all think that; but I am saying that here is a rationale that even the most hard nosed positivist should acknowledge.

The man who demands 'a more objective answer' to his question, 'How ought men to live?' or 'What is the meaning of Life?' may not be just muddled. If he is *just* making a 'category mistake' and this is pointed out to him, he will desist, but if he persists, his limiting question probably expresses some anxiety. In demanding an answer to an evaluative question that can be answered independently of any attitudes he might have or choices he might make, he may be unconsciously expressing his fear of making decisions, his insecurity and confusion about what he really wants, and his desperate desire to have a Father who would make all these decisions for him. And it is well in such a context to bring Weston LaBarre's astute psychological observation to mind. "Values," LaBarre said, "must from emotional necessity be viewed as absolute by those who use values as compulsive defenses against reality, rather than properly as tools for the exploration of reality."[14] This remark, coming from a Freudian anthropologist, has unfortunately a rather metaphysical ring, but it can be easily enough de-mythologized. The point is, that someone who persists in these questions, persists in a demand for a totally different and 'deeper' justification or answer to the question 'What is the meaning of Life?' than the answer that such a question admits of, may be just expressing his own insecurity. The heart of rationalism is often irrational. At such a point the only reasoning that will be effective with him, if indeed any reasoning will be effective with him, may be psychoanalytic reasoning. And by then, of course, you have left the philosopher and indeed all questions of justification far behind. But again the philosopher can describe the kinds of questions we can ask and the point of these questions. Without advocating anything at all he can make clearer to us the structure of "the life of reason" and the goals we human beings do prize.

VI

There is another move that might be made in asking about this haunting question: 'What is the meaning of Life?'. Suppose someone were to say: 'Yes I see about these "limiting questions" and I see that moral reasoning and reasoning about human conduct generally are limited modes of reasoning with distinctive criteria of their own. If I am willing to be guided by reason and I can be reasonable there are some answers I can find to the question: "What is the meaning of Life?". I'm aware that they are not cut and dried and that they are not simple and that they are not even by any means altogether the same for all men, but there are some reasonable answers and touchstones all the same. You and I are in perfect accord on that. But there is one thing I don't see at all, "Why ought I to be guided by reason anyway?" and if you cannot answer this

---

[14]Weston LaBarre, *The Human Animal* (University of Chicago, 1954).

for me I don't see why I should think that your answer—or rather your schema for an answer—about the meaning of Life is, after all, really any good. It all depends on how you *feel*, finally. There are really no answers here.'

But again we have a muddle; let me very briefly indicate why. If someone asks: 'Why ought I to be guided by reason anyway?' or 'Is it really good to be reasonable?' one is tempted to take such a question as a paradigm case of a "limiting question", and a very silly one at that. But as some people like to remind us—without any very clear sense of what they are reminding us of—reason has been challenged. It is something we should return to, be wary of, realize the limits of, or avoid, as the case may be. It will hardly do to take such a short way with the question and rack it up as a category mistake.

In some particular contexts, with some particular people, it is (to be paradoxical, for a moment) reasonable to question whether we ought to follow reason. Thus, if I am a stubborn, penny-pinching old compulsive and I finally take my wife to the 'big-city' for a holiday, it might be well to say to me: 'Go on, forget how much the damn tickets cost, buy them anyway. Go on, take a cab even if you can't afford it.' But to give or heed such advice clearly is not, in any fundamental sense, to fly in the face of reason, for on a deeper level—the facts of human living being what they are—we are being guided by reason.

It also makes sense to ask, as people like D. H. Lawrence press us to ask, if it really pays to be reasonable. Is the reasonable, clear-thinking, clear-visioned, intellectual animal really the happiest, in the long run? And can his life be as rich, as intense, as creative as the life of Lawrence's sort of man? From Socrates to Freud it has been assumed, for the most part, that self-knowledge, knowledge of our world, and rationality will bring happiness, if anything will. But is this really so? The whole Socratic tradition may be wrong at this point. Nor is it obviously true that the reasonable man, the man who sees life clearly and without evasion, will be able to live the richest, the most intense or the most creative life. I hope these things are compatible but they may not be. A too clear understanding may dull emotional involvement. Clear-sightedness may work against the kind of creative intensity that we find in a Lawrence, a Wolfe or a Dylan Thomas.

But to ask such questions is not in a large sense to refuse to be guided by reason. Theoretically, further knowledge could give us at least some vague answers to such unsettling questions; and, depending on what we learned and what decisions we would be willing to make, we would then know what to do. But clearly, we are not yet flying in the face of reason, refusing to be guided by reason at all. We are still playing the game according to the ground rules of reason.

What is this question, 'Why should I be guided by reason?' or 'Why be reasonable?' if it isn't any of these questions we have just discussed? If we ask this question and take it in a very general way, the question is a limiting one and it does involve a category mistake. What could be *meant* by asking: 'Why ought we *ever* use reason at all?' That to ask this question is to commit a logical blunder, is well brought out by Paul Taylor when he says:

> . . . it is a question which would never be asked by anyone who thought about what he was saying, since the question, to speak loosely, answers itself. It is admitted that no amount of arguing in the world can make a person who does not want to be reasonable want to be. For to argue would be to give reasons, and to give reasons already assumes that the person to whom you give them is *seeking* reasons. That is it assumes he is reasonable. A person who did not want to be reasonable in any sense would never ask the question, 'Why be reasonable?' For in asking the question, Why? he is seeking reasons, that is, he is being reasonable in asking the question. The question calls for the use of reason to justify *any* use of reason, including the use of reason to answer the question.[15]

In other words, to ask the question, as well as answer it, commits one to the use of reason. To ask: 'Why be guided by reason at all?' is to ask 'Why be reasonable, ever?' As Taylor puts it, "The questioner is thus seeking good reasons for seeking good reasons," and this surely is an absurdity. Anything that would be a satisfactory answer would be a "tautology to the effect that it is reasonable to be reasonable. A negative answer to the question, Is it reasonable to be reasonable? would express a self-contradiction."

If all this is pointed out to someone and he still persists in asking the question in this logically senseless way there is nothing a philosopher *qua* philosopher can do for him, though a recognition of the use of limiting questions in discourse may make this behavior less surprising to the philosopher himself. He might give all five volumes of *The Life of Reason* or *Vanity Fair* and say, 'Here, read this, maybe you will come to see things differently.' The philosopher himself might even sing a little song in praise of reason, but there would be nothing further that he could say to him, philosophically: but by now we have come a very long way.

VII

Ronald Hepburn is perceptive in speaking of the conceptual "darkness around the meaning-of-life questions".[16] We have already seen some of the reasons for this; most generally, we should remark here that people are not always asking the same question and are not always satisfied by answers of the same scope when they wrestle with meaning-of-life questions. And often, of course, the questioner has no tolerably clear idea of what he is trying to ask. He may have a strong gut reaction about the quality and character of his own

---

[15]Paul Taylor, "Four Types of Relativism," *Philosopical Review* (1956).
[16]Ronald W. Hepburn, "Questions About the Meaning of Life." [This volume, p. 123 (Eds.)]

life and the life around him without the understanding or ability to concep-
tualize why he feels the way he does. Faced with this situation, I have tried to
chart some of the contexts in which 'What is the meaning of Life?' is a coherent
question and some of the contexts in which it is not. But there are some further
contexts in which 'meaning-of-life questions' get asked which I have not
examined.

There are philosophers who will agree with me that in a world of people
with needs and wants already formed, it can be shown that life in a certain
'subjective sense' has meaning, but they will retort that this is not really the
central consideration. What is of crucial importance is whether we can show
that the universe is better with human life than without it. If this cannot be
established then we cannot have good reason to believe that life really has
meaning, though in the subjective senses we have discussed, we can still
continue to say it has meaning.[17]

If we try to answer this question, we are indeed brought up short, for we
are utterly at a loss about what it would be like to ascertain whether it is better
for the universe to have human life than no life at all. We may have certain
attitudes here but no idea of what it would be like to know or have any reason
at all to believe that 'It is better that there is life' is either true or false or
reasonably asserted or denied. It is quite unlike 'It is better to be dead than to
live with such a tumor'. Concerning this last example, people may disagree
about its correctness, but they have some idea of what considerations are
relevant to settling the dispute. But with 'It is better that there be life' we are
at a loss.

We will naturally be led into believing that 'What is the meaning of Life?' is
an unanswerable question reflecting 'the mystery of existence', if we believe
that to answer that question satisfactorily we will have to be able to establish
that it is better that there is life on earth than no life at all. What needs to be
resisted is the very acceptance of that way of posing the problem. We do not
need to establish that it is better that the universe contains human life than not
in order to establish that there is a meaning to life. A life without purpose, a
life devoid of satisfaction and an alienated life in which people are not being
true to themselves is a meaningless life. The opposite sort of life is a meaningful or significant life. We have some idea of the conditions which must obtain
for this to be so, i.e. for a man's life to have significance. We are not lost in an
imponderable mystery here and we do not have to answer the question of
whether it is better that there be human life at all to answer that question.
Moreover, this standard non-metaphysical reading of 'What is the meaning of
Life?' is no less objective than the metaphysical reading we have been
considering. There are no good grounds at all for claiming that this metaphysi-

---

[17]See in this context Hans Reiner, *Der Sinn unseres Daseins* (Tubingen, 1960). This view has
been effectively criticized by Paul Edwards, "Meaning and Value of Life," *The Encyclopedia of
Philosophy*, Paul Edwards, ed. (Macmillan, 1967), Vol. 4, pp. 474–476.

cal 'question' is the real and objective consideration in 'What is the meaning of Life?' and that the more terrestrial interpretations I have been considering are more subjective. This transcendental metaphysical way of stating the problem utilizes unwittingly and without justification arbitrary *persuasive* definitions of 'subjective' and 'objective'. And no other grounds have been given for *not* sticking with the terrestrial readings.

A deeper criticism of the account I have given of purpose and the meaning of life is given by Ronald Hepburn.[18] It is indeed true that life cannot be meaningful without being purposeful in the quite terrestrial sense I have set out, but, as Hepburn shows, it can be purposeful and still be meaningless.

> One may fill one's days with honest, useful and charitable deeds, not doubting them to be of value, but without feeling that these give one's life meaning or purpose. It may be profoundly boring. To seek meaning is not just a matter of seeking justification for one's policies, but of trying to discover how to organise one's vital resources and energies around these policies. To find meaning is not a matter of judging these to be worthy, but of seeing their pursuit as in some sense a fulfillment, as involving self-realisation as opposed to self-violation, and as no less opposed to the performance of a dreary task.[19]

A person's life can have significance even when he does not realize it and even when it is an almost intolerable drudge to him, though for human life generally to have significance this could not almost invariably be true for the human animal. But one's own life could not have significance *for oneself* if it were such a burden to one. To be meaningful to one, one's life must be purposive *and* it must be a life that the liver of that life finds satisfactory in the living of it. These conditions sometimes obtain and when it is also true that some reasonable measure of an individual's purposive activity adds to the enhancement of human life, we can say that his life is not only meaningful to him but meaningful *sans phrase*.[20]

This is still not the end of the matter in the struggle to gain a sense of the meaning of life, for, as Hepburn also points out, some will not be satisfied with a purely terrestrial and non-metaphysical account of the type I have given of 'the meaning of Life'.[21] They will claim "that life could be thought of as having meaning only so long as that meaning was believed to be a matter for discovery, not for creation and value-decision.[22] They will go on to claim that

---

[18]["Questions About the Meaning of Life," this volume (Eds.)] Hepburn's criticisms are directed toward an earlier version of this essay, "Linguistic Philosophy and "The Meaning of Life' ", *Cross-Currents*, 14 (Summer 1964).

[19]*Ibid.* [This volume, p. 116 (Eds.)]

[20]*Ibid.* [See also the two articles by Ilham Dilman cited in the Bibliography of this volume (Eds.)]

[21]"Questions About the Meaning of Life." For arguments of this type see F.C. Copleston, "Man and Metaphysics I," *The Heythrop Journal*, I, 2 (January 1960), p. 16. See in addition his continuation of this article in successive issues of *The Heythrop Review* and his *Postivism and Metaphysics* (Lisbon: 1965).

[22]"Questions About the Meaning of Life." [This volume, p. 128 (Eds.)]

"to be meaningful, life would have to be *comprehensively* meaningful and its meaning invulnerable to assault. Worthwhile objectives must be ultimately realisable despite appearances."[23]

However, even if they are not satisfied with my more piecemeal and terrestrial facing of questions concerning the meaning of life, it does not follow that life can only have meaning if it has meaning in the more comprehensive and less contingent way they seek. It may be true that life will only have meaning *for them* if these conditions are met, but this does not establish that life will thus lack meaning unless these conditions are met. That is to say, it may be found significant by the vast majority of people, including most non-evasive and reflective people, when such conditions are met and it may be the case that everyone *should* find life meaningful under such conditions.

It is not the case that there is some general formula in virtue of which we can say what the meaning of life is, but it still remains true that men can through their purposive activity give their lives meaning and indeed find meaning in life in the living of it. The man with a metaphysical or theological craving will seek 'higher standards' than the terrestrial standards I have utilized.

Is it rational to assent to that craving, to demand such 'higher standards', if life is really to be meaningful? I want to say both 'Yes' and 'No'.

On the one hand, the answer should be 'No', if the claim remains that for life to be meaningful at all it must be comprehensively meaningful. Even without such a comprehensive conception of things there can be joy in life, morally, aesthetically and technically worthwhile activity and a sense of human purpose and community. This is sufficient to give meaning to life. And as Ayer perceptively argues and as I argued earlier in the essay, and as Hepburn argues himself, the man with a metaphysical craving of the transcendental sort will not be able to succeed in finding justification or rationale for claims concerning the significance of life that is any more *authoritative* and any more certain or invulnerable to assault than the non-metaphysical type rationale I have adumbrated. In actuality, as we have seen, such a comprehensive account, committed, as it must be, to problematic transcendental metaphysical and/or theological conceptions, is more vulnerable than my purely humanistic reading of this conception.

On the other hand, the answer should be 'Yes' if the claim is reduced to one asserting that to try to articulate a comprehensive picture of human life is a desirable thing. However, it should be noted that this is quite a reduction in claim. In attempting to make such an articulation, the most crucial thing is not to wrestle with theological considerations about the contingency of the world or eternal life, but to articulate a comprehensive normative social and political philosophy in accordance with which we could set forth at least some of the

---

[23]*Ibid.* [This volume, p. 128 (Eds.)]

conditions of a non-alienated life not simply for a privileged few but for mankind generally. We need to show in some general manner what such a life would look like and we need to attempt again, and with a reference to contemporary conditions, what Marx so profoundly attempted, namely, to set out the conditions that could transform our inegalitarian, unjust, vulgar and—as in countries such as South Africa and the United States—brutal capitalist societies into truly human societies.[24] Linguistic philosophers and bourgeois philosophers generally have been of little help here, though the clarity they have inculcated into philosophical work and into political and moral argument will be a vital tool in this crucial and yet to be done task.[25] When this task is done, if it is done, then we will have the appropriate comprehensive picture we need, and it is something to be done without any involvement with theology, speculative cosmology or transcendental metaphysics at all.[26]

[24]For a contemporary Marxist account see Adam Schaff, *A Philosophy of Man* (London: 1963). But also note the criticism of Schaff's views by Christopher Hollis in "What is the Purpose of Life?", *The Listener*, 70 (1961), pp. 133–136.

[25]The strength and limitations here of linguistic analysis as it has been practiced are well exhibited in Ayer's little essay "Philosophy and Politics".

[26]If what I have argued above is so, many of the esoteric issues raised by Milton Munitz in his *The Mystery of Existence* and in his contribution to *Language, Belief, and Metaphysics*, Kiefer and Munitz, eds. (New York: 1970) can be bypassed.

XII

The Absurd

Thomas Nagel

Most people feel on occasion that life is absurd, and some feel it vividly and continually. Yet the reasons usually offered in defense of this conviction are patently inadequate: they *could* not really explain why life is absurd. Why then do they provide a natural expression for the sense that it is?

I

Consider some examples. It is often remarked that nothing we do now will matter in a million years. But if that is true, then by the same token, nothing that will be the case in a million years matters now. In particular, it does not matter now that in a million years nothing we do will matter. Moreover, even if what we did now *were* going to matter in a million years, how could that keep our present concerns from being absurd? If their mattering now is not enough to accomplish that, how would it help if they mattered a million years from now?

Whether what we do now will matter in a million years could make the crucial difference only if its mattering in a million years depended on its mattering, period. But then to deny that whatever happens now will matter in a million years is to beg the question against its mattering, period; for in that

From Thomas Nagel, "The Absurd," *The Journal of Philosophy* (October 21, 1971), pp. 716–27; reprinted by permission of Thomas Nagel and the Editors of *The Journal of Philosophy*.

sense one cannot know that it will not matter in a million years whether (for example) someone now is happy or miserable, without knowing that it does not matter, period.

What we say to convey the absurdity of our lives often has to do with space or time: we are tiny specks in the infinite vastness of the universe; our lives are mere instants even on a geological time scale, let alone a cosmic one; we will all be dead any minute. But of course none of these evident facts can be what *makes* life absurd, if it is absurd. For suppose we lived forever; would not a life that is absurd if it lasts seventy years be infinitely absurd if it lasted through eternity? And if our lives are absurd given our present size, why would they be any less absurd if we filled the universe (either because we were larger or because the universe was smaller)? Reflection on our minuteness and brevity appears to be intimately connected with the sense that life is meaningless; but it is not clear what the connection is.

Another inadequate argument is that because we are going to die, all chains of justification must leave off in mid-air: one studies and works to earn money to pay for clothing, housing, entertainment, food, to sustain oneself from year to year, perhaps to support a family and pursue a career—but to what final end? All of it is an elaborate journey leading nowhere. (One will also have some effect on other people's lives, but that simply reproduces the problem, for they will die too.)

There are several replies to this argument. First, life does not consist of a sequence of activities each of which has as its purpose some later member of the sequence. Chains of justification come repeatedly to an end within life, and whether the process as a whole can be justified has no bearing on the finality of these end-points. No further justification is needed to make it reasonable to take aspirin for a headache, attend an exhibit of the work of a painter one admires, or stop a child from putting his hand on a hot stove. No larger context or further purpose is needed to prevent these acts from being pointless.

Even if someone wished to supply a further justification for pursuing all the things in life that are commonly regarded as self-justifying, that justification would have to end somewhere too. If *nothing* can justify unless it is justified in terms of something outside itself, which is also justified, then an infinite regress results, and no chain of justification can be complete. Moreover, if a finite chain of reasons cannot justify anything, what could be accomplished by an infinite chain, each link of which must be justified by something outside itself ?

Since justifications must come to an end somewhere, nothing is gained by denying that they end where they appear to, within life—or by trying to subsume the multiple, often trivial ordinary justifications of action under a single, controlling life scheme. We can be satisfied more easily than that. In fact, through its misrepresentation of the process of justification, the argument makes a vacuous demand. It insists that the reasons available within life are incomplete, but suggests thereby that all reasons that come to an end are incomplete. This makes it impossible to supply any reasons at all.

The standard arguments for absurdity appear therefore to fail as arguments. Yet I believe they attempt to express something that is difficult to state, but fundamentally correct.

II

In ordinary life a situation is absurd when it includes a conspicuous discrepancy between pretension or aspiration and reality: someone gives a complicated speech in support of a motion that has already been passed; a notorious criminal is made president of a major philanthropic foundation; you declare your love over the telephone to a recorded announcement; as you are being knighted, your pants fall down.

When a person finds himself in an absurd situation, he will usually attempt to change it, by modifying his aspirations, or by trying to bring reality into better accord with them, or by removing himself from the situation entirely. We are not always willing or able to extricate ourselves from a position whose absurdity has become clear to us. Nevertheless, it is usually possible to imagine some change that would remove the absurdity—whether or not we can or will implement it. The sense that life as a whole is absurd arises when we perceive, perhaps dimly, an inflated pretension or aspiration which is inseparable from the continuation of human life and which makes its absurdity inescapable, short of escape from life itself.

Many people's lives are absurd, temporarily or permanently, for conventional reasons having to do with their particular ambitions, circumstances, and personal relations. If there is a philosophical sense of absurdity, however, it must arise from the perception of something universal—some respect in which pretension and reality inevitably clash for us all. This condition is supplied, I shall argue, by the collision between the seriousness with which we take our lives and the perpetual possibility of regarding everything about which we are serious as arbitrary, or open to doubt.

We cannot live human lives without energy and attention, nor without making choices which show that we take some things more seriously than others. Yet we have always available a point of view outside the particular form of our lives, from which the seriousness appears gratuitous. These two inescapable viewpoints collide in us, and that is what makes life absurd. It is absurd because we ignore the doubts that we know cannot be settled, continuing to live with nearly undiminished seriousness in spite of them.

This analysis requires defense in two respects: first as regards the unavoidability of seriousness; second as regards the inescapability of doubt.

We take ourselves seriously whether we lead serious lives or not and whether we are concerned primarily with fame, pleasure, virtue, luxury, triumph, beauty, justice, knowledge, salvation, or mere survival. If we take other people seriously and devote ourselves to them, that only multiplies the problem. Human life is full of effort, plans, calculation, success and failure: we *pursue* our lives, with varying degress of sloth and energy.

It would be different if we could not step back and reflect on the process, but were merely led from impulse to impulse without self-consciousness. But human beings do not act solely on impulse. They are prudent, they reflect, they weigh consequences, they ask whether what they are doing is worth while. Not only are their lives full of particular choices that hang together in larger activities with temporal structure: they also decide in the broadest terms what to pursue and what to avoid, what the priorities among their various aims should be, and what kind of people they want to be or become. Some men are faced with such choices by the large decisions they make from time to time; some merely by reflection on the course their lives are taking as the product of countless small decisions. They decide whom to marry, what profession to follow, whether to join the Country Club, or the Resistance; or they may just wonder why they go on being salesmen or academics or taxi drivers, and then stop thinking about it after a certain period of inconclusive reflection.

Although they may be motivated from act to act by those immediate needs with which life presents them, they allow the process to continue by adhering to the general system of habits and the form of life in which such motives have their place—or perhaps only by clinging to life itself. They spend enormous quantities of energy, risk, and calculation on the details. Think of how an ordinary individual sweats over his appearance, his health, his sex life, his emotional honesty, his social utility, his self-knowledge, the quality of his ties with family, colleagues, and friends, how well he does his job, whether he understands the world and what is going on in it. Leading a human life is a full-time occupation, to which everyone devotes decades of intense concern.

This fact is so obvious that it is hard to find it extraordinary and important. Each of us lives his own life—lives with himself twenty-four hours a day. What else is he supposed to do—live someone else's life? Yet humans have the special capacity to step back and survey themselves, and the lives to which they are committed, with that detached amazement which comes from watching an ant struggle up a heap of sand. Without developing the illusion that they are able to escape from their highly specific and idiosyncratic position, they can view it *sub specie aeternitatis*—and the view is at once sobering and comical.

The crucial backward step is not taken by asking for still another justification in the chain, and failing to get it. The objections to that line of attack have already been stated; justifications come to an end. But this is precisely what provides universal doubt with its object. We step back to find that the whole system of justification and criticism, which controls our choices and supports our claims to rationality, rests on responses and habits that we never question, that we should not know how to defend without circularity, and to which we shall continue to adhere even after they are called into question.

The things we do or want without reasons, and without requiring reasons—the things that define what is a reason for us and what is not—are the starting points of our skepticism. We see ourselves from outside and all the contingency and specificity of our aims and pursuits become clear. Yet when we take this view and recognize what we do as arbitrary, it does not disengage us from life, and there lies our absurdity: not in the fact that such an external view can be taken of us, but in the fact that we ourselves can take it, without ceasing to be the persons whose ultimate concerns are so coolly regarded.

III

One may try to escape the position by seeking broader ultimate concerns, from which it is impossible to step back—the idea being that absurdity results because what we take seriously is something small and insignificant and individual. Those seeking to supply their lives with meaning usually envision a role or function in something larger than themselves. They therefore seek fulfillment in service to society, the state, the revolution, the progress of history, the advance of science, or religion and the glory of God.

But a role in some larger enterprise cannot confer significance unless that enterprise is itself significant. And its significance must come back to what we can understand, or it will not even appear to give us what we are seeking. If we learned that we were being raised to provide food for other creatures fond of human flesh, who planned to turn us into cutlets before we got too stringy— even if we learned that the human race had been developed by animal breeders precisely for this purpose—that would still not give our lives meaning, for two reasons. First, we would still be in the dark as to the significance of the lives of those other beings; second, although we might acknowledge that this culinary role would make our lives meaningful to them, it is not clear how it would make them meaningful to us.

Admittedly, the usual form of service to a higher being is different from this. One is supposed to behold and partake of the glory of God, for example, in a way in which chickens do not share in the glory of coq au vin. The same is true of service to a state, a movement, or a revolution. People can come to feel, when they are part of something bigger, that it is part of them too. They worry less about what is peculiar to themselves, but identify enough with the larger enterprise to find their role in it fulfilling.

However, any such larger purpose can be put in doubt in the same way that the aims of an individual life can be, and for the same reasons. It is as legitimate to find ultimate justification there as to find it earlier, among the details of individual life. But this does not alter the fact that justifications come to an end when we are content to have them end—when we do not find it necessary to look any further. If we can step back from the purposes of individual life and doubt their point, we can step back also from the progress of human history, or of science, or the success of a society, or the kingdom, power, and glory of God,[1] and put all these things into question in the same way. What seems to us to confer meaning, justification, significance, does so in virtue of the fact that we need no more reasons after a certain point.

What makes doubt inescapable with regard to the limited aims of individual life also makes it inescapable with regard to any larger purpose that encourages the sense that life is meaningful. Once the fundamental doubt has begun, it cannot be laid to rest.

Camus maintains in *The Myth of Sisyphus* that the absurd arises because the world fails to meet our demands for meaning. This suggests that the world might satisfy those demands if it were different. But now we can see that this is not the case. There does not appear to be any conceivable world (containing us) about which unsettlable doubts could not arise. Consequently the absurdity of our situation derives not from a collision between our expectations and the world, but from a collision within ourselves.

IV

It may be objected that the standpoint from which these doubts are supposed to be felt does not exist—that if we take the recommended backward step we will land on thin air, without any basis for judgment about the natural responses we are supposed to be surveying. If we retain our usual standards of what is important, then questions about the significance of what we are doing with our lives will be answerable in the usual way. But if we do not, then those questions can mean nothing to us, since there is no longer any content to the idea of what matters, and hence no content to the idea that nothing does.

But this objection misconceives the nature of the backward step. It is not supposed to give us an understanding of what is *really* important, so that we see by contrast that our lives are insignificant. We never, in the course of these reflections, abandon the ordinary standards that guide our lives. We merely observe them in operation, and recognize that if they are called into question

[1]CF. Robert Nozick, "Teleology," *Mosaic*, XII, 1 (Spring 1971) 27/8.

we can justify them only by reference to themselves, uselessly. We adhere to them because of the way we are put together; what seems to us important or serious or valuable would not seem so if we were differently constituted.

In ordinary life, to be sure, we do not judge a situation absurd unless we have in mind some standards of seriousness, signifiance, or harmony with which the absurd can be constrasted. This contrast is not implied by the philosophical judgment of absurdity, and that might be thought to make the concept unsuitable for the expression of such judgments. This is not so, however, for the philosophical judgment depends on another contrast which makes it a natural extension from more ordinary cases. It departs from them only in contrasting the pretensions of life with a larger context in which *no* standards can be discovered, rather than with a context from which alternative, overriding standards may be applied.

V

In this respect, as in others, philosophical perception of the absurd resembles epistemological skepticism. In both cases the final, philosophical doubt is not contrasted with any unchallenged certainties, though it is arrived at by extrapolation from examples of doubt within the system of evidence or justification, where a contrast with other certainties is implied. In both cases our limitedness joins with a capacity to transcend those limitations in thought (thus seeing them as limitations, and as inescapable).

Skepticism begins when we include ourselves in the world about which we claim knowledge. We notice that certain types of evidence convince us, that we are content to allow justifications of belief to come to an end at certain points, that we feel we know many things even without knowing or having grounds for believing the denial of others which, if true, would make what we claim to know false.

For example, I know that I am looking at a piece of paper, although I have no adequate grounds to claim I know that I am not dreaming; and if I am dreaming then I am not looking at a piece of paper. Here an ordinary conception of how appearance may diverge from reality is employed to show that we take our world largely for granted; the certainty that we are not dreaming cannot be justified except circularly, in terms of those very appearances which are being put in doubt. It is somewhat far-fetched to suggest I may be dreaming; but the possibility is only illustrative. It reveals that our claims to knowledge depend on our not feeling it necessary to exclude certain incompatible alternatives, and the dreaming possibility or the total-hallucination possibility are just representatives for limitless possibilities most of which we cannot even conceive.[2]

Once we have taken the backward step to an abstract view of our whole system of beliefs, evidence, and justification, and seen that it works only, despite its pretensions, by taking the world largely for granted, we are *not* in a position to contrast all these appearances with an alternative reality. We cannot shed our ordinary responses, and if we could it would leave us with no means of conceiving a reality of any kind.

It is the same in the practical domain. We do not step outside our lives to a new vantage point from which we see what is really, objectively significant. We continue to take life largely for granted while seeing that all our decisions and certainties are possible only because there is a great deal we do not bother to rule out.

Both epistemological skepticism and a sense of the absurd can be reached via initial doubts posed within systems of evidence and justification that we accept, and can be stated without violence to our ordinary concepts. We can ask not only why we should believe there is a floor under us, but also why we should believe the evidence of our senses at all—and at some point framable questions will have outlasted the answers. Similarly, we can ask not only why we should take aspirin, but why we should take trouble over our own comfort at all. The fact that we shall take the aspirin without waiting for an answer to this last question does not show that it is an unreal question. We shall also continue to believe there is a floor under us without waiting for an answer to the other question. In both cases it is this unsupported natural confidence that generates skeptical doubts; so it cannot be used to settle them.

Philosophical skepticism does not cause us to abandon our ordinary beliefs, but it lends them a peculiar flavor. After acknowledging that their truth is incompatible with possibilities that we have no ground for believing do not obtain—apart from grounds in those very beliefs which we have called into question—we return to our familiar convictions with a certain irony and resignation. Unable to abandon the natural responses on which they depend, we take them back, like a spouse who has run off with someone else and then decided to return; but we regard them differently (not that the new attitude is necessarily inferior to the old, in either case).

The same situation obtains after we have put in question the seriousness with which we take our lives and human life in general and have looked at ourselves without presuppositions. We then return to our lives, as we must, but our seriousness is laced with irony. Not that irony enables us to escape the

---

[2]I am aware that skepticism about the external world is widely thought to have been refuted, but I have remained convinced of its irrefutability since being exposed at Berkeley to Thompson Clarke's largely unpublished ideas on the subject.

absurd. It is useless to mutter: "Life is meaningless; life is meaningless . . ." as an accompaniment to everything we do. In continuing to live and work and strive, we take ourselves seriously in action no matter what we say.

What sustains us, in belief as in action, is not reason or justification, but something more basic than these—for we go on in the same way even after we are convinced that the reasons have given out.[3] If we tried to rely entirely on reason, and pressed it hard, our lives and beliefs would collapse—a form of madness that may actually occur if the inertial force of taking the world and life for granted is somehow lost. If we lose our grip on that, reason will not give it back to us.

VI

In viewing ourselves from a perspective broader than we can occupy in the flesh, we become spectators of our own lives. We cannot do very much as pure spectators of our own lives, so we continue to lead them, and devote ourselves to what we are able at the same time to view as no more than a curiosity, like the ritual of an alien religion.

This explains why the sense of absurdity finds its natural expression in those bad arguments with which the discussion began. Reference to our small size and short lifespan and to the fact that all of mankind will eventually vanish without a trace are metaphors for the backward step which permits us to regard ourselves from without and to find the particular form of our lives curious and slightly surprising. By feigning a nebula's-eye view, we illustrate the capacity to see ourselves without presuppositions, as arbitrary, idiosyncratic, highly specific occupants of the world, one of countless possible forms of life.

Before turning to the question whether the absurdity of our lives is something to be regretted and if possible escaped, let me consider what would have to be given up in order to avoid it.

Why is the life of a mouse not absurd? The orbit of the moon is not absurd either, but that involves no strivings or aims at all. A mouse, however, has to work to stay alive. Yet he is not absurd, because he lacks the capacities for

---

[3]As Hume says in a famous passage of the *Treatise:* "Most fortunately it happens, that since reason is incapable of dispelling these clouds, nature herself suffices to that purpose, and cures me of this philosophical melancholy and delirium, either by relaxing this bent of mind, or by some avocation, and lively impression of my senses, which obliterate all these chimeras. I dine, I play a game of backgammon, I converse, and am merry with my friends; and when after three or four hours' amusement, I would return to these speculations, they appear so cold, and strain'd, and ridiculous, that I cannot find in my heart to enter into them any farther" (Book 1, Part 4, Section 7; Selby-Bigge, p. 269).

self-consciousness and self-transcendence that would enable him to see that he is only a mouse. If that *did* happen, his life would become absurd, since self-awareness would not make him cease to be a mouse and would not enable him to rise above his mousely strivings. Bringing his new-found self-consciousness with him, he would have to return to his meagre yet frantic life, full of doubts that he was unable to answer, but also full of purposes that he was unable to abandon.

Given that the transcendental step is natural to us humans, can we avoid absurdity by refusing to take that step and remaining entirely within our sublunar lives? Well, we cannot refuse consciously, for to do that we would have to be aware of the viewpoint we were refusing to adopt. The only way to avoid the relevant self-consciousness would be either never to attain it or to forget it—neither of which can be achieved by the will.

On the other hand, it is possible to expend effort on an attempt to destroy the other component of the absurd—abandoning one's earthly, individual, human life in order to identify as completely as possible with that universal viewpoint from which human life seems arbitrary and trivial. (This appears to be the ideal of certain Oriental religions.) If one succeeds, then one will not have to drag the superior awareness through a strenuous mundane life, and absurdity will be diminshed.

However, insofar as this self-etiolation is the result of effort, will-power, asceticism, and so forth, it requires that one take oneself seriously as an individual—that one be willing to take considerable trouble to avoid being creaturely and absurd. Thus one may undermine the aim of unworldliness by pursuing it too vigorously. Still, if someone simply allowed his individual, animal nature to drift and respond to impulse, without making the pursuit of its needs a central conscious aim, then he might, at considerable dissociative cost, achieve a life that was less absurd than most. It would not be a meaningful life either, of course; but it would not involve the engagement of a transcendent awareness in the assiduous pursuit of mundane goals. And that is the main condition of absurdity—the dragooning of an unconvinced transcendent consciousness into the service of an immanent, limited enterprise like a human life.

The final escape is suicide; but before adopting any hasty solutions, it would be wise to consider carefully whether the absurdity of our existence truly presents us with a *problem*, to which some solution must be found—a way of dealing with prima facie disaster. That is certainly the attitude with which Camus approaches the issue, and it gains support from the fact that we are all eager to escape from absurd situations on a smaller scale.

Camus—not on uniformly good grounds—rejects suicide and the other solutions he regards as escapist. What he recommends is defiance or scorn. We can salvage our dignity, he appears to believe, by shaking a fist at the world which is deaf to our pleas, and continuing to live in spite of it. This will not make our lives un-absurd, but it will lend them a certain nobility.[4]

This seems to me romantic and slightly self-pitying. Our absurdity warrants neither that much distress nor that much defiance. At the risk of falling into romanticism by a different route, I would argue that absurdity is one of the most human things about us: a manifestation of our most advanced and interesting characteristics. Like skepticism in epistemology, it is possible only because we possess a certain kind of insight—the capacity to transcend ourselves in thought.

If a sense of the absurd is a way of perceiving our true situation (even though the situation is not absurd until the perception arises), then what reason can we have to resent or escape it? Like the capacity for epistemological skepticism, it results from the ability to understand our human limitations. It need not be a matter for agony unless we make it so. Nor need it evoke a defiant contempt of fate that allows us to feel brave or proud. Such dramatics, even if carried on in private, betray a failure to appreciate the cosmic unimportance of the situation. If *sub specie aeternitatis* there is no reason to believe that anything matters, then that doesn't matter either, and we can approach our absurd lives with irony instead of heroism or despair.

[4]"Sisyphus, proletarian of the gods, powerless and rebellious, knows the whole extent of his wretched condition: it is what he thinks of during his descent. The lucidity that was to constitute his torture at the same time crowns his victory. There is no fate that cannot be surmounted by scorn" (*The Myth of Sisyphus*, Vintage edition, p. 90).

Notes on Contributors

LEO TOLSTOY was the celebrated nineteenth century Russian novelist, whose works include *Anna Karenina, War and Peace,* and *The Death of Ivan Ilyich.* In later life, he renounced his aristocratic title and its trappings in pursuit of an ascetic existence devoted to social and moral reform. His philosophical writings of this period include *What I Believe, What is Art?* and *My Confession.*

ARTHUR SCHOPENHAUER was a nineteenth century German pessimist and critic of the Enlightenment. His principal work is *The World as Will and Representation,* which presents the theory that will, not intellect, is the fundamental feature of man and nature. His other writings include *On the Fourfold Root of the Principle of Sufficient Reason, On the Basis of Morality,* and *Parerga and Paralipomena.*

WALTER T. STACE served with the British Civil Service in Ceylon before becoming Professor of Philosophy at Princeton University. He published extensively in the areas of metaphysics, epistemology, and philosophy of religion. In addition to a book of poetry, he wrote *Mysticism and Philosophy, The Concept of Morals, Religion and the Modern Mind,* and *The Theory of Knowledge and Existence.* He died in 1967.

KURT BAIER is Professor of Philosophy at the University of Pittsburgh and has also taught at the University of Melbourne, the Australian National

University, and Cornell University. His best known work in moral philosophy is *The Moral Point of View* and he has co-edited *Values and the Future.*

ALBERT CAMUS left his native Algeria for France, where he became the editor of *Le Combat,* an underground newspaper of the French Resistance during World War II. *The Stranger, Caligula,* and *The Plague* are among his fictional works, and his philosophical essays include *The Rebel* and *The Myth of Sisyphus.* In 1957 Camus was awarded the Nobel Prize for Literature. He died in 1960.

RICHARD TAYLOR is Professor of Philosophy at the University of Rochester and has taught at Columbia University and Brown University. He is the author of *Action and Purpose, Metaphysics,* and *Good and Evil.*

PAUL EDWARDS is Professor of Philosophy at the City University of New York, Brooklyn College. He has also taught at Columbia University, New York University, and the University of Melbourne. He is Editor-in-Chief of the *Encyclopedia of Philosophy* and the author of *The Logic of Moral Discourse.*

R. M. HARE is White's Professor of Moral Philosophy at Oxford University. He has published a number of widely influential works in moral philosophy including *The Language of Morals* and *Freedom and Reason.* Four volumes of his philosophical essays on concepts and applications of moral philosophy, practical reasoning, and philosophical method have recently appeared.

HAZEL E. BARNES is Professor of Classics at the University of Colorado and has taught at the University of Toledo, Ohio State University, and Pierce College in Greece. She is a prominent American exponent of existentialist thought, the author of *Humanistic Existentialism* and *An Existentialist Ethics,* and is perhaps best known for her translation of Jean-Paul Sartre's *Being and Nothingness.*

RONALD W. HEPBURN has taught at New York University, the Universities of Aberdeen and Nottingham, and is Professor of Philosophy at the University of Edinburgh. He has written extensively in the areas of philosophy of religion and aesthetics. He is the author of *Christianity and Paradox* and co-author of *Metaphysical Beliefs*.

KAI NIELSEN is Professor of Philosophy at the University of Calgary and has taught at New York University and Amherst College. He has written widely in ethics and philosophy of religion. His books include *Quest for God, Ethics without God, Contemporary Critiques of Religion,* and *Reason and Practice*.

THOMAS NAGEL is Professor of Philosophy at Princeton University. He is an Associate Editor of *Philosophy and Public Affairs,* and author of *The Possibility of Altruism* and *Mortal Questions*.

Bibliographical Essay

This bibliography is intended as a comprehensive guide to readers who wish to pursue the themes and problems of this book. It cites not only alternative positions, but also further developments of, and responses to, the views found in our selections.

I. Raising Questions about Life's Meaning

The question of the psychology of the meaning of life is not explicitly examined in our readings. For psychological theories relating to the problems of the meaning of life, see Alfred Adler, *What Life Should Mean to You* (G.P. Putnam's Sons, 1958); Bruno Bettelheim, *The Uses of Enchantment* (Knopf, 1976); Viktor Frankl, *Man's Search for Meaning* (Beacon, 1963); Sigmund Freud, *The Future of an Illusion* (Cape and Smith, 1928) and *Civilization and its Discontents* (Cape and Smith, 1930); Erich Fromm, *Man for Himself* (Holt, Rinehart and Winston, 1947); C.G. Jung, *Modern Man in Search of a Soul* (Harcourt Brace Jovanovich, 1955), and "Psychotherapy and a Philosophy of Life," *The Collected Works of C.G. Jung*, Vol. 16 (Princeton, 1966); Rollo May, *Man's Search for Meaning* (Norton, 1953).

Questions about the meaning of life often arise in conjunction with diagnoses of the human condition. The following assessments of the human condition may be of interest: G.J. Warnock in *The Object of Morality* (Methuen, 1971) writes that the human condition constitutes a *predicament* in which "the inherent liability of things to go badly" derives mainly from limitations in human rationality and sympathy. Robert Heilbroner's grim prognostications in *An Inquiry into the Human Prospect* (Norton, 1974) portend "a continuation of the darkness, cruelty, and disorder of the past" with worse impending for the future. The novels of Louis-Ferdinand Celine, especially *Journey to the End of the Night* (New Directions, 1960) and *Death on the Installment Plan* (New Directions, 1962) describe a world in which everybody is an alien—hopelessly isolated or immobilized in contrived and mechanical relationships. A brief discussion of similar themes in the fiction of Bernard Malamud and Albert Camus is found in Oscar Mohl, "Man's Search for Significance in Recent Literature," *Journal of Critical Analysis*, 2 (April 1970): 21–27.

For further statements of Schopenhauer's views on the meaning of life, see "The Vanity and Suffering of the World," in his *The World as Will and Representation*, 2 Vols. trans. E. F. J. Payne (Dover, 1966), Vol. 2, and sections 56–59 of Vol. 1, as well as some of the essays in *The Pessimist's Handbook* (Nebraska, 1964).

The impact of modern science and the place it leaves for purpose and value in life is explored in Bertrand Russell's "A Free Man's Worship," in *Mysticism and Logic* (Allen & Unwin, 1917). For Stace's further ideas concerning science and values, see his *Religion and the Modern Mind* (Lippincott, 1960) and the volume of essays entitled *Man Against Darkness* (Pittsburgh, 1967). Replies to the Stace essay which appears in the present collection have been made by J. J. Maguire, "The Illogical Dr. Stace," *Catholic World*, 168 (November 1948): 102–5; and T. M. Greene, "Man Out of Darkness," *Atlantic* 183 (April 1949): 45–49. The Russell-Stace contention that science rules out purpose has also been challenged by Etienne Gilson in *God and Philosophy* (Yale, 1941), Ch. 4.

The teleological argument (argument from cosmic purpose or design) for the existence of God is relevant to the question of the purpose of life. Almost any general work on the philosophy of religion discusses this argument—for example, John Hick, ed., *The Existence of God* (Macmillan, 1964). The classic challenge to the design argument is stated by David Hume in his *Dialogues Concerning Natural Religion* (London, 1779, many editions). Recent challenges to the design argument from the fact of evil can be found in *God and Evil*, Nelson Pike, ed. (Prentice-Hall, 1964).

II. The Search for Meaning

Discussions of the meaning of life and the Western theistic tradition, with its roots in Judaic and Christian thought, can be found in the following writings: Paul Althus, "The Meaning and Purpose of History in the Christian

View," *Universitas* 47 (1967): 197–204; Karl Britton, *Philosophy and the Meaning of Life* (Cambridge, 1969), Ch. 2; Delwin Brown, "God's Reality and Life's Meaning," *Encounter* 28, 3 (Summer 1968): 252–62; Emil Fackenheim, "Judaism and the Meaning of Life," *Commentary* 39 (1965): 49–55; Abraham Heschel, *Man is Not Alone* (Farrar, Straus & Giroux, 1951); C.S. Lewis, "De Futilitate," *Christian Reflections* (Geoffrey Bles, 1967); Reinhold Niebuhr, *The Nature and Destiny of Man*, Vol. II (Scribner's, 1943), *The Godly and the Ungodly* (Faber, 1958), Ch. 9; Eugene Troubetzkoy, "The Reign of Nonsense in the World" and "The Meaning of Life," *The Hibbert Journal* 16 (1918); J.S. Whale, *Christian Doctrine* (Fontana, 1957). The Hindu, Islamic and Buddhist traditions (as well as Judaism and Christianity) are discussed in *The Meaning of Life in Five Great Religions*, R.C. Chalmers and J.A. Irving, eds. (Westminster, 1965). For metaphysical theories with a religious basis, see Rudolf Eucken, *The Meaning and Value of Life* (Black, 1910) and W.E. Hocking, "Meanings of Life," *Journal of Religion* 16 (July 1936).

Humanistic alternatives (especially to Christianity) are advanced by Kai Nielsen, "Ethics Without Religion" and Kurt Baier, "Meaning and Morals," both in *Moral Problems in Contemporary Society*, Paul Kurtz, ed. (Prentice-Hall, 1969). On humanism and life's meaning, see also H.J. Blackham, "The Pointlessness of it All," *Objections to Humanism*, H.J. Blackham, ed. (Lippincott, 1963) and Paul Kurtz, *The Fullness of Life* (Horizon, 1974), Ch. 5. An atheistic attempt to answer questions about the meaning of life is put forward by Richard Robinson, *An Atheist's Values* (Oxford, 1964), esp. pp. 54–57, 114, 155–57.

Atheistic existentialist views can be found in the writings of Jean-Paul Sartre, especially "Existentialism," and the other selections in *Existentialism and Human Emotions* (Philosophical Library, 1957). See also Simone de Beauvoir, *The Ethics of Ambiguity* (Philosophical Library, 1948). Non-atheistic existentialist views can be found in Gabriel Marcel, *The Mystery of Being* (Henry Regnery, 1960), Vol. I: 199–215; and Karl Jaspers, *Philosophy* (Chicago, 1971), Vol. 3: 192–207. Concern about the meaning of life is often a theme in the literary work of existentialists. See, for example, Sartre, *Nausea* (New Directions, 1959) and *The Wall* (New Directions, 1948); Albert Camus, *The Stranger* (Knopf, 1946), *The Fall* (Random House, 1956), and *The Plague* (Random House, 1948). Robert Solomon's *The Passions* (Doubleday, 1976) connects an inquiry into the meaning of life with a theory of human emotions from an existentialist perspective. A critique of existentialist themes concerning the meaning of life is offered by Sidney Hook in "The Quest for Certainty—Existentialism Without Tears," *Pragmatism and the Tragic Sense of Life* (Basic Books, 1974).

Contemporary concern with nihilism and absurdity derives largely from the writings of Friedrich Nietzsche and Albert Camus. Many of Nietzsche's works touch on the issue of the meaning of life. See especially *The Will to Power* (Random House, 1967), Book One; *The Gay Science* (Random House,

1974), Book Four; and *Twilight of the Idols* in *The Portable Nietzsche,* Walter Kaufmann, ed. (Viking 1954). Nietzsche's ideas are explored in Karl Jasper's *Nietzsche* (Arizona, 1965), Ch. 6, and in R.J. Hollingdale, *Nietzsche* (Routledge & Kegan Paul, 1973), Ch. 1. For a sustained study of nihilism, see Stanley Rosen, *Nihilism: A Philosophical Essay* (Yale, 1969). Several interesting essays on nihilism and absurdity are collected in Part Two of *New Essays in Phenomenology,* James Edie, ed. (Quadrangle, 1969). Camus' ideas on absurdity are to be found in *The Myth of Sisyphus,* from which the present selection is drawn, and also in *The Rebel* (Knopf, 1956). A criticism of Camus that places his views in their ontological setting is Herbert Hochberg's "Albert Camus and the Ethics of Absurdity," *Ethics* 75 (1964–65): 87–102.

Discussions of death and the meaning of life can be found in William James, "Is Life Worth Living?" in *The Will to Believe* (New York, 1897, many editions); Jacques Choron, *Death and Modern Man* (Collier, 1972); and Bernard Williams, "The Makropulos Case: Reflections on the Tedium of Immortality," *Problems of the Self* (Cambridge, 1973).

III. Analyzing Questions about the Meaning of Life

Wittgenstein's remarks on questions of the meaning of life can be found in his *Notebooks, 1914–16* (Harper & Row, 1961), pp. 72–83, and his *Tractatus Logico-Philosophicus* (Routledge & Kegan Paul, 1961), sections 6.4–7. Wittgenstein's view of the problem of the meaning of life and his approach to philosophy generally can be contrasted with the view taken by Karl R. Popper, *The Open Society and Its Enemies,* 2 Vols. (5th rev. ed., Princeton, 1966), esp. Vol. 2, Ch. 25.

A full-length study of the meaning of life which includes a critical examination of various answers as well as an analysis of questions about the meaning of life is Karl Britton, *Philosophy and the Meaning of Life* (Cambridge, 1969).

John Wisdom considers various meanings of 'the meaning of life' in *Paradox and Discovery* (California, 1965), Ch. 4.

L.J. Russell challenges the assumption that only eternal life or immortality gives life meaning in "The Meaning of Life," *Philosophy* 28 (1953): 30–40. The distinction between thinking one's life is meaningful and its actually being meaningful is discussed by Ilham Dilman, "Life and Meaning," *Philosophy* 40 (1965): 320–333. Dilman also responds to the paper by Ronald Hepburn in this volume in "Professor Hepburn on Meaning in Life," *Religious Studies* 3 (April 1968): 547–554. Circumstances contributing to meaninglessness are explored by W.D. Joske, "The Meaning of Life," *Australasian Journal of Philosophy* 52, 2 (1974): 93–104.

Three books by contemporary analytic philosophers relate questions about the meaning of life to problems in ethics and philosophy of religion generally: Ronald Hepburn, *Christianity and Paradox* (Pegasus, 1968), esp. 151ff.; Antony Flew, *God and Philosophy* (Dell, 1966), esp. 104ff.; and Kai Nielsen, *Ethics Without God* (Prometheus, 1973), Chaps. 2 and 3. An analysis of questions of the meaning of life as well as an attempt to meet certain challenges to Christian theism is found in Delwin Brown, "Process Philosophy and the Question of Life's Meaning," *Religious Studies* 7 (1971): 13–29.

Questions about the meaning of life are related to questions concerning the individual's place in nature and society, the nature of the good life, and so on. Three works which discuss the voluminous literature on this topic and put forward views of their own are C.D. McGee, *The Recovery of Meaning— An Essay on the Good Life* (Random House, 1966); Alfred Stern, *The Search for Meaning: Philosophical Vistas* (Memphis, 1971); and David L. Norton, *Personal Destinies* (Princeton, 1976).

Index